50
MASTERS OF
GOLF

50 MASTERS OF GOLF

Michael Hobbs

MOORLAND PUBLISHING

British Library Cataloguing
in Publication Data

Hobbs, Michael, 1934-
    50 masters of golf.
    1. Golfers — Biography
    I. Title
    796.352'092'2   GV964.A1

    ISBN 0 86190 076 6

Illustrations have been provided by:
The US Golf Association p 8, 30, 44, 58, 154,
192; H.W. Neale p 16, 22, 36, 62, 72, 90, 98,
101, 106, 135, 150, 165, 169; Professional
Golf Association p 19, 39, 41, 55, 127, 142,
162; Michael Hobbs p 12, 25, 69, 77, 87,
104, 110, 116, 132, 158, 177, 180, 184; Pete
Dazeley p 33, 51; Phil Sheldon p 47, 82, 93,
120, 124, 129, 189; Pringle of Scotland
147; George Beldam p 173.

Printing by Redwood Burn Ltd, Wiltshire
for the publishers
Moorland Publishing Co Ltd,
9-11 Station Street, Ashbourne,
Derbyshire, DE6 1DE England.
Telephone: (0335) 44486

Contents

Introduction

It has been a pleasure, through.writing, to renew a kind of acquaintance with so many of the great golfers of all time. I think readers will agree that all the very greatest players can be found in these pages from as far back as Young Tom Morris and John Ball, the earliest players included, through the Great Triumvirate (Vardon, Taylor and Braid), Jones, Hagen, Cotton, Hogan up to such moderns as Lyle and Norman.

Comparing golfers of different periods is at least difficult and, I think, ultimately impossible. It can be done, if at all, only by looking at their records in the major championships: the American and British Opens, the US PGA and the Masters. More run-of-the-mill tournaments come and go to the extent that 1983 saw the end of the oldest European sponsored event (after 37 years), the Dunlop Masters. The quality of fields also varies far more than it does for the major championships: the great players restrict their schedules but seldom indeed fail to compete in the events that can provide immortality.

So, this book, although a collection of the great players of all time, does not pretend to be a selection of the top fifty of all time. That would be unnecessary arrogance. I have also felt a slight bias towards players active during the last forty years, because of a greater depth of knowledge and personal experience of seeing them play. Nevertheless, twenty of the players in this book had either completed their careers or become major players before the beginning of World War II.

American golf quickly became dominant after World War I, which also saw the virtual end of the Triumvirate of Vardon, Taylor and Braid, and thanks to this dominance claims about half of the entries. Britain, with its earlier pre-eminence, also claims a good share, though, if population sizes are compared, Australia has a fair claim to be considered the best golfing nation of all. Golfers from South Africa, Argentina, New Zealand and Spain are also included. In Severiano Ballesteros, the latter country has one of the most prolific tournament winners ever of the last few years, and also a winner of three major championships, with more likely to come. It is perhaps not surprising, however, that the name of Nicklaus occurs so often. I have not allowed him to take up too massive a space in his own piece because he naturally forces his way into the deeds of others. In their different eras, Vardon, Jones, Hogan and then Nicklaus were always the men to beat in their best years and others gained far more glory if they managed to hold off a challenge from these players.

A few amateurs have been included, but golf at the top has now long been a professional matter: for a good many years now, no golfer has given himself the time to establish a great amateur career before joining the professional ranks. Perhaps only Michael Bonallack in Britain and Henri de Lamaze in France have built records formidable enough to compare with such earlier players as John Ball. In modern times, the only player to have established a great record as both amateur and professional is a woman: JoAnne Gunderson Carner.

Michael Hobbs, Bristol, June 1983

John Ball

Born Hoylake, Lancashire, England, 1861

'I should get more aesthetic ecstasy out of watching him than Bobby Jones and Harry Vardon put together.' So did Bernard Darwin dismiss the claims of Jones and Vardon and, had he lived to a greater age, no doubt such moderns as Weiskopf, Snead, Sneed and Littler would have been similarly treated. As John Ball last competed more than 60 years ago, there must be few now alive who saw him play. He is mostly remembered for his record of having won the British Amateur eight times, a total unapproached and unapproachable.

On a world scale, his total of nine wins in major championships is bettered only by Nicklaus, Jones and Hagen and equalled by Player and Hogan. Ball had only two majors available to him: the British Open and Amateur Championships. Even here, his collection of championships was impeded by outside influences. He missed three years due to his service in the South African War and several more during World War I. Earlier, although the Open Championship was in existence, it was not decided to have a counterpart for amateurs until 1885, by which time Ball might have won a handful, judging by his early attempts at the Open, in which he first competed in 1878, coming only a few shots behind the winner. At the age of seventeen, he had finished equal 4th. This was a considerable feat.

The first Amateur Championship was seven years away, and Ball had put his amateur status in jeopardy by his achievements at the age of seventeen. In the 1878 Open he had accepted a few shillings in prize money, an event which caused a few heart-searchings, as no one had expected an amateur to feature and it was shortly enacted that no amateur could accept prize money.

John Ball won his first Amateur in 1888 and his greatest year followed closely in 1890. He then won the Amateur again and took the Open with a two-round total of 164, with a pair of 82s, three better than his runner-up. Today, it may not sound at all impressive but previous winners at the same course, Prestwick, had recorded 161, 160, 170, 157, 166, 166 back to 1872. Only Young Tom Morris had done better, with winning scores successively of 157, 154, 149 and 166.

By his win in 1890, John Ball became the first amateur and the first Englishman to win both championships and the only man, other than Bobby Jones in 1930, to win both in the same year. He was also the first Englishman to win the Open.

As year followed year, he continued long to dominate the Amateur Championship, winning again in 1892, 1894, 1899, 1907, 1910 and 1912. The gap of 24 years between his first and last wins easily remains a record.

Few details have come down in golf history of the features of his play that made all this possible. J.H. Taylor, for instance, is often credited with being the first man to develop the ability to hit high, stopping iron shots to the flag. It is more likely that it was John Ball who led the way, in an age when golf was primarily a game played with wooden clubs of various lofts. I believe that he was the first man to abandon the notion that you should keep the ball low under the wind from a closed stance and instead struck irons from a notably open stance with a high flight. Despite this, he relished playing in wind and during his last entry in the Amateur Championship at the age of 60 he had the feeling that he might win it again if only the winds would sweep over Hoylake from the Welsh Hills. Alas, it stayed calm, but John Ball still reached the 6th round.

How well Ball's abilities survived into middle age can be seen by his achievements in the years leading up to World War I. In the semi-finals of 1910, Ball faced the 23-year-old Abe Mitchell, who was soon, with George Duncan, to be recognised as the best British golfer, either amateur or professional. Ball defeated him by 5 and 4. Then he met C.C. Aylmer, not one of the great names of amateur golf but a man who had just knocked out Harold Hilton, who the following year was to become the only British player to take the British and US amateur championships in the same year. Ball, at nearly 50, had a long walk back to the clubhouse: he won by 10 and 9!

John Ball

The year 1912 saw his last victory. His ability to fight back was well illustrated in a 5th round match. Standing five down with just seven holes to go, his win remains one of the most dramatic recoveries of golf history in so little breathing space. In the final, again against Abe Mitchell, Ball won on the 38th.

By these two wins, Ball had provided two proofs that I think we need to judge the supreme stature of a golfer: his game had lasted and, by beating Mitchell twice, he had bridged a generation gap. Ball had beaten his great contemporaries repeatedly and in his victories over Abe Mitchell he had overcome one of the two great British golfers of the 1920s, arguably the best player not to win the Open.

Ball's almost unprecedentedly long career at the top of amateur golf must have been greatly assisted by his long, free swing: if in youth you do not take the club back far there is little to be played with when the joints and sinews stiffen. This long swing enabled him to hit the ball a long way. He was perhaps about 35 yards shorter with his driver than Douglas Rolland, the longest hitter at the turn of the century. This meant that Ball moved it along about 200 yards, which was extremely good with the gutta percha ball in use till the revolution caused by the wound Haskell ball from 1902 onwards.

By chance, Ball had a little to do with the popularisation of the new ball. He gave one to Sandy Herd, who declared he would not use the thing; had a practice drive with it; found he had produced the longest drive he had ever hit and was an instant convert! He used it throughout the 72 holes of the 1902 Open and at the end had become Open Champion for the only time in his long career. I wonder what his fellow competitors thought about it because Sandy was the only player with a Haskell but there is nothing to wonder about in the consequences: the gutta percha was dead and golf a more pleasant if easier game.

There are few stories of John Ball, however. He let his clubs do the talking and was often shy and of few words when he did speak. His opinions, nevertheless, were strong. Throughout his career he refused to use a niblick (the rough equivalent of a heavier 8 or 9 iron) which he referred to as 'another bloody spade'. For bunker and other lofted shots Ball preferred to lay back the face of a mid iron. If we were to see him in action today, no doubt we should relish the fluency and rhythm of his game but in many essentials his swing was typical of his era and would have needed modification for today's equipment. The clubhead went far back beyond the horizontal and the shaft appeared to touch the right shoulder, while the shoulder turn itself was so full that Ball was just able to see the ball from the corner of his left eye when the near 180 degree turn was complete. The hip turn was about 90 degrees and he came up on the toes of his left foot and rocked over on the edge of his right. His left-hand grip would meet the conventions of today but the grip rested in the palm of his right hand and in the vee between thumb and forefinger. Nearly all this, of course, derived from the characteristics of hickory as opposed to steel shafts: the swing had to be exceptionally full by modern standards so that speed to impact could be built up in a gradual and unforced way. If there was brute force, the whip of hickory was impossible to control consistently.

Severiano Ballesteros

Born Pedrena, Spain, 1957

With the slight decline in the successes of Jack Nicklaus in world golf there is plenty of argument about who is the current best golfer in the world. Is it still Nicklaus, who now has far greater variety of shot than in his earlier years and is the most consistent from tee to green? Has the consistency of Ray Floyd in the past couple of years and a 1982 that included a dominant performance in the US PGA and victory in the Sun City $1 Million Challenge entitled him to consideration? (Many of his contemporaries think he is playing the best consistent golf of anyone.) Or is it Tom Watson, miles ahead as a money winner cumulatively in the period 1977-82, who in 1982 won his first US Open and his fourth British since 1975 and brought his major championship total to seven. Or Severiano Ballesteros, the best of the younger generation beyond dispute and with two major championships under his belt by the age of 23, followed in 1983 by a second US Masters?

Everyone will have his own opinion but few other names could be added to our query list. There is, however, surely no dispute about who is the most exciting. It is Ballesteros all the way, perhaps in golf history matched only by the engaging recovery play and charm of Walter Hagen in the 1920s or the crash, bang drama of Arnold Palmer in the 1960s.

So in what lies the appeal of the young Spaniard? First there is the full golf swing. When he first appeared on the scene it was thought by some students of the game to be rather a bad one. The problem, such people thought, was the flying right elbow. Conventional instruction has said since the lore began to be set down in writing (though early Scottish golfers did not practise it) that the right elbow should stay close to the side in the backswing. One tip was that, to check on this, the golfer should place a handkerchief in this position, where it should remain. Few criticised Nicklaus, however, when he broke the rule. The man was too immediately successful for that. Ballesteros also was thought to stand too far from the ball. In club golfers, this produces a groping lean-forward from the hips, accompanied by a bent back. In Ballesteros, however, the result was to allow him space for what was soon recognised to be the most uninhibited lash at the ball yet seen in a major player. He is amongst the longest drivers in the world and is rated by Jack Nicklaus as the longest hitter with a 1-iron that he has seen.

However, the Spaniard's swing is seen at its best when he is not hitting at full throttle. When, for instance, he is playing a shaped approach shot, perhaps a drifting right to left mid-iron or a high-floating sand iron approach. In these instances, the free, full swing may still be there but more apparent to onlookers is the easy acceleration into the ball, the deft use of hands and perfect balance through the hitting zone. When he hits, full out, the shot is still well balanced but club velocity at the end of the follow-through seems to cause a bounce off the full finish.

There is, indeed, a very great contrast between Ballesteros full out and the short game expert. In the latter, one can see how much of a 'hands' player he is, able to control trajectory and draw or fade shots more effectively than any other current player. Indeed, he is almost an oddity in these days when even club golfers strive to be a golf machine playing the same swing for every stroke, letting the number on the clubhead decide the distance achieved. All this breaks down when a full shot is not required, the point at which Ballesteros's feel for the clubhead and hand-eye co-ordination most come into effect. Youthful practice and competition with his fellow caddies for pesetas developed touch and experience. Wherever Ballesteros gets himself on a golf course near the green he has past experience of how to coax a ball from every kind of lie to draw on. Similarly, in bunker play he has the ability to play a considerable variety of shots, rather than the one standard stroke relied on by so many players.

In the future, his putting is, I think, quite likely to prove troublesome. More of the acknowledged present leading experts, Ben Crenshaw, Bob Charles, Bill Rogers, Tom Watson and Jerry Pate, favour a basically straight-arm action. This draws its feel for distance not from the hands but forearms, upper arms and even shoulders. Ballesteros poises himself fairly low over the ball and the arms are bent. There is no harm at all in this while the nerves last but when the wear and tear of tournament play has its effect this method, which relies on the small muscles, is very likely to be affected by stress.

Ballesteros first appeared on the European scene in 1974 and began to make some impression on his fellow players at the end of that season. He was unnoticed by the British press, who were naturally more on the look-out for British promise, or the Spanish, who were little interested in golfing. However, as Peter Oosterhuis was finishing his European career with wins in the Italian and El Paraiso Opens, the 17½-year-old Spaniard was finishing 5th and 17th in those two events and following with another 5th place behind Gary Player, Peter Townsend, Jerry Heard and Tony Jacklin in the Ibergolf tournament in Madrid. Characteristically, in the two-round event he had a 79 and 69 to be three behind the winning total, his 69 at Las Lomas being the best round. He was 118th in the year's Order of Merit and had won himself £2,915. He had played just 13 tournament rounds, averaging a little under 75 a time.

His apprenticeship continued through 1975, though his brother Manuel continued to be the better known player. Severiano moved up to 26th in the Order of Merit and about £5,000 in money winnings. In 1976 he began with good finishes in the Portuguese, Spanish, Madrid and French Opens, but for a while did less well when the Tour moved to Britain. Suddenly at Royal Birkdale he became a name. After one round he was tied for the lead with the Japanese Norio Suzuki and Christy O'Connor Junior. In the second round they both fell away but Ballesteros did not. He had another 69 to lead Johnny Miller by two strokes, and kept the same margin after another round. Could the impossible happen and a player three months past his nineteenth birthday win the Open?

Ballesteros had been playing the kind of golf that was shortly to become well known. Huge drives were sometimes followed by a trudge into the sand hills, but his recoveries from wild country were prodigious. If, like Miller, he had switched to his 1-iron from the tee victory might have come. Yet Miller played finely for his 66 that final day. After eleven holes Ballesteros was out of it. Miller cruised serenely home and Ballesteros secured a joint second place with Jack Nicklaus by finishing eagle, birdie.

He was now on his way and was the most successful European player for the rest of the season, winning first the Dutch Open, then the Lancome and being leading money winner, with the best stroke average. With Manuel Pinero, Spain won the World Cup. He

Severiano Ballesteros PGA, Sandwich, 1983

followed by again being number 1 in Europe in 1977, but became truly an international star by winning outside in New Zealand and taking the Japan Open and the Japan Dunlop Phoenix. The pattern was the same the following year. Again he took the Japan Open, won in Africa and had his first US Tour victory, the Greater Greensboro'. By the end of 1978 he had won fifteen events in his career.

By the standards he had been setting, 1979 was a bad year. He won only twice: in the English Golf Classic and the British Open Championship. It had been thought that an accurate driver would win at Royal Lytham because the rough was particularly testing. Ballesteros hit few fairways, as did the neat Hale Irwin; but it was an American that cracked this time, Irwin subsiding to a 78 in the final round. Ballesteros was the first continental European to win the Open since Arnaud Massy in 1907 and the youngest since Young Tom Morris won in 1872.

Well within the year, he was US Masters champion also, giving perhaps his best performance in any event. He began with a 66 to share the lead and was three ahead after a second round 69 and then seven with a 68. Obviously the Masters was his and a breaking of the record total 271 set by Jack Nicklaus and Ray Floyd was in prospect. In the fourth round, Ballesteros pushed his lead to ten and then from the 11th to 13th holes dropped five shots, being twice in water. The gap with the rest of the field, all playing for second place, had narrowed fast but there were no more alarms. Ballesteros was soon the youngest ever wearer of the green jacket as Masters champion.

By this time, some of Ballesteros's publicity was beginning to be less favourable. In a long television interview, for example, he made one remark to the effect that he owed golf nothing. This did not go down well. There seems to be a convention that those who win fame or fortune from a sport 'owe' it something. Ballesteros's opinion was that he had worked very hard for his success and that the interest in golf he aroused had done quite a lot for the sport. He also declined to play for Spain in the World Cup. Those that thought this unpatriotic were often unaware that in several golfing nations this was becoming almost the norm as the event declined in prestige. In 1982, for instance, Faldo and Lyle did not play for England and Scotland respectively and the first to accept for the USA were Calvin Peete and Bob Gilder, who were well up the money list but not of the class of Stadler, Floyd, Watson, Nicklaus, Wadkins, and Kite; these golfers were mostly playing in the Sun City £1 Million Challenge, as was Severiano Ballesteros.

In Europe, there were quarrels about appearance money, to which Ballesteros was not entitled under the rules as from 1979 he ceased to be top money winner. In 1981, he resigned from the Tournament Players Division though he was soon back.

After the US Masters, his highest-ranking successes have been in the World Matchplay Championship at Wentworth. In 1981 he crushed Hale Irwin, Greg Norman and Berhard Langer in succession and was champion after a close final with Ben Crenshaw. Ballesteros had consistently played easily the best golf of the week and had taken some shine from any thoughts that Greg Norman and Berhard Langer might be acknowledged as the best players on the European Tour. Ballesteros was around 25 under par for the eight rounds he played at Wentworth and had become the first European golfer to win the event, previously dominated by Americans and Gary Player.

His next Matchplay win in 1982 saw a less dominant performance from the Spaniard. He beat Clampett 2 and 1, Wadkins 3 and 1 and then faced Sandy Lyle in the final, who had gone round Wentworth in an approximate 63 to turn a six hole deficit against Nick Faldo into victory. With six holes left in the 36 hole final, Ballesteros was 3 up but Lyle suddenly began sinking unlikely putts for a 3, 2, 4, 2 sequence and the match was square, as it remained after the full 36 holes. The 1st hole at Wentworth, a long par 4, with an uphill second shot that must carry all the way to the green, had not been birdied all week and the green had seldom been hit in two. Lyle outdrove Ballesteros by some 20 yards, as he had done frequently in the match, and put a long iron some 5 yards from the hole while Ballesteros's 3-wood was some 10 yards away. He holed for a birdie; Lyle missed.

At the end of 1982, Ballesteros had won some twenty-eight major events and his total world money winnings were well over $1½ million. His game had changed. The driving remained long, but the full fling of the club at the ball was less evident and he used an iron for safety far more often. Some also felt that his short game was not so outstanding. On the other side of the balance, he was much less likely to fling strokes away with wild shots.

He is, then, at a point of transition from young gallant to mature campaigner. It will be a matter of some fascination to see how his golfing character and performance develop. Twenty-six in 1983, he had won some dozen more professional tournaments than Nicklaus at the same age, but Nicklaus had four major championships to Ballesteros's two Masters and British Open. Perhaps motivation — which Nicklaus has long directed towards the major championships — will decide. If Ballesteros has the desire to be one of the great golfers of history then certainly none in the past has so young demonstrated more outstanding natural gifts and seasoned ability.

At Augusta on 19 April 1983 he scattered the pride of America when he started the final round birdie, eagle, par, birdie and went to the turn in 31. He did not falter during the final stretch in contrast to his performance in the 1980 Masters, and when he outrageously chipped in on the last hole he was champion by the same emphatic four-stroke margin as his previous victory.

Ballesteros was a contender throughout the championship and his driving, very long and much straighter than it is often though to be, was a key to the victory. It led to his being no less than ten under par for the four rounds on the par 5s.

The US golf world was then much taken aback when the Spaniard apologised for being unable to play in the Tournament of Champions which began shortly afterwards. He explained that he had a prior engagement for the Madrid Open. In fact, he planned to play little more in the US for the rest of the season, just the US Open, US PGA and the Westchester Classic, taking the last of these on his next US appearance shortly after winning the European PGA!

Americans regard the US Tour as the centre of the golf stage but Ballesteros sees himself as an international golfer, as do few except the top Australians and South Africans.

Ballesteros is gifted with more variety of shot than any of his contemporaries. He has a particular gift for curving the ball, and the ability to hit high or low at will. There are many judges that would argue that no contemporary or indeed predecessor has been so outstanding for the contrasting talents of prodigious power and subtlety.

If Tom Watson is the world's number 1, Ballesteros is comfortably his closest rival and poised to overhaul him.

Michael
Bonallack

Born Chigwell, Essex, England 1934

On Saturday, 29 July 1968 in the final of the English Amateur Championship
Michael Bonallack played perhaps the finest round of golf ever produced by an
Englishman. The setting was Ganton near Scarborough, a course of 6,905 yards at
the time, with a par of 71. This is how Bonallack went: 3, 3, 3, 4, 3, 4, 4, 4, 4, 2, 3, 3,
3, 4, 4, 3, 3, 4. He had gone round in 61: out in 32, home in 29. Yet it was still not
a perfect round, which is almost always assessed in terms of hitting all the
fairways and reaching all the greens in the right number of strokes. Nowadays,
this includes hitting the par 5s in two, making Ganton a theoretical par of 69.

Bonallack marred his round by missing the 4th, 7th, 9th and 15th greens. We
might also think he ought to have hit the 14th with his drive for it is definitely
reachable, even though tightly bunkered. In golf, what seems to be perfect can
always be improved upon. The round highlights Bonallack's single greatest
strength: putting. He took only 24 putts and he got down five times from a
distance that he would not usually expect. Of course, the 24 was and is by no
means a record. Tom Watson, who has had years of averaging only a little over 28
for his efforts on the US Tour, has achieved the figure several times. The
minimum, as far as I have been able to discover, is held for US events by Sam
Trahan, with 18, who qualified for the US Tour for a single year only; and in
Europe, where such records have only recently been kept, I suspect an Open
Championship round by a little known golfer called Stan Taggart some fifty years
ago, again using 18 only, probably holds the unofficial field.

Bonallack's putting method was very distinctive. He spread his legs wide, bent
over his club shaft and had his nose almost touching the end, giving the
appearance almost of sniffing at both ball and line to the hole. Thereafter, his
'method' was extremely simple: he believed that the golfer should 'will' the ball
into the hole. There may well be more to this theory than appears at first sight.
For most golfers, most of the time, approach most putts with fear as the main
emotion. They are afraid, on long putts, of hitting the ball too far or too short,
while in the 2 foot to 4 foot range fear of missing predominates. At best, there is
the hope of getting the thing to drop, not the Bonallack tunnel-visioned exercise
of will power.

Of course, he won that English Amateur. His opponent, David Kelley, had
decided that his match strategy would be to ignore Bonallack and concentrate on
trying to play strict par golf. If he could manage that, Kelley though, he could not
go far wrong. Kelley succeeded very well, not dropping his first stroke until the

Michael Bonallack (left) wins the 1969 Amateur Golf Championship

14th, but by that time, Bonallack, as can be seen from his card, had just produced a sequence of five holes in birdies and an eagle and had also begun his round with three birdies in a row. Kelley was seven down. Shortly after the lunch break Bonallack was champion by 12 and 11, a record margin of victory in the English Amateur, his hole-by-hole figures only equalled by the golf of the American Lawson Little when eclipsing James Wallace by 14 and 13 in the final of the 1934 British Amateur at Prestwick.

There is no question of Bonallack's 61 being in itself a record, for it was played under match not stroke play rules (little though they differ) and a couple of little putts were conceded by his opponent. Nevertheless, he established many records in British amateur golf: outstandingly so in the British Amateur, the championship which Jones thought the most difficult of the major championships to win, making several unsuccessful attempts before he came through after close matches in 1930. Bonallack won this five times, against what most would agree was stiffer competition than prevailed in Jones's day. His first win came in 1961 at Turnberry and in 1965 he won a close match at Royal Porthcawl over Clive Clark, now a TV golf commentator. In 1969, he began an unparalleled sequence of three wins in a row. First he beat Irishman Joe Carr, then aged 46 and the finest amateur of the previous generation, by 7 and 6, being about eight under par for the holes played. His victim in both 1969 and 1970 was the fine American amateur, Bill Hyndman, who went down at Hoylake by 3 and 2 and at

Newcastle, County Down, by 8 and 7. No one in the history of the event had managed to win three consecutive times and since World War II only Joe Carr has been a three-times winner. The overall record belongs to John Ball with eight wins, the last of which came in 1912. Even he did not win two in a row.

Even if Nicklaus had remained an amateur and contested this championship throughout his career he might not have bettered Bonallack's record. My reason for what might seem to be an extreme opinion is that many of the matches are played over 18 holes. Over so short a stretch, our master golfer has to be only a little below his sharpest or an opponent enjoy a spurt of good play or luck to find himself using his most gracious loser's smile. Even over 36 holes, matchplay is still highly unpredictable, so much so that many of today's superstars have a marked distaste for it. They prefer the more prolonged test of 72 holes of consistent strokeplay and, perhaps, saying 'I came fourth, just two strokes behind the winner', rather than the simpler and more humiliating 'I was beaten' of matchplay.

Bonallack had an equally fine record in the English Amateur, also a matchplay event. He reached six finals from 1959 to 1968 and lost only in the first of these years, to Guy Wolstenholme. His five victories are a record and he is also the only man to have won two in succession twice with his 1962-3 and 1967-8 championships.

The remaining key event for amateurs in Britain is the English Amateur Strokeplay Championship, an event open to all nationalities (formerly known as the Brabazon Trophy). Bonallack finished in first place in 1964, 1968, 1969 and 1971. His four victories are, again, a record.

His only failure was in the Walker Cup, in which he won only three singles and lost eight. Despite being the best amateur over the years 1959-73 in Britain or America he must have suffered from always being a man expected to win and had also usually to play at the top of the order. Also, perhaps, there was the fact that his opponents were particularly on their mettle when facing Bonallack.

It is interesting to speculate on what Bonallack might have achieved had he turned professional. The gap between top amateur golf and top professional is not as great as has sometimes been argued. In the recent past, such players as Townsend, Clark, Faldo and James have quickly made the transition and we saw Gordon Brand Jnr and Ronan Rafferty win events in their first 1982 season. Bonallack has given his own reason: he did not become a good enough player until past 25 and he felt he was by then 'too old'.

Few doubt that he would have been a great success: he brought to competitive golf mental toughness that no modern British professional has excelled. He was also able to compile a good score when playing comparatively badly through the green. During the week of the English Amateur that climaxed with the 61, he complained that his swing had so many faults in it that he didn't know where the ball was going. But in this state (by which Bonallack really meant that he was not striking the ball well and, for example, could not produce a consistent fade) he still always scored quite well because he was seldom wild and, when he missed the greens, was remorseless to an opponent in getting down in two. This was something he once did no fewer than twenty-two times in the final of one English Amateur!

James Braid

Born Elie, Fife, Scotland, 1870

While both Taylor and Vardon won the Open Championship as unknowns, the third member of the Great Triumvirate, James Braid, had to struggle for some years before he broke through. One reason was that they both began as good to fair putters and, in Vardon's case, deteriorated, while Braid had his difficulties on the greens. These difficulties were not overcome until he suddenly discovered an aluminium-headed putter that suited him, and thereafter he rapidly became just about the best putter in the country.

Braid was brought up in prime golfing country and was apprenticed to a joiner. He was a scratch golfer by his mid-teens and his game improved further when he moved to St Andrews and had the opportunity to play with some of the leading players of the time.

In 1893 he moved to London and a job as clubmaker in a famous department store, the Army and Navy. His play further improved as he was able to play on Sundays, having escaped from the Scottish Sabbath. He played an exhibition match against Douglas Rolland, not an Open champion but very nearly one (second in 1894) and played his first Open at Sandwich, the first time the championship was staged outside Scotland, in 1894. He finished well up the field in the year of Taylor's first win.

By 1896, Braid was a professional with a club job at Romford and in that year's Open at Muirfield he finished sixth, seven strokes behind the play-off between Vardon and Taylor. The following year, at Hoylake, he did more to establish himself. With a 74, he had the lowest round amongst the high finishers and had a last-green putt to tie Harold Hilton, a great amateur who had won already in 1892. He failed but had at least come in five strokes ahead of Vardon, the previous year's champion.

He had good placings the following two years and in 1900 the Great Triumvirate occupied the top three places for the first time. Alas for Braid, it was Taylor, Vardon and Braid, thirteen strokes separating first and third places.

In 1901, the same three led the field, but this time with Braid's name at the head of the list. He was the longest hitter of the trio, credited with 'divine fury' when he struck the ball and, having found his putter, was about to embark on his great years. From 1901 to 1910, Braid won the Open five times, becoming, incidentally, the first man to do so. Each time his margin of victory was a comfortable one. In 1901 he beat Vardon by three and in his second championship at St Andrews in 1905, Taylor was five strokes in his wake. When he won

James Braid

consecutively at Muirfield in 1906 it was by four from Taylor and five from Vardon. Perhaps just as significant, however, had been his performance at Sandwich while coming second in 1904. Braid began moderately with 77, 80 but in the third round became the first man to break 70 in the Open. He followed with a 71 and a total of 297, a good enough score to have won any previous Open. A lesser known figure, however, Jack White of Sunningdale, played the golf of his life to finish 72, 69 and win by a stroke. It is said that Braid thought he had to finish with four pars for a 71 to tie, and did so.

His finest performance came in 1908 at Prestwick. He began with a couple of 3s, got to the turn in 33 and finished in 70. He didn't lead with this score for an unknown had surprised himself with a 68. More important was the fact that Vardon, Taylor and Ray had all taken 79. In the second round, Braid was again at the turn in 33, including four successive 3s, and was round in 72 for a six-stroke lead on Sandy Herd and an unknown. Taylor was out of it and Vardon fifteen behind. On the morning of the final day Braid suffered his only crisis, being both bunkered and out of bounds, and recording an 8. Nevertheless he was still round in about par for that period, 77, and few gained on him. He took a six stroke lead into the final round and a 72 saw him winner by the very large margin of eight strokes. His 291 was only the fourth time that 300 had been broken in the Open and can be compared to Vardon's winning score of 300 on the same course in 1903. It remained the Open record until equalled by Bobby Jones at Royal Lytham in 1926 and beaten by him with 285 at St Andrews the year after.

Braid finished second to Taylor in the following year and won his final championship at St Andrews in 1910. His score of 299 was ten strokes lower than the St Andrews record and gave him a win by four from Sandy Herd.

At about this time James Braid's eyesight, thought to have been damaged by lime in his late teens began to give him trouble. His best finish, in the years before World War I put a stop to championship golf and brought the careers of all the Great Triumvirate to a virtual end, was third at Muirfield in 1912 — eight behind Ted Ray's winning score.

However, he was by this time past forty and it likely that both his long hitting and putting were on the wane. He had enjoyed an unparalled run of success when competition was at its keenest in British golf. Besides his pre-eminence in the British Open in 1901-10, he had been just as effective in the PGA Matchplay Championship. He won the first time it was staged in 1903 and his fourth win came in 1911. With the far greater public interest in matches, rather than stroke tournaments, the event ranked little below the Open in status. During his peak years, James Braid was as formidable competitor in either form of the game. He was also beaten finalist in 1913 and 1927. The latter occasion was particularly remarkable, for Braid was 57. It was perhaps not surprising that he lost heavily there to Archie Compston, at the time one of the very best British players and 1925 champion.

During and after his playing days, Braid was highly active, as were many players, as a golf course architect, concentrating on making the best use of the natural landscape in days when horse, cart and plough were the tools of the trade. Unlike today, he would expect only to shape greens, site bunkers and build teeing areas. Most of his courses have been much changed from his original designs, to suit longer hitting.

After his early professional years at Romford, Braid moved to Walton Heath Golf Club in 1904 and thereafter was part of the scenery, being also made an honorary member twenty-five years before his death in 1950. He was also amongst the group of three professionals who were the first to be made honorary members of the R and A.

As Braid's performance in the 1927 PGA Matchplay shows, he kept his game into late middle age and, when in good form, was able to compete with far younger men. This indicates that such players as Vardon, Taylor, Sandy Herd and himself, who reached an early peak in the Victorian Age, were not a whit inferior to those who came after.

At Walton Heath, there was the annual 'ceremony', at which the press would gather, to see whether or not he could 'beat his age' on his birthday. More often than not he did and was several strokes under at the age of 78.

Billy
Casper

Born San Diego, California, 1931

'As colourless as a glass of water.'

'If you couldn't putt, you'd be selling hotdogs outside the ropes.'

The first is a remark by the highly colourful tournament player Dave Hill; the second is ascribed to Ben Hogan. In both cases the subject was William Earl Casper Jnr and both comments go some way towards explaining why this golfer has never quite achieved the status and renown that his playing performances entitled him to.

Casper had a matter-of-fact approach to each shot: a walk up to the ball, a couple of casual practice flicks and then away it went. There was little drama in the performance; watchers tended to feel they were witnessing little more than a journeyman going about his everyday business. Those interviewing Casper found him similarly bland and, if not unquotable, certainly not memorably quotable. The fact that he was allergic to a wide variety of foods, but could tolerate buffalo steaks, came to be seen as the most interesting characteristic of one of the last generation's great golfers. He also followed the Mormon religion and was rather active in the work of that church at a local level. It was difficult indeed out of these straws to build a hero image.

Hogan's judgement was even more cruel and perhaps, coming in that maestro's later years, it reflected his bitterness at his own increasing failure on the greens and some envy of Casper's famed prowess there.

For Casper was a master, ranked with Bob Charles and Deane Beman, as the best putter in the game from the late 1950s to early 1970s. His technique was, in part, highly unorthodox. Many, earlier this century, used primarily a wristy stroke for the difficult business of getting the ball into the hole but by Casper's time it had become almost universally accepted that such a method was unreliable in a crisis, involved the added complication of the player having to combine both arm and wrist action for longer putts and, worst of all, meant that it was impossible for the putter head to be kept close to the ground on the backswing.

Casper felt that, provided the palms of both hands were precisely opposed, with the back of the left and palm of the right directly on line with the hole, the hingeing wrist movement is near infallible for directing a golf ball along the chosen line. It also, he considered, gives the player a greater sense of 'feel' than does the basically arm method of, say, Crenshaw or Watson, or the Bob Charles shoulder action. He further thought that his method of striking imparted overspin to the ball. In this opinion he was certainly wrong for it is impossible to

Billy Casper

putt a ball with overspin. However the ball is struck it will skid away just off the ground for the first part of its journey and then roll.

Any club imparts various amounts of backspin, removed quickly or on the second and third bounce when the ball hits the ground. However, it is certainly possible to impart more backspin to a putt by use of an above standard putter loft or hitting a descending blow. Casper believed he imparted overspin; in fact he had succeeded in keeping backspin to a level which felt like overspin to him, and the less backspin the better, especially in judging length.

These technicalities apart, whatever Casper thought he did to the ball, he certainly got it into the hole very consistently indeed. While winning the 1959 US Open he used his putter only 114 times and, in his repeat 1966 win, 117 times. That represents 28.25 and 28.75 per round respectively, figures that Casper himself has quoted with some pride. They can be compared with what another great putter, Bobby Locke, thought represented an exceptionally good round, and the year's low averaging putter on the US Tour for the years 1980-2 has produced similar figures.

Casper turned professional in 1954 and joined the US Tour in 1956. After a couple of years of acclimatising himself, he became a prolific money winner. Between 1958 and 1970 he was eleven times amongst the leading four money winners and several times won four or more Tour events in a year. Twice, in 1966 and 1968, he was the year's leading money winner, in the latter year topping $200,000, the first man to do so (Nicklaus first accomplished this increasingly easier feat as late in his career as 1972). Casper's first US tournament win came in 1956 and his last in 1975. Most significantly, he was winner of the Vardon Trophy in 1960, 1963, 1965, 1966 and 1968. The Vardon is awarded for the year's lowest stroke average and Casper's five awards are a record he shares with Lee Trevino, while in comparison, Nicklaus, hardly an inconsistent player, has not won it.

In the major championships, Casper achieved rather less than the level of his other performances would have suggested. The US Open came to him early in his career at Winged Foot. After rounds of 71, 68, 69, he went into the last round with a four stroke lead on Palmer and Bob Rosburg (an equally good putter) and held on to beat Rosburg by a single stroke. He was next well placed in this event in 1964, when he finished fourth; then came the remarkable 1966 encounter with Arnold Palmer, recalled in my account of that far more charismatic figure. Casper's other high placing came with another fourth place in 1967.

Casper did not make a real effort to win the British Open until towards the end of his best years, and only once came close to winning. This was in 1968 at Carnoustie, in a year dominated by Player, whom Casper led by five after two rounds and by two going into the last round before collapsing to a 78 and fourth place.

The Augusta National course was said to highlight the disadvantages of Casper's conservative style of play. On the four par 5s, it is usually considered that the player must go for the green with his second shot, usually over water, in order to pick up the birdie that is then on offer. Casper's approach was to play short with his second and then try to lob his pitch close enough for him to single putt. Winners are usually well under par (though not always — Craig Stadler was not in 1982, while Ray Floyd in 1976 was thirteen under). This is one of the more thrilling aspects of championship golf at Augusta: the golfer is not merely 'trying to get up' in two; he will be in water if he fails.

Casper was fourth in 1960 and then in 1969 he led for three days after an opening 66 before taking 40 to the turn on the last day and finishing joint second. In 1970, he made amends. Again he led into the last round with scores of 72, 68, 68 (going for the greens with his second shot on the par 5s) and eventually tied with Gene Littler, beating him in the play-off fairly conclusively by 69-74.

He did not succeed in winning the US PGA — though he was three times second — so his tally of only three major championships is in contrast to his 51 US Tour wins, a total which puts him behind only Snead, Nicklaus, Hogan, Palmer and Nelson. As a money winner, he was the second man (after Arnold Palmer) to reach $1 million in career winnings on the US Tour.

Whatever his failings and achievements there is little doubt that Billy Casper proved himself the most consistent player of modern times.

Bob
—— Charles ——

Born Carterton, New Zealand, 1936

When Bob Charles first began to swing a golf club, like most other beginners, he had to beg a club from his father, a man who happened to be left-handed. From this chance grew the career of the only man to win a major championship who swung on the left side of his body. An irony is that Bob Charles is not a natural left-hander at all: in everything else, he uses the right.

Probably because I am a left-sided player myself, I have given some idle hours to wondering what can explain an almost total lack of success by my brethren. In any other sport, it will be found that left-handed performers of the highest quality crop up about in proportion to their lower numbers. Tennis, for instance, has what many consider the best ever in Rod Laver; and on today's scene Connors, Navratilova, McEnroe and Tanner make up as good a group as you can find. The famous left-handers in such sports as baseball and cricket, which are at least similar to the extent that something is swung or flung from the same side of the body, are legion and include some of their most legendary performers: the same applies to virtually every sport.

Why does this not occur in golf, which is almost unique in that an opponent's play has no direct physical influence? A golfer merely stands on a patch of ground and moves a ball on to another. The course has no opinion of its own about the rightness or wrongness of a left-hander treading its greens and fairways. Yet there must be something that has denied left-handers more than minimal successes.

Until recent years, the explanation was a simple one. If twenty or so years ago you had gone to visit a professional and informed him that you had decided to take up the game and that you were left-handed, the chances are he would have said (a) golf was a bit like hockey and only right-hand sticks were made; (b) few makers produced left-hand clubs and those available were of inferior quality; (c) if you bought left-hand clubs you'd never be able to sell them; (d) (by far the most frequent) the left hand is by far the more important and most golfers never escape from being excessively right-side dominant. Why not begin correctly with a head start? Swing from the right-side but lead into the ball with your naturally dominant left.

I've seen nineteenth-century left-hand clubs so objection (a) has, for our purposes, been dismissed and (b) and (c), though less extreme, are subject to the same criticism. But (d) was and is an enticing one. Were not both the great guru Hogan and Johnny Miller left-handed?

They were indeed, but what of the countless who appeared on our professional's doorstep as self-confessed right-handers? Did he ever give them the benefit of the same words, but substituting 'left' for 'right'? Never. So, with some regret, we can leave our not at all mythical professional's preaching out of this.

The answer, briefly, is that it *must* be the golf courses which are 'against' left-handers. Golf is a highly sensual game, its prime appeal being to the sight. In most sports, the action occupies but a split second. There is no time to stand and stare, not at least without risking a sharp crack on shin or knuckle or being more comprehensively swept aside. Yet this is what good, or even moderate, golf is mainly concerned with: the contemplation of the drive bold against the sky, a crisply struck iron shot plummetting down on the flag, even a long putt precisely following the calculated undulations of a green and slowing to nestle at the holeside.

The courses are designed by right-handed golfers, with the result that the perspective from tee to fairway, place-ment of bunkers and even decisions as to which trees to leave in situ are all calculated to please the eye of the man and woman who stand with the left leg advanced before the right. The influ-ence this has is probably most clear on par-3 holes. Invariably, from the tee a green appears offset to the right, leaving a left-hander feeling that he is required to aim at a target which has a tendency to be hiding away behind his

Bob Charles

back. All this ought to have only a slight influence, for, as I said earlier, the aim of each stroke in golf is the clear-out one of hitting a ball from one point to another. But golfers as a group whether left or right handed, are affected by such slight distractions. How often have you heard a player complain that he has hit his drive off line, for instance, because the tee markers were 'pointing in the wrong direction'? It would be my argument that for most of the time these subtle distractions lower the performance of left-handers and it is only on the greens that they are fully equal with the rest.

Perhaps it is no coincidence, then, that Bob Charles is thought by many to be the best putter who has ever lived; aspects of his method are the most imitated of any. What, however, is the Charles method? It is a very simple one; and simplicity is a great deal of the secret of his success. His action is one-piece. Charles himself feels that the putting stroke is a pivoting action from a point in the middle of the back of his neck. The shoulders tilt and the arms go back in unison; no wrist break is perceptible. The absence of wrist action is a common factor today in the method of all the great putters, the ball being hit via the muscles of the upper arms rather than by an unhingeing movement of the wrists. Observe Tom Watson and Ben Crenshaw, currently the two best putters in the world.

Bob Charles's finest hour was of course his one major championship victory in the 1963 British Open at Royal Lytham and St Anne's. He began finely with 68, 72 to be no fewer than five behind American Phil Rodgers, himself a short-game expert, and who later gave a series of lessons to Jack Nicklaus before his 1980 revival. Peter Thomson (four strokes), Jack Nicklaus (two) and Kel Nagle (one) were also ahead of him. Third rounds have often been said to be particularly vital in major championships though this has become less true since champions have had to produce four good rounds to win. In the morning of the third and final day (36 holes were played the last day until 1966), Charles swept through the field with a 66, while of the contenders mentioned, the next lowest round came from Jack Nicklaus, with a 70. Rogers and Nagle fell away to 73s and Thomson had a 71. Charles went into the last hours with a lead of one stroke on Thomson, two on Rogers, while Nicklaus was also poised a couple of strokes behind and in good form. Nicklaus was the year's Masters champion and later took the US PGA.

The betting men's money was mostly on Nicklaus, who was recognised as a golfing phenomenon and who at twenty-three already had two major championships to his credit. Peter Thomson, who had been placed first or second in the Open every year from 1952 to 1958, was also favoured and had one more championship left in him, the 1965 Open. However, this year Thomson fell away badly and eventually finished with a 78 in fifth place. Nicklaus did not and finished in 70 for a 278 total. However, he had made up only a stroke on Bob Charles's 71 and finished a stroke behind the play-off between Charles and Phil Rodgers, who had a 69.

This was the last year that a play-off was over 36 holes. After it was all over, Charles suggested that perhaps 18 holes was a fair enough test on which to award a championship. So it has been ever since. The Rodgers and Charles totals of 277 are still the lowest record in a Lytham Open, five and six strokes respectively lower than Player's 1974 score and Ballesteros in 1979.

Charles had putted consistently throughout, to average 30 a round but he did better in the play-off and has been said to have 'putted Phil Rodgers to death'. In the morning, he used his putter just 26 times and led Rodgers by three, with 69 to 72; later, Rodgers fell even further behind and Charles was champion eventually by an emphatic eight strokes.

Perhaps in part because of his success as a putter, Bob Charles's long game has tended to be devalued. One reason has been his left-handedness. No one thinks a Connors or a McEnroe looks 'odd' and seldom subjects a left-handed batsman at cricket to such criticism, but a golfer is a rarer and stranger bird. Charles has always been thought an awkward-looking swinger of a club though I do recall one observer reporting that he had watched the fellow in a mirror and, with the image reversed, all looked quite normal.

Perhaps the truth lies halfway. He is neither an elegant nor a powerful swinger but he has a workmanlike action, an exceptionally simple up, and down again, movement. He is a short hitter by modern standards, endures spells of poor striking sometimes but is not often seen deep in the woods.

Charles first achieved prominence when he won the New Zealand Open as an amateur (a very young one at that) in 1954. It has long attracted a strong field in spite of the fact that it is not in the forefront of world golf. In this period Thomson was very much the man to beat, winning the Open seven times in the period 1950-61.

Charles did not immediately rush into the professional ranks, being by no means over-confident of his ability; a feeling perhaps reinforced by the fact that when he did eventually turn professional in 1960 he had still not succeeded in winning his national Amateur Championship.

In 1961, he won the New Zealand PGA and competed in Europe both that year and the following, being fourth in the Order of Merit in 1962, the year he began to concentrate on the US Tour. In America, in 1963, he became the first left-hander to win a Tour event, and performed strongly for the rest of the decade. In all his years on the US Tour he was 34th or better in 1963-5 and 1967-70, his highest achievement being to take the 1968 Canadian Open, only just below a major championship in status. Eventually, he came to feel that his game was unsuited to US conditions as he was constantly battling against longer hitters. In all he won five times in 1963 to 1974 and totalled more than $\$\frac{1}{2}$ million in his career. He then gave up his American home and moved to a South African base, concentrating his summers on the European Tour. By the end of 1982, his bank balance had benefited to a sum of well over £150,000 with eight career wins. In 1972, he won the John Player Classic and the Dunlop Masters in succession and was the 1969 winner of the World Matchplay, giving in that event one of his most formidable putting displays, in which he beat Maurice Bembridge, Tommy Aaron and Gene Littler in the final in the first extra hole, having holed a 30 foot putt on the last to keep in the game.

By 1982, he was an old man in golfing terms, of forty-six, and confessed that his steady putting stroke was at long last subject to the twitch but he was still good enough to amass £19,715, the most he had won in any single year in Europe.

He is still recognised as the best left-hander playing though there is a Japanese player called Yatuka Hagawa in his early twenties, with a win in the Japan Open behind him, who may soon take over.

Henry Cotton

Born Holmes Chapel, Cheshire, England, 1907

When Tony Jacklin took both the British and US Open within the space of a single year, it was thought that here was a player who might rival the deeds of the great triumvirate of Vardon, Braid and Taylor. As Jacklin's form declined from year to year, however, it became clear that the triumvirate still have just one successor: Henry Cotton.

If we take as a measure performance in major championships there are a dozen or more British players who have won a single major championship. In a streak of good form Havers, Perry, Burton, Faulkner or others have taken the Open. The occasional player has threatened to do so again — and that is all. Henry Cotton's achievements are spread over many years. He played his first Open in 1927 and was still good enough to finish 6th at Hoylake 29 years later. Even though he had long been semi-retired from tournament and championship golf by that time, the Press still largely spoke of him first when considering British hopefuls for the Open.

Longevity at the top must be a prime test of a golfer's nerve and method and Cotton, despite a suspect constitution, remained a master from his teens to his eventual departure from the competitive scene.

Born of middle-class parents, Cotton turned professional at 17 and took assistants' jobs at Fulwell, Rye and Cannes (where he developed a taste for living in warm climates that was to remain with him). At 19½ he was appointed full professional at Langley Park, where he practised all day, went home for dinner and then practised some more in a garage net. By 1928 he was beginning to make his mark, finishing 8th behind Jones in the Open that year and 2nd in the News of the World tournament.

Already, he had become aware that US players had that something which their British counterparts had lost. Cotton decided to go to America to see what he could learn, which was very unusual in those days. In his first event in California, Cotton finished 3rd but found that he was shorter off the tee than US players. Tommy Armour convinced him that he would have to abandon his fading pattern of shot and learn to draw the ball because of the extra roll he would get. For the rest of his tour, Cotton's game suffered as he tried to absorb the new method, but by the time he sailed for England in the following spring he still had the £300 with which he had started out.

After a winning on his first appearance that summer in the Ryder Cup, Cotton wintered in Argentina, teaching, giving exhibitions and winning the only tournament in which he competed.

His sights were now on the Open Championship and a long haul it was to be. In 1930, a Jones Grand Slam year, he led after one round and at Carnoustie the following year was in front after two. In 1933, now from a Belgian base, he shared the lead after three rounds and eventually finished three behind Densmore'Shute and Craig Wood.

In 1934, he arrived at Royal St George's with four sets of golf clubs and, as Henry Longhurst put it, 'couldn't hit his hat with any of them'. Cotton decided that as he had made the journey he might as well play. In the first qualifying round he went round in 66, '18 of the most perfect holes I have ever played'. Two days later, in the first round proper, the magic was still there and he went to the turn in 31 and came back in par for a 67. He was three strokes in the lead. The next day he named a golf ball. The Dunlop 65, still in production today, derives from a record-breaking round that was not to be beaten in Open Championship play for 43 years. That was a nine-stroke lead. On the final day there was a stiff breeze and scoring rose. Cotton's 72 gave him a ten-stroke lead going into the final round. When Cotton reached the 13th tee in his last round the jubilance of the swarming and partisan British crowds was long stilled. The Messiah of British golf had gone to the turn in 40 (there were three par 3s in that half) and had started back 5, 5, 5. Nerves had attacked Cotton in the form of stomach cramp. Indeed, if his putting had not served him well, his score might have been one to disgust an 18-handicapper.

On the 13th, he got down a putt of 10 foot or so for a 4 to break the sequence. Suddenly he was himself again. The collapse was past, the cramp gone and he cruised home in level par for an unpicturesque 79 to win, however, by five clear strokes. He had broken a sequence of ten American victories in the Open; indeed no American was to win again until Snead in 1946.

In 1937 the United States first won the Ryder Cup on British soil and players such as Byron Nelson, Sam Snead, Walter Hagen, Horton Smith, Ed Dudley, Gene Sarazen and Densmore Shute moved on to Carnoustie to decide which of them would take the Open trophy. In practice they were superb; in the qualifying rounds no less so. Smith led on 138 followed by Sarazen, 141, and then Snead, Hagen and Nelson on 142. Cotton was the leading British player on 145.

When the championship proper began, Carnoustie had been stretched to a full 7,200 yards. Now the Americans were less dominant. Horton Smith, for instance, declined to a 77 and, though Ed Dudley led with a 70 on the first day, British players were close behind. After two rounds, a future champion, R.A. Whitcombe, led on 142 with Cotton four strokes behind. Perhaps this was for the best: Cotton had the reputation of being a poor front-runner, perhaps a result of his near disastrous last round at Sandwich three years before, but he had also faded in other Opens. In the third round he played steadily for a 73, ending with an eagle on the last hole. With the afternoons to come he was three behind R.A. Whitcombe and one behind Charles Whitcombe, both members of a brotherly triumvirate. But Cotton knew none of this. It was long, long before the days of giant score boards, walkie-talkies and all the paraphernalia of a modern Open. When he went out for the last time, he knew little more than that he was probably not far behind but that he would need a good final round to have a chance of victory.

He began 4, 3, 4, 4, 4, 4, two under par. Immaculate golf? Not quite. On five of those holes he had needed a chip and a putt for a par. Nevertheless, two under was good going in incessant rain.

During this spell, Cotton, who knew how easy it was to lose, had a spurt of confidence and turned to a friend saying, 'Don't worry, I'll win this thing.' With nine holes to go Cotton knew what he had to do to win: achieve a 72. His driving continued long and straight, the irons were fair and his chipping and putting continued excellent. With three holes to go he had the severe task of finishing 4, 4, 5 on holes whose strict par is something like 3½, 4½, 4½. The 16th, for instance, is about 230 yards to a slightly domed green. A near perfect wood is needed if the ball is not to run away off the green. The 17th offers the choice of playing safely short of the Barry Burn and having a very long shot to the green or going for

Henry Cotton

glory and having only a mid-iron left, if the carry is safely made. Cotton negotiated the problems and playing the 72nd hole, needed just a 6 to win. He drove long and safe, hit a 2-iron deliberately right to avoid the out of bounds and got his 5. One problem remained: puddles had formed on the greens. It was possible that the final round would have to be repeated if the course became unplayable. However all was well in the end. Cotton took the championship claret jug and a cheque for £100, a far cry from the current £30,000. However, then as now, the prize money was of far less importance than the prestige, endorsement contracts, enhanced exhibition fees, golf club retainer, and so on. Cotton himself said that he would have been happy to pay over £10,000 for an Open title. But there was more to it than that. By this victory, Cotton had set himself beyond dispute at the summit of British golf. Between the wars, no other home-grown player succeeded in winning the Open more than once; six other players between 1920 and 1939 won once, but not one came close to a repeat victory. Similarly, since World War II, Daly, Faulkner and Jacklin were one-time winners.

During the period leading up to the war, Cotton followed Walter Hagen, though less flamboyantly, in enhancing the status of the British professional. They were regarded as necessary employees of golf clubs, but humble ones, when Cotton came to the fore. They tended to live out their days in a wooden shed a little removed from the clubhouse, which they were not permitted to enter. In that shed, they made and repaired clubs, repainted golf balls, fixed nails in shoes and emerged to give lessons at a ludicrously low hourly rate. Frequently they doubled as greenkeeper and/or steward at smaller clubs. Even as late as 1958 I can remember such a man at a club to which I then belonged, and eventually the poor man was sacked because the standard of his golf was thought to have fallen below the required level! This was partly why Cotton chose to spend a few years as a club professional in Belgium during the 1930s: the money was better as was the status. However, he had returned to Britain in 1937, complete with a Mercedes cabriolet; this at a time when very few professional golfers had a car of even humble make and model. He now began to charge far more than had been the norm for lessons, exhibition matches and all the rest of the activities that go to supplement a tournament winner's income.

He still, however, looked for opportunities outside the British Isles. It is significant perhaps that he won almost a dozen European national titles during the 1930s, particularly towards the end of the decade.

War came and Cotton went into the RAF but was invalided out after suffering stomach ulcers and a burst appendix. The end of the war found him in a weak state and with little money. In the first Open after the war he led after two rounds but faded to a 79 in the last as he physically weakened. A part of the answer was some winter work in Monte Carlo, followed by a visit to the USA, to play the tour and also to get plenty of good red meat. Though the golf was subsidiary, Cotton did win an event, the White Sulphur Springs Invitational but, more importantly, came back restored to full fitness.

Cotton was delighted when he surveyed Muirfield before the 1948 Open, particularly because the fairways were narrow and the rough long. It would suit his particular qualities and dismay many others.

Most golfers, increasingly so in recent times, do not try to hit the ball straight. They feel that to hit down the left-hand side of a fairway and fade the ball back towards the middle or, less often, do the reverse and draw it from right to left is far safer than to attempt a straight shot. Whether it's a right-to-left or left-to-right pattern, there is far more room for error. Cotton's method allowed little room for error yet that week, in the four rounds, he claims to have hit an unprecedented 52 fairways out of 56. (For comparison, at the other extreme, Severiano Ballesteros, in winning the 1979 Open, hit seven fairways throughout!)

Cotton began with a pair of 69s to lead the qualifiers and then began the championship proper with a 71 before spread-eagling the field with a 66. He faltered in the third round, going to the turn in 39 and dropping shots at the next two holes but came back immediately with two birdies. He finished in 75 and 72 to win by five strokes. The first prize was £150 but his future was financially secure once more.

Cotton played no more in the Open until 1952 and during this time played tournament golf only occasionally. Increasingly he devoted himself to journalism, authorship and golf course architecture. Even so, he was good enough still to finish 4th, on his next appearance in 1952.

He won his last major tournament, the Penfold, in 1954 and had long since proved himself to be the greatest British golfer since Vardon, Taylor and Braid, a position he still holds with none to dispute it.

Bruce
Crampton

Born Sydney, Australia, 1935

There would be few to dispute that Gary Player has been the most successful foreigner of all time to play the US Tour, but his contemporary Bruce Crampton runs him close.

Bruce followed the normal pattern of Australian golfers in having his first successes at state level (he won the New South Wales junior title in 1952-3) and he turned professional before allowing himself to have much further impact on amateur golf. It is said that he was disappointed at being omitted from an Australian international team and promptly turned professional. There was soon to be some compensation, for while still under eighteen he was chosen to represent his country's professionals against New Zealand.

That was the country which saw some of his early successes, as has been the case with many Australians, Peter Thomson included. He was second in the 1954 New Zealand Open (to Bob Charles) and won their PGA.

Norman von Nida has always interested himself in promising Australian talent. He coached Crampton and was soon partnering him to win a foursomes title — again in New Zealand.

In 1956, Crampton obtained his first really significant title when he won the Australian Open at Royal Sydney, establishing himself as a successor to such post-war Australian winners as Ossie Pickworth, Eric Cremin, Norman von Nida and Peter Thomson, though the latter still had many good years ahead of him.

The following year he set out to test himself in Europe but in Britain found that the contemporary scene did not suit him. Having entered a tournament at Killermont, Glasgow, he was highly annoyed to find himself not allowed to practise on the course, only a couple of days before the event began. He did not return to Britain for ten years.

The same year he made his debut on the US Tour in the Houston Open and finished 13th to win nearly $700, not a huge amount of money by today's standards but which nevertheless compared favourably with the $520 cheque for being Australian Open champion.

Crampton decided to settle in America and did not, as have many others, commute between the two countries. He did not play in Australia for some ten years.

Despite his promising enough start, Crampton was no overnight success in the US; indeed, the reverse was the case. In 1957-60, he earned less than $14,000 and 1961, with some $8,000 banked, was little better. He had, however, surmounted

Bruce Crampton

the obstacle of his first Tour win, the Milwaukee Open.

His main problem had been inconsistent driving. Although excellent iron play is essential to winning golf at any level, many would argue that driving and the short game are more important. No one can hit for the green from the middle of a lake and few from deep in the woods. If, however, the drive is on the fairway, a good short game can have the player down in two strokes even if he misses the green. With his slow measured swing, it was inevitable that Crampton would eventually become a sound driver and, that achieved, he began to forge ahead. He already had an excellent short game and was a particularly good putter.

In 1962, he first became a significant Tour player, being 13th on that year's money list. At about that time he earned himself the nickname 'The Iron Man'. This arose because he moved relentlessly from tournament to tournament, never missing an event. In one 1962-3 spell he played thirty-seven. Many might think that this is not particularly unusual. It is a matter of common knowledge that Jack

Nicklaus has for long had a strictly limited interest in run-of-the-mill tournaments and has centred his year on the major championships. It is, perhaps, less well known that his fellow Tour players follow a similar pattern, though for different reasons. They do not concentrate on the majors; they realise that it is impossible to keep their game at a high level for the ten months that make up the US season. If they play week after week it is normally for one of two reasons: either they are moderate players enjoying a spell of good form and fear to break the spell, or they are making a living — more or less — week by week and plod onwards, untroubled by the stresses of being in winning positions. Otherwise, about three-quarters of the tournaments available would be a fair average.

So Crampton continued upon his inexorable way. 1965 was a good year, when he won three events, but he reached a peak not as a young man but after the hardening of many years of experience at about the age of thirty-three in 1968. This was the first year he won over $100,000, a very considerable target at the time but no longer so; 38 players topped that figure in 1981 and 36 in 1982.

From then until the end of 1975, he continued to top $100,000 each year, his best seasons being 1969-70, 1973 and 1975, when he had money list placings of 5th, 3rd, 2nd and 10th. His outstanding year was 1973, when he won four US Tour events, was second five times and amassed $274,000. He also became only the fifth man to pass a career $1 million on the US Tour.

In writing of Crampton, I have mentioned money frequently; the main reason being that he was a particularly consistent player yet his career was not crowned by a major championship victory. In his best years, however, he did come close, especially in 1972, when he finished runner-up to Jack Nicklaus in both the US Masters and Open. Later, in 1973 and 1975, he was runner-up for the US PGA. By chance, it was also to Nicklaus on both these occasions.

This consistency showed itself particularly in 1973 and 1975, with his victory in the Vardon Trophy for the lowest stroke average both years at about 70.5 per round. But this consistency won him little popularity in America. Crampton saw tournament golf as his personal equivalent of going to the office or factory bench and he played with cold, humourless concentration, seldom exchanging more than a curt word with his playing partners. In fact it is said that he once played a round with three rich men who had paid $1,000 for the privilege; he didn't talk to them at all.

Suddenly it was all over. He had a poor year in 1976 and retired in 1977, having spent three months in hospital with what was diagnosed as depression. Very likely the relentless wear and tear of competitive tournament play had caught up with him, the first foreigner to top that magic $1 million on the US Tour.

It was by no means a tragedy in the long run. Crampton had been sacrificing time with his family which he could now make up and he had a variety of business interests in Texas in banking, oil, property and farming. When he felt that his nerve for golf had gone, he merely changed from his golf course 'office' to others.

He left behind the record of having won fifteen US tournaments and $1,374,294 (still 17th all-time). Almost all of his winnings came from his adopted home, for he added only about $125,000 from performances outside and a very few other tournament wins.

Ben
Crenshaw

Born Austin, Texas, USA, 1952

During the first few months of the 1983 US season, Crenshaw re-established himself as one of the premier players in modern golf. By mid-April, he was sixth in the money list, with more than $130,000 in the bank. He was also achieving consistent high placings, lying second to Tom Kite in the Seiko Grand Prix, an award that seeks to reward the player who performs best in this respect.

He also looked good in the official US PGA statistics, which try to single out the men who are performing best in various categories of the game: driving distance and accuracy, stroke average, birdie totals, hitting greens in 'par', average number of putts per round, getting down in two from sand and frequency at breaking par.

Crenshaw was fifth in scoring, first in 'sand saves', second in breaking par and tied first in birdie total. My guess is that these statistics were introduced a few years ago as a means of 'proving' who was the best putter, most accurate driver, best bunker player, longest hitter, and so on. In fact, most of the categories prove rather little. At the time, the longest hitter seemed to be a certain John McComish, who, at 276.9 yards was five yards clear of his nearest rival, Tom Weiskopf (while languishing at 123rd on the money list). The truth of the matter is more likely to be that McComish is certainly a long hitter and relishes the distinction of ranking highest. Meanwhile other, more talented, players probably left their drivers in the bag more often, in favour of a safe iron.

What of putting? Ben Crenshaw is recognised as just about the best putter in modern golf. As he led the birdie total, you would expect to find him featuring strongly amongst the putting leaders. Not so. He did not register in the top ten! The reason is that Ben had been playing much better golf than in the previous year, when he headed the putting category with an average of 28.65 per round. The putting leader is likely to be a man who misses a very large number of greens, pitches or chips quite close and then gets down in single putts; but that would be for pars rather than birdies.

Despite his apparently impressive putting in 1982, Crenshaw had a very bad year, finishing 83rd on the US money list, nearly fifty places worse than any other season of his ten year professional career. Improvement came shortly after the end of the American season, when in Australia he finished tied for second in the PGA Championship, having opened up 69, 65 at Royal Melbourne, a course that some have rated the best in the world. The 65 gave him a new record and he was no fewer than seven under par after the opening seven holes.

Crenshaw won his first US event for three years, The Byron Nelson Classic, in

May 1983 and had managed another of his famous second place finishes in the US Masters, moving up from 15th place after three rounds with a final 68, best score of the day, but still four strokes behind the glittering achievement of Severiano Ballesteros.

Crenshaw is well-known for his love of golf history, thus more aware than most of the pre-eminence of victories in major championships; try as he might, he has not yet won such a victory.

His nearest approach was in the 1979 US PGA. Scores of 69, 67, 69, 67 — at Oakland Hills of all places — should have been amply good enough to win but David Graham produced a last round 65 (nearly a 63) and then won the play-off with Crenshaw on the third extra hole. Crenshaw does not do well in play-offs; he has taken part in five and lost the lot.

This second place followed closely on another narrow failure, this time in the British Open at Royal Lytham and St Anne's. Crenshaw produced more consistent scoring than anyone else

Ben Crenshaw

with 72, 71, 72, 71 but faltered on the 71st hole, where he dropped two strokes and eventually finished joint second with Jack Nicklaus, three behind Ballesteros's up-and-down winning score of 73, 65, 75, 70. During this spell, Crenshaw played five tournaments and was second in four of them.

Just as Sam Snead eventually came to regard it as fore-ordained that he would never win a US Open, I wonder if Crenshaw may be arriving at the same conclusion as regards the four major championships. As the years pass, the feat becomes more rather than less difficult. Though experience is held to be vital to winning, the most valuable experience to look back on is that of having won.

Crenshaw nearly did it early in his professional career, in the 1975 US Open. Although he only tied for third at Medinah with four others, he was just a stroke behind the play-off between Lou Graham and John Mahaffey, and on the 71st hole put a shot into water.

The following year, he was second in the Masters but eight behind Raymond Floyd, who had opened 65, 66 and continued to give one of the most dominant performances in a major championship of the modern era.

That year, his love affair with the history of golf and historic courses was enhanced by his win at Portmarnock in the Irish Open. Some said that it was the first time he had seen a linksland course.

The following year, at Turnberry, he was the only player who kept within reach of Nicklaus and Watson for three rounds, but could not sustain his pressure as the Titans fought out one of the most memorable of all British Opens.

Undeterred, Ben was again in the thick of it in the same event at St Andrews in 1978 but he was again rewarded with only second place, with three others, behind Jack Nicklaus.

On the US Tour, Crenshaw has been a winner, however, from the beginning of his professional career. He came into the professional arena after perhaps the most promising amateur career of anyone since Jack Nicklaus. His first event was the San Antonio-Texas Open. He led throughout and followed by second placing in the marathon World Open, played over eight rounds for a huge prize. He seemed the new Messiah, destined for a very high placing indeed amongst our masters of golf.

Yet there were flaws in his game that held him back. Crenshaw has an extremely long backswing that takes him well past the horizontal. Most great players have found this leads to some loss of control. Certainly Ben Hogan did not begin to make his mark until he had drastically shortened his, while Henry Cotton always employed what he called a three-quarter swing, except when going for extreme length.

In consequence, Crenshaw was known as an erratic driver early in his professional career. The other side of the coin was that he tended to be voted by his fellow professionals as the best player of recovery shots. Additionally, there was the stiff-armed, wristless putting stroke that quickly came to be considered as just about the most effective in modern golf, as the best putters came to expect to average 28 or 29 putts a round, a figure that not so long ago would have been considered a near freak achievement in one round.

After his outstanding professional start, Crenshaw coasted for the next two seasons as he adapted to the different stresses of the professional game. In 1976, he took three American titles and over a quarter of a million dollars to finish second to Jack Nicklaus on the season's money list, only some $9,000 behind. Since then, 1982 is the only year he has failed to pass $100,000 while he approached $¼ million in both 1979 and 1980 and is sure to do so in 1983 also.

His US Tour wins now total nine and his foreign wins are on the same level, the most recent coming in the 1982 Mexican Open while in 1983 he passed $1½ million, a total which means he is nearing the top 10 of all-time.

However, even so massive a money-winner as Bruce Crampton fades in the memory as the years pass. Only the major championships convey immortality. Here, Crenshaw, at thirty-one, may have his best years ahead of him. He has largely overcome his tendency to be erratic and the biggest question mark lies against his nerve. There are too many second places in his record, and he has lapsed at crisis points in the major championships.

Jimmy Demaret

Born Houston, Texas, USA, 1910

Jimmy Demaret was a star in a golden age of American golf, when the names on all lips were Hogan, Snead, Nelson, Little, Mangrum, Guldahl and Wood. In one respect, his record was unusual: he won three major championships but all in one event, the US Masters. In a spell from 1940 to 1950 he became the first player to take this title three times, a record which remained until Arnold Palmer achieved his fourth win in 1964, followed by Nicklaus's fifth in 1975.

Demaret had turned professional in 1927, so his early competitive career coincided with the Depression, when money was not much easier to come by in professional golf than outside. In the second half of the 1930s, he brought off the occasional victory but did not become a force to be reckoned with until 1940, a year when he had several victories, the most important by far being the Masters. He entered the event in a streak of good form and in the first round went to the turn in 37 — nothing spectacular there — but on the second nine he set a mark of 30 that has never been bettered; golfers to equal it being Gene Littler (1966), Ben Hogan (1967), Miller Barber (1970), Maurice Bembridge (1974) and Gary Player (1978). One player, Johnny Miller, has had a 30 on the first nine. Of all the players named, only Gary Player also won the tournament, his 30 coming on the last nine holes of the event to make up a 64 final round.

Demaret totalled 67 and, even in days when scoring was a little higher than it is today, this was not enough to give him the first round lead. Lloyd Mangrum shot a 64, to set a championship record that has since been equalled but not bettered. However, in the following round Mangrum fell away to a 75 and Demaret's 72 brought the pair level. After a third round 70 he led Mangrum by one with the rest further away by four and more strokes. In the final round, Demaret made no serious errors and won by four clear strokes, a record at the time and one that was to stand until 1948.

He featured strongly in each year to 1947. Then he tied with Byron Nelson for the first round lead with a 69 and went ahead in the second round by one from Nelson. The tournament remained a duel between the two until the end, Demaret's 71, 70, 71 over Nelson's 72, 72, 70 bringing him home against the greatest player of the day by two strokes. The formidable amateur, Frank Stranahan, joined Nelson in second place after a concluding 68.

Demaret had won his second Masters at the age of thirty-seven and his most remarkable victory in the championship came when he had reached forty. This time the principal victim was the former Australian Amateur and Open Champion

Jim Ferrier, who held a lead of five on Demaret after two rounds and of four after the third round. With just six holes to play he led Demaret by a commanding five strokes. Demaret played those holes in two under par while Ferrier dropped shot after shot and eventually finished two behind the Texan.

Undoubtedly some of Jimmy Demaret's best years were lost to World War II, which came when he had reached a peak. However, it is not mere years that determine the decline of a golfer but the wear and tear of tournament play. The history of golf is full of examples of men who have come to the fore in their early twenties but have been burnt out in a decade. Usually, it is the putting that is most affected and Demaret himself confesses that he first suffered 'the jumps' in 1954, fought them off and played successfully again until they returned in 1963 to finish his career.

Jimmy Demaret

For Demaret to be thought as one of the great golfers rather than a near great, he should have gained the laurels of a US Open Championship, but it was a case of so near yet so far. In 1946, he produced a fine last round 68 as the best of the contenders, but was still two behind the play-off between Mangrum, Nelson and Vic Ghezzi. At Riviera in 1948 he broke the US Open record with 278, having the fine finish of 68, 69 but Ben Hogan was two strokes better. His last real chance came in 1957, when he was forty-seven, and he finished just a shot behind the play-off between Cary Middlecoff and Dick Mayer.

Perhaps the US Tour was his true metier. After confining much of his early play to his home state of Texas, he went on to total 31 PGA Tour wins and twice had five in a year, being the leading money winner in 1947. He was elected to the US PGA Hall of Fame in 1960.

Although money did not pour into the hands of eager golfers in the profusion of today (Demaret totalled $173,982 in his career, about the same as the man in 19th place for 1982 earned) he achieved his own ultimate ambition when with Jack Burke, a fellow Tour player, he set up and now jointly owns the Champions Golf Club near his home town of Houston.

George Duncan

Born Methlick, Aberdeenshire, Scotland, 1883

The careers of George Duncan and Abe Mitchell were almost inextricably joined for many years just as the names of Braid, Vardon and Taylor were often mentioned in one breath.

Duncan, indeed, was very much a link between the days of Victorian golf and golfers and the 1920s world of Walter Hagen and Bobby Jones. With Mitchell, he was throughout the 1920s the leading British hope to keep the Americans at bay in the Open Championships, which was at those times even more than today the centrepiece of the golf season.

Of course, tournaments were few and far between at that time and there was in no sense a professional 'Tour'; no-one had thought of a leading money winners' list. Instead, exhibition and challenge matches excited a great amount of public interest. This is in great contrast to today. Golf is the poorer for the change. Think of the hordes who would have gathered at various times during the last twenty years as rivals to Nicklaus appeared: Palmer, Player, Weiskopf, Miller and Watson in succession.

As I remember, such a match, doubtless for $1 million, was proposed between the new star, Johnny Miller, and Jack in about 1974. Neither was at all keen on the notion. They probably felt there was just too much at stake: the winner would have been regarded as Mr World Number One. Otherwise, exhibition matches do occur, but they are that and nothing more and often played as a four, not as a man-against-man confrontation.

The Victorians and Edwardians loved them, though, and I don't think that a loser was thought to have fallen many rungs down the golf ladder. He had merely been beaten on the day. Duncan took part in many in the early years of this century. In 1906, he and C.H. Mayo challenged Braid and Vardon over 72 holes for a £100 stake (much more than was available for an Open winner who was taking home only £150 even in the late 1940s). Duncan and Mayo lost and suffered the same fate in 1909 against Braid and Taylor, this time for £200. In another big match in 1908, however, Duncan, as always loyal to Mayo, beat Ted Ray and Tom Vardon (no this is not a misprint, Harry's brother Tom was a good enough player to finish second in the Open but his abilities were almost totally obscured by his brother's far greater achievements).

Duncan, then, grew up in golf as a future rival of the Great Triumvirate and before World War I had many achievements to his credit, despite the comparative lack of tournaments. He had been a Scottish international from 1906 in the

George Duncan wins the 1929 Ryder Cup

matches against England that took place annually and aroused great interest (as they well might today and more indeed than those strange Hennessy Cup events between Great Britain and Ireland, Europe and the assorted collection known as the Rest of the World).

In 1909, Duncan won the North Berwick 300 Guineas Tournament. In 1912 he won the Belgian Open and the following year the French. The premier event after the Open was the PGA Matchplay Championship, in which Duncan reached the semi-finals in 1906, probably the achievement which first earned him recognition at the age of twenty-three. He progressed to being beaten finalist in 1920 and beat James Braid for the 1913 title.

In the Open, he had also made a mark. He was third in 1910, fourth in 1912 and tenth in the last year before the war, 1914, ten strokes behind Harry Vardon, the last of the Great Triumvirate to win an Open.

When golf resumed in 1919, the days of Braid, Vardon and Taylor were over due to their age. Duncan himself had lost what might have been his best years, thanks to the war. He reached 36 in 1919. The main tournaments that year were the Matchplay and the 'Professional Golfers' Championship'. In both of these Duncan was bested by Abe Mitchell: (in the final of the Matchplay, while Mitchell also took this championship intended to celebrate victory in the war). The top 60 players in the 1914 were invited; in all but name it was the Open. Mitchell and Duncan tied and agreed that their scores in the Eden Tournament the following day should decide the matter. Mitchell won but was never to win the Open proper.

Duncan, on the other hand, did so the following year. Again his name was paired with that of Mitchell, who began 74, 73 to lead, while Duncan languished thirteen strokes behind after a pair of 80s. Amazingly, all Mitchell's lead went in the third round, with Duncan round in 71 to Mitchell's 84. Mitchell heard that Duncan had had a very good round as he set off himself and putted appallingly all the way. In the afternoon, though Mitchell pulled himself together for a 76, Duncan had 72. Over the last 36 holes he had gone round in seventeen fewer strokes.

After Duncan had achieved a fifth place in the 1921 Open which was won by Jock Hutchison, a Scot who had emigrated to the USA, he produced one of the most dramatic performances in Open history in 1922 at Sandwich. Duncan began 76, 75 against Walter Hagen's 76, 73 and fell further behind with 81 to 79. Hagen then produced one of the lowest rounds of the championship, a 72. Well-wishers gathered to congratulate the man who had outscored all his close rivals as champion. Then came news that George Duncan was playing what could be the greatest winning last round ever played in the championship. He came to the last needing a four for a 68 and a tie with Hagen. Alas he missed the green, did not chip very close and missed the putt. Hagen had his first of four Opens in the period 1922-9.

By this time, Duncan was approaching forty, an age by which most golfers have faded as major figures; but he continued to feature for a little while in the Open, though he never again came close to winning. He did, however, twice win the *Daily Mail* event in 1920 and 1922, the Gleneagles in 1920 and 1924 and had a late flowering in his mid forties when he won both the French and Irish Opens in 1927.

He played in all the matches against the USA in the period 1921 to 1931 and in all played four singles, winning the lot. The photograph shows him accepting the trophy as captain from Samuel Ryder after a 6 to 4 British victory. In the background, Walter Hagen can be seen, as the US captain who was obviously undismayed by the defeat. He had arranged informally to play against Duncan in the singles and then told his team 'Well boys, that's a point for our side.' Duncan won by 10 and 8, the biggest margin in Ryder Cup history!

Duncan was an extraordinary player to watch on a golf course and how he would have tolerated today's weighing up of which iron to use and lining up of putts is difficult to imagine. The consensus was that Duncan played *too* fast, coming close at times to hitting the ball on the walk. It is said that even when he had that putt in 1922 to tie Hagen he still gave scarcely a glance at the hole before putting. Many wondered that if perhaps just a little more care had been taken . . . but Duncan was a highly-strung, vital man and probably played at the pace that suited him. He argued his case in a book aptly entitled *Golf at the Gallop*.

Jim
—— Ferrier ——

Born Manley, Sydney, Australia, 1915

The oldest existing golf club in Australia was founded in 1882, with more rapid development coming in the 1890s. The game is therefore of roughly the same age as it is in the USA. But whereas America experienced an early influx of British professionals — mainly from Scotland — to develop the game, Australia was much more out on a limb. Until the advent of fast modern travel, golf grew much more slowly, with the tours of such players as Walter Hagen and Gene Sarazen in the 1930s an exception rather than the rule. Without the spur of international competition, standards grew rather more slowly than those, for example, in America, which was already producing home-grown open champions before the First World War.

Jim Ferrier was the first Australian to become an international superstar and, like his successors, he had to leave his homeland to do it. He can be said to have 'arrived' at the age of sixteen. In the Australian Open that year he began 79, 77. Although that scoring was not as disastrous as it would be today, he was still nine strokes behind the leader, another sixteen-year-old, Harry Williams. Ferrier then produced the round of the championship, a 70, and with the afternoon's round of the day's final 36 holes to come had pulled to within three of the leader — still Williams.

In the end, however, it was a much older man, Ivo Whitton, aged 38 and also an amateur, who was to rival Ferrier that day. From well back in the field he seized the lead with an outward nine in 33 and finished on 301, which was to be the winning score. On the final hole, Ferrier needed a par 5 to tie and took 6.

For Whitton it was a last fling and his fifth Australian Open success; the 6 foot 3½ inch Ferrier was at the beginning. That year he had to be satisfied with winning the New South Wales Amateur; he was also semi-finalist in the Australian Amateur, outstanding results for one so young.

He had to wait a few more years for his first dramatic success. In 1934 he won the Queensland Open and Amateur Championships and his second New South Wales Open. The following year he took his first major championship, the Australian Amateur and in 1936 went to Britain. While there, he won the Gleneagles Silver Tassie and the *Golf Illustrated* Gold Vase, the latter a competition that Bobby Jones had won some years before. His aim was, though, the British Amateur. His attempt on this title was foiled by a miracle shot from his opponent in the final, Hector Thomson. One down on the 36th hole at St Andrews, Jim put his second shot on the green safely but Thomson followed with

Jim Ferrier

an approach to 6 inches, one of the most conclusive golf shots ever struck. Ferrier lost by two down.

Back in Australia his successes piled up, culminating in his achievements in 1938-9. In those two years he won both the Amateur and Open Championships of his country and suddenly there were no more Australian championships for him to take. In his own country there was little point in his turning professional. At that time, a tournament win was worth just a few dollars and Ferrier did not want to become a club professional but to compete on the world stage.

That meant America. He left Australia in 1940 to compete in the US Amateur but was disbarred under the rules of amateurism, when it was discovered that he had written a golf instruction book. Shortly afterwards, he officially turned professional but his new career was cut short by war. He served as a sergeant in the US Army.

From 1944 he became a tournament winner in the US, and by 1947 was fifth on the year's money list. More importantly he had won a world major championship, the US PGA, then played as a matchplay event which, alas, has not been the case for many years. In the earlier rounds he beat such stars as Claude Harmon and Lloyd Mangrum and faced Chick Harbert in the final, and a remarkable one it was.

Ferrier was a great competitor but not a great striker of the golf ball. He was a winner because he had a strong nerve, fine determination and, an equaliser in any match, he was a superb putter.

He used a putter several inches longer than standard which he had obtained by swapping it for a few golf balls. He then hunched himself over the ball. Many very tall men have had a better short game than long; Ferrier was an outstanding example.

Harbert went into an early lead and continued to match his 300 yard drives against Ferrier's short game. It is said that in the whole match Ferrier never had to putt twice: his short irons were at their most accurate and so his first putts were either in or dead. If he had a long putt he coasted it up close enough so that Harbert had to concede. This precision was in some contrast to his long game: Ferrier is said to have hit no fewer than eight spectators en route to victory by 2 and 1.

Three years later, he had the US Masters in his grasp. He opened 70, 67 to lead and with six holes to go in the final round had only to coast home for victory. But there followed a collapse as complete and dramatic as Ed Sneed's in 1979. On the par 5 13th he hit his second shot into the creek and followed up by dropping shots on each of the next four holes. A surprised Jimmy Demaret found himself Masters champion for the third time Consolation came later, when Ferrier took the Canadian Open and was second on the US money list that year, worth not much short of $400,000 today but then a matter of a little over $27,000.

The following year, he won the Canadian Open again and in what was his best season won a total of five events including the rare feat (only ten players have done it in US Tour history) of winning three in a row. He was third in the money list this time, when such players as Hogan, Snead, Mangrum, Demaret and Middlecoff were at their best. With the exception of Locke in his one great year (related elsewhere), he was the first man who had learned his golf in another country to become a dominant force on the US Tour, then as now offering the most daunting competition in the world.

Jim Ferrier remained a leading money winner into the mid-1950s and had also one of the best golfing addresses in America as professional at Lakeside in Hollywood. In the years that followed before he left tournament competition in the early 1960s he continued to win occasionally and once came close to another major championship.

Again it was the US PGA, by then a strokeplay event. His 66 at Firestone in the third round was the lowest that year and put him one stroke behind Doug Sanders, but level with Sam Snead and Jay Herbert. The latter won with a closing 70, and Ferrier came in second, a stroke behind.

Ray
——Floyd——

Born Fort Bragg, North Carolina, USA, 1942

During the 1982 World Matchplay at Wentworth, while Ray Floyd was being despatched by Sandy Lyle, a BBC commentator remarked that the year's US PGA champion and number two money winner had been a top player for only a couple of years or so.

It was a pardonable mistake. Floyd's earlier career has been obscured by his massive winnings in both 1981 and 1982: near to $400,000 in both seasons; but that career is little shorter than Jack Nicklaus's. He was first a tournament winner in the same period — 1963, after a bad start during which he made the 36 hole cut in just one of ten entries. On his eleventh, he took the St Petersburg Open.

Nicklaus's first victory was in the US Open of 1962 and from there on he marched to a different tune: he began by wanting to be the greatest golfer who had ever lived. No one has ever suggested that was Ray's objective yet by 1983 it could be said that he is a better player than Nicklaus; certainly a bigger money winner by far, he is now a more likely tournament and major championship winner.

In the twenty years of his professional career, Floyd did not build quickly on that early win pursued by many for so long. He had no particular difficulty in remaining in the Top 60 after he entered it in 1963, but for the next several years only one more win came his way and he was no better than 24th in the money list until 1969, when he broke through to the top ranks and on a major championship stage first showed his trait of being able dramatically to dominate an event.

At Dayton, Ohio, he opened 69, 66, enough in most years to distance the field, but Gary Player hung only a stroke behind. Floyd then threw a 67 into the ring and that was about that. He did, however, play rather too conservatively in the last round, avoiding risks, and his 74 was only just good enough to win the US PGA by a stroke from Player.

For the US professional, a Tour win is a first essential, while a major championship elevates the winner to a star position. Floyd had undoubtedly arrived at the age of 27. Winning two other events that year, he was 8th on the money list and had comfortably topped $100,000, a far greater feat then than the routine achievement it has since become.

Having reached the centre stage, Floyd retreated to the wings once more. He lost his Ryder Cup place and in 1972-3 had the kind of years that a little later were to cause golf writers by the dozen to speculate on the decline of Miller's game.

Ray Floyd

Floyd had been finding it difficult to motivate himself. Golf had already brought him enough money and this ex-manager of the first topless girls' band was more interested in spending it, often into the early hours, than in an arid dedication to golf. Anyway, he had that kind of inner self-assurance which gave him the belief that he could do it again when he chose to.

In the mid-1970s, marriage, children, and, perhaps, the knowledge that time for everyone must run out brought to him a new will to win and that tunnel-visioned concentration that most see as a necessary part of the equipment of the winning golfer.

In 1975, he won a tournament for the first time since 1969 and in the following year gave one of the most dominant performances of all time in a major championship. The scene was Augusta National Golf Club in Atlanta, Georgia; the championship the US Masters.

Floyd's use of two clubs that week in April 1976 has gone down into mini-legend. First, there was the 'old man's' 5-wood, normally most used by those who can't hit a long iron to save their life: fairly seldom by top professionals. But to Ray Floyd it was the answer to a problem. At the Augusta par-5s, the greens can be reached with a variety of clubs — woods or long irons — but the trick to hold them is to hit a shot that is both long *and* high. How can these two aims be achieved? The 5-wood, thought Floyd, was the answer, though it meant discarding one of the long irons that the Tour players find far more useful.

On the par-5s, Floyd was no fewer than thirteen under par, which roughly means that he was averaging birdies, so the 5-wood proved its worth in 1976, as did the second club I referred to. This was a Zebra putter, for which the claim is made that it is perfectly balanced and that the face automatically returns to a square position. It helped Floyd to twenty-one birdies and one eagle during the four rounds of play.

Floyd began with a 65, the lowest round by a winner, and followed with a 66. Barring the kind of collapse that Ray Floyd does not allow to happen to him, the championship was already his. His 36-hole total was a record; so also his 54 hole mark as he added a 70 in the third round. He went into the last round with no one in pursuit, Nicklaus being closest at eight strokes behind. Without alarms, Floyd played out the championship for a last round 70. Nicklaus had drifted further away with a 73 and only Ben Crenshaw made up real ground with a 67 to finish in second place, eight strokes behind. Floyd's 271 total tied Nicklaus's 1965 record, though the latter retained his record margin of victory that year, by nine over Arnold Palmer and Gary Player.

Floyd moved up the money list that year to 7th and kept his place in 1977 but then faded again in the next couple of years, at an age when the careers of many players come to an end. Not Floyd. After a couple of fallow years he was a big money winner again in 1980 with $192,993 and the following year he became one of an exclusive band of eight players to top $300,000 in a year on the US Tour. His actual winnings were much higher for in the spring, by winning the Doral-Eastern Open and the Tournament Players Championship, he earned a bonus of $200,000 because these wins were consecutive.

The superb qualities of Ray Floyd as a front-runner were to be seen at their clearest in the 1982 US PGA championship at one of the most respected courses in America, Oklahoma's Southern Hills. Floyd began with one of the lowest rounds ever produced in a major championship, a 63, and continued running with the ball for 69, 68, 72. After three rounds, players with such scores as Greg Norman's 66, 69, 70 or Calvin Peete's 69, 70, 68 were almost out of touch when they would normally have been looking behind them to see how far off the pursuers were.

Floyd played the last hole, knowing the championship to be won and needing a par 4 to beat the four round record for the PGA. He missed the green with his second and then was faced with a little pitch shot which he dumped into a bunker in front of his nose and an unmajestic 6 was the eventual result.

During the rest of the season, Floyd's play paralleled his 1981 standard and he was again number 2 on the US Tour money list, with around $400,000. He was outdistanced by Craig Stadler but equally far behind him were such players as Watson, Kite, Wadkins and Nicklaus. At the end of the year he won a massive $300,000 for his win in the $1 Million Challenge in Sun City.

The Zebra putter with which he holed out so infallibly during the 1976 Masters has long since disappeared but, with a Ping, he remains one of the best putters in the game. More enduring is his swing which, though ungainly and even lurching, has about it a ponderous conviction.

David
——— Graham ———

Born Windsor, Australia, 1946

Peter Thomson's record of having been the first Australian to win the British Open and of having established near dominance over the event in the 1950s assure him of a perpetual place amongst golfing immortals. David Graham's achievements are of a lesser stature but include achievements in the United States that outdistance anything Thomson achieved there. Most memorable is his 1981 US Open victory at Merion Cricket Club, Pennsylvania, where he produced one of the great winning final rounds of major championship golf.

Merion is the shortest course, at 6,544 yards, used at this level of golf. Indeed, few are used for run-of-the-mill tournaments which are not at least approximately 6,800, but Merion is feared by competitors as much as any course in the world. The winning score of the greatest shot-maker of all time, Ben Hogan, when he won the 1950 Open was 287 from rounds of 72, 69, 72, 74, while Olin Dutra in 1934 took 293, giving some idea of the difficulty of the course. In a more recent year, 1971, Trevino and Nicklaus improved on those totals when they finished level at 280. Graham far outmatched this scoring and indeed came within a stroke of Nicklaus's 272 US Open scoring record, set at Baltusrol in 1980.

Early on, attention had centred on George Burns, who had been having a terrible year on the US Tour but began 69, 66 to Graham's 68, 68, while Jack Nicklaus was ominous with 69, 68. Burns was expected to crack but followed with a 68 which, at 203 for 54 holes, set a new US Open record. During the round he had one of those pieces of luck which most champions need but which irritate the golf purist. On the 11th, he hooked his tee shot into thick rough and then pulled his next even further left into bushes and trees. If he was lucky, he might be able to find a stance and a gap and force his ball back to the fairway and then be out of range of the green for his next. But, lo and behold, there was a temporary immovable obstruction on the line of sight from where his ball lay to the green. He was able to move away from all the trouble and should have been rather happy to drop only one shot on the hole.

Graham, on the other hand, had a piece of bad luck. To be bunkered near the green is usually a minor problem for a tournament player. True, he would rather have sent his approach near the hole and be putting for a birdie, but even from sand is often slightly hopeful of holing out and expecting to get down in two more. Graham's misfortune on the 14th was that he was bunkered to the right of the 14th green not in sand but in a bush of Scots broom. He had the choice of dropping it out, in which case the large bush would still have obstructed his next shot after a one-stroke penalty for an unplayable lie, or he could mount the bush and hope that the disturbance did not move the ball. All was well. He managed to chop it out onto the green.

Graham finished his round without further alarms in 70, three strokes behind George Burns. A stroke further away was Bill Rogers, not expected to win a major championship at that time. Five behind were Nicklaus, John Schroeder and Rodriguez, while Ben Crenshaw had soared up the field with a 64, having made the 36-hole cut none too comfortably.

How then did Graham's great final round go? He began by missing his only fairway during the round but had only a short iron to play from the difficult Merion rough. He birdied the hole and did better on the next, sending another short iron only a matter of inches from the hole. He was now just a stroke behind George Burns, with whom he was paired for the last round.

On the 4th, at 600 yards one of the longest par-5s in golf, Burns dropped a shot through putting a shot in a burn and the pair were level. The next, Graham three-putted for the only time in the round, yet putting was not the factor behind his eventual success. He used 33, which can be compared with what Tour players regard as a 'par' of 30 and Watson's recent average of only 28 and a bit. With Burns again in a one-shot lead the pair matched par with par over the next several holes, yet Burns no longer looked the likely winner. Although using an iron from the tee most of the time, he was still unable to find the fairway, pulling and hooking towards the left rough: he was having to struggle, Graham was hitting his tee shots into the fairway and his irons from the resultant good lies.

On the 10th, again in the left rough, Burns missed the green with his approach and did not get down in two this time. Level again, pars were exchanged up to the 14th, the first hole of Merion's famous finish, which Graham birdied from about 2 yards and repeated from a little further away on the next. On the 16th he had a chance of finishing the championship but hit the edge of the hole from about 3 yards. This is a hole of 455 yards with a green protected by a grassed over quarry, the second shot over it being one of the most testing on the nerve in golf. Graham finished with a par 3 and a par 4, again having birdie chances, for a 67 and a three-stroke victory over Burns and Bill Rogers, the latter encouraged enough by his performance to win the British Open at Royal St George's shortly afterwards.

Graham had missed only the first fairway and had been on, or on the edge of, every green in regulation strokes. Merion had forced him to use every club in his bag except one, a rare experience for pro or club golfer.

Why, though, is this round of golf considered fit to rank with, for example, Johnny Miller's 63 to win the 1973 US Open, Hogan's last round 67 at Oakland Hills to win in 1951 or the 65, 65 and 65, 66 that Watson and Nicklaus threw at each other for *two* rounds at the end of the 1977 Turnberry British Open? The answer is the quality of striking. Crenshaw, after his earlier 64, honestly did not regard it as a great round at all. He thought he'd hit more than his share of poor shots but his putter had been working very well. Not a few think that the quality of David Graham's ball control and precision of strike that last day has never been bettered.

Crenshaw figured also in Graham's other major championship victory, the

David Graham, US Open, Merion 1981

1979 US PGA at Oakland Hills, Michigan, a course that Ben Hogan once — and he intended it as no compliment — called a 'monster' after his win in the 1951 US Open. Hogan's distaste was mainly occasioned by changes Robert Trent Jones had made to the original design and by 1979 some of these had been moderated. A more recent change did nothing to ease the battle for par. Except for rabbits who blanch when they see the number '500', par 5s ought to be the easiest holes on any golf course: hit a couple of shots 200 yards each and you cannot be far away for your short pitch. Substitute these figures for a 450 yard par 4 and the golfer has already in theory dropped a shot after his two wooden club shots. Two of the par 5s at Oakland Hills were shortened the necessary distances and they became 4s.

Otherwise, the course was not at its most testing: the rough was not severe and the greens were comfortably holding. Watson, seeking his first US PGA (he still was at the beginning of the 1983 season) led after the first round with a 66, with Crenshaw taking over after with a 36 hole total of 136. At this point Graham was a stroke behind, with Jay Haas and Rex Caldwell, the latter a little known player with some strong, but not winning, performances on his record.

You would expect that as Crenshaw repeated his scores of the first two rounds, 69, 67, he ought to have won. He did not, however. Again the most consistently unsuccessful challenger of recent times for major championships missed out. (I omit Jack Nicklaus. In this respect, with twenty runner-up finishes he is the most pipped-at-the-post golfer of all time.)

Graham played out a steady 70 in his third round and therefore went into the last round two behind, a considerable deficit with Oakland Hills playing at its easiest.

On the last day he began with two birdies (Crenshaw opened with three) and added two more to be out in 31. He then birdied the 10 and 11th and put a medium iron inches from the hole on the 15th to be seven under par and, more significantly, into a two stroke lead in the championship. He now needed par over the last three holes for a 63. He passed the 16th and 17th safely but the proceedings on the last bordered on farce.

On this par 4 of 459 yards, David Graham lost concentration and pushed his shot to the right into trees. Finding his ball and a line to the green, he was unsure what club to play from so unfrequented a place. Graham thought a 7-iron, his caddie a 6 and no doubt the caddie would have been correct had the circumstances been normal, as the shot was just over 200 yards. But he reckoned without the extra distance a top golfer hits the ball when 'pumped up' by the thrill of a successful chase. Graham played the 6-iron and hit it well through the back of the green. Then the farce began. To win he had only to get the ball on the green and two-putt. He had the choice of a lofted shot that would probably run a little past the hole, which was set well towards the back, or to run it through the fringe grass at just the right pace to coast up to the hole. David Graham coasted it up to just short of the green. Winning was no longer a formality. He had a testing downhill chip, which didn't stop until a couple of yards past the hole. He then putted firmly for his 5 uphill, missed, and had to hole a testing downhiller of a little less than 2 feet. A formality? Not when you are playing for your first major championship and have just produced five mishit or misjudged shots in a row.

However, his nerve did not crack. The putt was holed and a sudden death play-off with Ben Crenshaw followed. Graham, the man who had just thrown outright victory away after a brilliant round of golf against Crenshaw, whose four round score of 272 would have won the PGA any year except 1964, and who had won money in vast quantities in golf but not the prize he most passionately craved —

a major championship.

The 1st was a hole of 444 yards. Crenshaw was just short in two, Graham well short and he then pitched several yards past the flag whereas Crenshaw put his little third shot almost dead to 2 foot. Graham holed the formidable putt. The story was much the same on the 521 yard 2nd. With Crenshaw 2 inches from the hole, Graham had to hole from 10 foot to stay in the match — and did. Suddenly it was all over, as Crenshaw was struggling. On a 202 yard par 3 he was bunkered but David Graham was only some 3 yards from the hole. Crenshaw hit a weak bunker shot and, having to putt first, missed. David Graham had two putts for the PGA but needed only one. He was the first Australian to win a major championship since Thomson took the 1965 British Open.

He had been playing the US Tour since 1971 and had won three events over the years there, with 1976 his best season, at 8th on the money list. Otherwise, America had been a hard grind. So had been David Graham's earlier golf life. When he decided to turn professional, his father had said he would never speak to him again should he do so. A few years later they did meet again but what should have been reconciliation turned into a quarrel and that was finally that.

He left school at fourteen for full-time work in golf and changed from playing left handed to right. In due course, he took a club professional's job, failed financially at it and worked at the Sydney PGF club factory while trying local tournaments. His first important victories did not follow until 1970, a year in which he won the French, Thailand, Victorian, Tasmanian and Yomiuri (Japan) Opens. With Bruce Devlin, a player who gave him much useful coaching help, he formed the winning pair in that year's World Cup.

The following year he won the Japan Open and his success in the 1976 World Matchplay may have had a significant effect on his career. In the final, Hale Irwin, winner the previous two years played almost flawless golf but towards the end Graham holed some monster putts and won in extra holes. The following year he won his national Open.

He does not entirely look the part as a great golfer, giving a rather mechanical impression as he sets up to hit. The head is tucked into drawn-up shoulders and the legs are straight so that the overall effect is of a stiffness utterly the opposite of the free swing of a Ballesteros. His walk also is on a par but handsome is as handsome does.

David Graham's most recent successes have been to take the Lancome Trophy in Paris in the consecutive years 1981-2 and the 1983 Houston Open.

Ralph
Guldahl

Born Dallas, Texas, USA, 1912

Mary Tudor had Calais engraved upon the heart and the name of Guldahl probably features similarly for Sam Snead. The pair were tied going into the last round of the US Open at Oakland Hills and Guldahl produced a 69 to Snead's 71. It was Snead's first season on the US Tour and the first time he had played the US Open, yet he was never to come any nearer to winning it (though he lost a play-off to Lew Worsham in 1947).

Guldahl had first been heard from in 1933 when he hunted the amateur Johnny Goodman home, scoring five strokes lower in the last round but still finishing second by a stroke, after missing a fairly short putt to tie.

Guldahl then virtually disappeared from the professional golf scene for a while, as the professional Tour was then very different from the regularly spaced sequence of events it eventually became. A player, as in Britain, was usually first and foremost a club professional, the Tour in the main a matter of winter events in the sunshine. Professionals could leave their clubs in the off season.

It is also said that Guldahl's game fell apart and that he spent the intervening years trying to put the pieces together again. As he had won a Tour event in 1932, the Phoenix Open, coupled with a strong US Open performance in 1933, the latter is probably the more likely explanation.

Eventually, Guldahl felt that he was performing more satisfactorily and he came back as a major golfer. He won three events from part way through the 1936 season and finished only $400 behind Horton Smith as the year's leading money winner. Today I suppose a man might expect to pocket more than $300,000 for that kind of season's work. Guldahl made $8,600.

Nevertheless he was well and truly on his way. Early the next year he led Byron Nelson by four strokes going into the last round of the Masters after 69, 72, 68 but the tournament swung on the par-3 12th and the par-5 13th. Guldahl went 5, 6, which was bad enough. Worse was that Byron Nelson recorded 2, 3 to leap-frog into a lead which he held to the end, winning by two strokes with 70 to 76.

However, it was not long before Snead's disappointment in the 1937 US Open. Snead had set a target, Guldahl knowing that he had to play from the 8th in level par to win. Guldahl promptly eagled that hole and held to par the rest of the way.

His 281 total was a US Open record that stood until his contemporary Hogan broke it in 1948. More important in the evolution of major championship golf was the fact that each of his scores was good (71, 69, 72, 69). Before, the US Open had normally been won with at least one poor score amongst the four. In Jones's four US Open wins, for example, his worst scores were 76, 79, 79, 75. From this time on, a more rigid consistency has been required, though there have been exceptions, such as Johnny Miller's 76, 63, finish in 1973.

Guldahl played at Southport and Ainsdale in the Ryder Cup that year, winning in both foursomes and singles. In the latter, playing top for the USA, he demolished Alf Padgham by 8 and 7. He earned a place in the 1939 match, which was cancelled because of war.

In 1938, he again looked a likely Masters winner, having tied with 'Light Horse' Harry Cooper but it was not to be. Henry Picard came in late to take the championship. Then came the US Open. Guldahl began 74, 70, 71 to be four strokes behind the leader, Dick Metz. Guldahl produced a closing 69

Ralph Guldahl

while Metz perpetrated one of the all-time collapses, a 79, but still finished second. Guldahl had become only the fourth man to take this title in successive years and only Ben Hogan has done it since.

Ralph Guldahl had just one more major championship left in him, the 1939 US Masters. Again the victim was Sam Snead. Guldahl went into the last round with a two stroke advantage but Snead came in with a total of 280, a new record for the event, after a last round 68. Guldahl got to the turn in 36, not a good enough score to win, but then came home in 33 to win by one.

That was nearly the end of Ralph Guldahl. He won two events in 1940 to take his career total to 14 and never won again. He left the Tour in 1942 and had another brief attempt in 1949.

What had happened? The usual tale is that Guldahl had 'lost his swing', something not in itself unusual but highly unlikely for a golfer of his eminence, having won three major championships in just over two years and the Western Open, little below them then in rank, three years in a row. Movie film was taken of his swing to see what faults might have developed in his method, a little difficult to tell in Guldahl's case for he always played with the rather extreme fault of falling back off the ball onto his right foot. In his good years, it hadn't mattered much.

Theories were many. The consensus was that Guldahl's swing was much the same but that the right things were no longer happening to the ball. Guldahl's explanation in later years was simple enough. He claimed that what he had lost was not his swing but his interest. He had made a name for himself and his motivation to play tournament golf was less than to live quietly with his family. The man born three months before Ben Hogan had come and gone several years before Hogan won his first major championship.

Walter ——— *Hagen* ———

Born Rochester, New York, 1892

'Hagin, a homebred American of whom no one seems to have heard much.' This was just about the first printed reference to a man who was soon to be the most famous golfer of his day. It came from the pen of Bernard Darwin, the most famous golf writer of them all, in the *Times* during September 1913 when he was over in the United States to watch either Harry Vardon or Ted Ray win the US Open. It is unlikely that he ever mispelled the man's name again.

At the time, Walter was uncertain as to whether or not his true metier lay in golf. He was sure he'd do pretty well as a baseball pitcher and there seemed to be more money and glory in that game. Meanwhile he'd made the trip to Brookline Country Club to see what this US Open Championship was all about.

A few days later, Walter had not won the thing but he had come close to ushering in the dominance of the New World over the Old. Until 1913, the US Open had usually been won by expatriate Scots and English and, even then, if the likes of Vardon, Ray, or Taylor chose to make the trip to the USA no US-based golfer was considered to have a chance. Vardon and Taylor had entered in 1900 and the result had been Vardon, first, Taylor second. Their nearest pursuers were seven and twelve strokes behind. In 1913 Ray and Vardon were on an exhibition and promotion tour and the US Open was postponed to fit in with their plans. The question was whether the poised, effortless and rhythmic swing of Vardon would win through, or the savage rather than elegant style of Ted Ray.

In the event, someone else came through of whom no one had heard much. His name rang out throughout America and the golf boom was on. Francis Ouimet was a shy 20-year-old amateur who was playing only because he lived near the course. He tied over four rounds with Vardon and Ray and in the 18-hole play-off, though no one thought he had a chance, won convincingly.

What of Walter Hagen? After three rounds he was two strokes behind the three who would play-off and knew by this time that he had the game to compete with anyone. However, he started his final round 6, 5, 7 on three par-4s. Having watched Vardon in practice, he thought he might as well try to emulate the feel of the Vardon swing. Much better: eagle, birdie, birdie and he was back with a chance. With nine holes to go he was level with Vardon and Ray with Ouimet apparently out of it: 43 to the turn, followed by a double bogey. But Walter perished on the 14th, having risked first a brassie then a long iron from doubtful lies. It was a 7 instead of a 4, the eventual margin by which he finished behind Ouimet, Vardon and Ray. There was, however, always next year.

Next year Hagen 'arrived'. In the first round he broke the US Open record with a 68: commonplace today, you may say, but consider the opening rounds of the three previous *winners*: 77, 74 and 81! There were no more sub-70 rounds for Walter and no bad ones either. He had led from start to finish and equalled the US Open record with 290.

In 1919, he did it again and with that second victory established himself as the premier golfer in America, until a man called Jones came along a few years later. Strangely, that was Walter's last US Open win. Again and again he featured amongst the leaders until as late as 1935, then well past his best, when he still finished third, in spite of the fact that his putting stroke had gone.

From 1919, Hagen's reputation derived from his achievements in the other two major championships (the US Masters did not begin until 1934): the US PGA and the British Open. In the first round, Hagen went to the turn in a useful 37 but his inward half was 48 for a total of 85. Not at all a good start and one he did little to improve on later. He finished 53rd. At the end of it all, his comment foreshadowed that famous one of General of the Armies Douglas Macarthur: 'I'll be back.' If there were wounds perhaps he healed them by crossing the Straits of Dover to win the French Open two weeks later.

Until American dominance over the British Open became almost total, from 1961 onwards, it used to be said that if the wind blew their chances were drastically lessened: US courses promote the technique of flying the ball long and high; punched low balls defeat the wind. Walter agreed. Later, he kept a special driver for use in windy linkland conditions. It had a particularly deep, straight face. At this time he was bothered by what had happened to his high pitch shots during that 48 inward half at Deal: they had been swept to either side of greens and away.

Back home he decided that he must add a particular shot to his armoury: the low pitch and run. The 1921 Open was held at St Andrews and Walter did *not* win, but sixth place was a considerable improvement.

In 1922 the Open returned to Kent at Royal St George's, Sandwich, and Hagen became the first American-born player to win both Opens. It was not without a fright. With a round to go, he was level with Jim Barnes and Charles Whitcombe, one behind J. H. Taylor and two behind Jock Hutchinson, champion the previous year. Hagen did a 72 and the championship was his, until the news began to come through that George Duncan was having the round of a lifetime. In 1920 George had begun with a pair of 80s and won. This time he had seemingly put himself out of it with a third-round 81. Yet as he approached the last he needed a 4 for a 68 and a tie with Hagen. Alas he missed the green and took three more to finish his round.

By this time, features of Hagen's game were making him a legend. For a start, his long game was the worst of any great player. On occasion, the drives and long irons would carve away to left and right. This gave Walter a stage on which to demonstrate one of his areas of mastery: the recovery shot. Here he always put on a show for the crowds. Deep in the woods, he would push his way back to the fairway to see exactly where the green was and then there would be much business of changes of mind about club before eventually the ball soared out and, as often as not, onto the green. Walter was then apt to ask: 'Did I make it look difficult enough?'

The ball had probably reached trouble in the first place not because of Walter's aversion to practice but due to two swing defects. He dragged the clubhead away from the ball, hands leading the backswing, an action which leads to wristiness and inaccuracy in the long game. He also bent his left leg in the backswing far more than would be acceptable today. All this came from the wide stance that leads to lack of balance. On the downswing, he had a pronounced sway into the ball, though much of this occurred after impact when it matters nothing.

With these flaws in his long game, Hagen had to make it up somewhere and it was from a hundred yards in to the flag that he did so. He was acknowledged as the finest short iron player of his day and his bunker play was equally good. Gene Sarazen invented the sand iron about 1931 by adding lumps of lead on the rear of the sole of his bunker iron. This caused the clubhead to ride through the sand. Overnight, once his idea had gone into production, the basic shot from sand became a matter of striking some two inches behind the ball and removing both a slash of sand and the ball from the bunker. Hagen, in his great days, played his shots with a thin-bladed club. If you hit behind the ball with

Walter Hagen

that, the head cut into the sand and the ball would squirt forward a few inches only. A Hagen bunker shot, then, had to take the ball clean. The strike had to be precise in the extreme and the touch sure. What was then perhaps the most difficult shot in golf has since become the easiest to both expert and average club golfer alike.

Once on the green, Hagen, with Bobby Jones, was the best putter of his day and so confident that once, when he had a putt to tie an Open Championship, he had his rival brought out of the clubhouse to watch it go in!

In 1924 Hagen won again, this time at Hoylake. He competed only once in the next three years, finishing third behind Jones in the latter's first Open win.

In 1928, the Haig's campaign in Britain began disastrously. He had contracted to play one of the best British players, Archie Compston, in a 72-hole match for

£500. Compston opened up with a 67, followed that with a 66 and then relaxed to a 70. Hagen had lost by the greatest margin I have seen recorded in a challenge match: 18 down with 17 to play. He was asked to continue in the second afternoon as a large crowd had gathered. He lost the bye and the bye-bye.

The following week Hagen won his third Open and Compston came third. In a return match fixed up in the US later that year Hagen won comfortably. I suspect that once Compston had built up an unassailable lead, Hagen was little concerned: he would have thought how much more publicity would result if the margin were really memorable. He was right: that 18 and 17 result is still remembered.

Hagen had one more Open left in him and it was his best. At Muirfield in 1929 Percy Alliss became the first player to break 70 over the course with a 69, to lead Hagen by six. At the end of the next day Hagen had brought about a nine-stroke swing over Alliss. He had gone round in 67, the best major championship round ever played by him or anyone else either up to that time. Nevertheless, Leo Diegel led him by two, having begun 71, 69.

The next day the winds were strong and there were to be no sub-par rounds for anyone. Hagen was right about Diegel: 82 in the morning and 77 in the afternoon, the latter about par for the day. Only one player broke 75 all day. Hagen took 75 and led the Open by four. In the afternoon he covered the first eight holes in 29 and the championship was over.

At this point, I think Hagen may have decided he'd done enough in the Open: he did not return for four years and played just twice before World War II. Increasingly, he travelled the world giving exhibition matches and the terms were usually the same: Hagen kept the gate money. On he went from country to country with the stuff thrust into suitcases.

Only one of Hagen's matches has so far been mentioned — the Compston débâcle — but it was as a match player that he excelled. Until 1958 the US PGA was decided by matchplay. Then the demands of TV for predictable timings caused a change to strokeplay. In it, Hagen set records that can now not be bettered.

Between 1916 and 1927 he won 32 of his 34 matches. In 1916 he lost in the semi-final on the last hole, did not play again until 1921, when he won. In 1923 he faced Gene Sarazen in a memorable final and lost on the 38th hole. He then proceeded to win 22 consecutive matches until beaten in the quarter finals of 1928. In between, he had won four consecutive titles, a record in major championships.

At the end of the 1920s Hagen had proved whatever it was that he wanted to prove. Golf for him was not, as for a Nicklaus or Hogan, a matter of establishing immortality. Hagen wanted the good things of life. Golf, rather than baseball, had proved to be the job that enabled him to 'Never worry, never hurry and be sure to smell the flowers along the way' for as he also said, 'I never wanted to be a millionaire, I just wanted to live like one.'

By 1982, only Jack Nicklaus, with 17, had exceeded Hagen's career record of 11 major professional championships. And no Masters existed in Hagen's best years.

Ben
——— Hogan ———

Born Dublin, Texas, USA, 1912

Just a few of our masters of golf became legendary during their playing careers. Hogan was thrice a legend. First there was the longest struggle of any major golfer to reach the top — that of Ben Hogan.

He turned pro in 1931 and the following year went to California with $75 for his expenses; he returned with nothing and his fate was similar the next year. His exceptionally full and lashing swing was the problem: too often the ball finished in what today's US players call 'Marlborough country' — the rough.

Though still a professional, Hogan turned to the conventional American pattern of earning a living in any way that presented itself: bank teller, oil field worker, car mechanic, croupier. The object was to save enough to try the US Tour again. In 1937 he did so. By January 1938 he had been living on little more than oranges for a month when he came out from his motel room one morning and found his car tyres stolen during the night. It was a turning point for Hogan. In despair, he went out to play the final round of the tournament and had a 69, which brought him up to second place and $380, which seemed a lot of money to a man with no tyres on his car. He was never so low again. That year he finished 15th in the money-winning list and improved to 7th the next year. He had found one of the 'secrets' of the golf swing: a consistent plane on the backswing, coupled with the feeling that at the top the club was fitting into a slot.

He was still not a name that counted for much: at that time Byron Nelson and Ralph Guldahl were carrying off the major championships and Sam Snead was the up and coming champion. By March 1940, Hogan had finished second six times in the previous 14 months and then set what was to be the first of many records. In the North-South Open at Pinehurst he began 66, 67, a record for the opening thirty-six holes of a US tournament. He went on to win and did much the same thing twice over the next two weeks. He finished the season as leading money winner and did so again in 1941, this time also winning the Vardon Trophy for the best stroke average. In 1942 he repeated the feat and also tied for the US Masters, though losing the play-off.

War had come though, and Hogan spent it in the US Army Air Force. Meanwhile, Byron Nelson, exempted as a haemophiliac from military service, was setting the records that earned him the soubriquet of 'Mr Golf'. Hogan was not amused.

In August 1945 he was released and won his second tournament and over the next 12 months shattered Nelson's dominance, winning eighteen tournaments to

Nelson's ten. He missed winning both the US Open and Masters by a single shot but did win his first major championship, the US PGA.

If in the late 1930s Hogan had found one of golf's secrets; by 1946 he had solved another problem, how to score competently when you are not playing well. He now felt for the first time that he could avoid disastrous rounds.

In 1947 he was slightly less successful and though Nelson had retired, his nerves gone, Hogan's friend Jimmy Demaret (*qv*) was the most successful player.

All the while, Hogan was at work, seeking to remove a basic threat to his technique. To all except the best club golfers, the main problem is a slice; but due to a far more natural athletic swing, most professional golfers fear a hook most. Hogan at this time was swinging back well beyond the horizontal and, though only 5ft 8½in tall and weighing just 135lb, he was able to lash the ball as far as any. Yet all his shots tended to hook at the end of flight. This kind of shot pattern holds neither greens nor fairways well.

He set to work to modify his method so that his basic shape of shot became a power fade: a ball which flies straight and at the end of flight 'fades' from left to right. This shot bites into receptive greens more readily and does not bound and roll along fairways. For tee shots it is also far more calculable. The player can aim along the left-hand side as his good shots will finish in the centre while his poor ones will drift further right — but still be in play and out of the rough.

Soon his fellow professionals were saying that Hogan had found 'the secret'. Hogan refused to discuss details, saying that he had not even told his wife. Hogan had, like Trevino years later, evolved a method that allowed him to hit full out without the fear of hooking, whereas a club golfer spends most of his time trying to avoid the opposite.

Hogan's method really involved just a few simple changes but they were changes that had to be drilled into muscle memory. He moved his left hand on the grip so that his thumb was directly on top and his right so that the V formed between thumb and forefinger pointed between chin and right shoulder: a method that almost all of his successors have followed.

Shortly he added a second US PGA to his record and then set out for a most significant course for his playing career, the Riviera Country Club in Los Angeles. There he beat the US Open record by five strokes and for the first time achieved the goal of an American professional: to be Open Champion. A new respect for him followed. The man known amongst his contemporaries as 'Bantam Ben' overnight became 'The Hawk'.

When the 1949 season opened, Hogan's dominance continued. He won two of the first four tournaments and tied in another. At 8.30 on the morning of 2 February 1949 the Cadillac he was driving was struck in fog by a Greyhound bus travelling on the wrong side of the road while overtaking a truck.

Hogan flung himself sideways to protect his wife. The move saved his life. The Cadillac steering wheel passed through the driver's seat, catching Hogan's left shoulder and breaking the collar bone. Its engine crushed his left leg and stomach. It was to be 5½ hours before an ambulance delivered the broken body to the Hotel Dieu Hospital in El Paso.

A preliminary examination showed that Hogan had suffered massive damage to his left leg, a fractured pelvis, broken ankle and collarbone, rib damage and

Ben Hogan

bladder contusions. Nevertheless a fortnight later it was arranged for him to leave hospital. Then he had a pulmonary embolism and it was realised that the crushed left leg might be the source of a coronary as further clots travelled towards the heart. The rare operation for the time of tieing off the vena cava to the heart from the lower body followed.

Two months after the accident a skeletal Hogan was thought fit enough to return to his home at Fort Worth, Texas. Throughout the ordeal, Hogan's thoughts had not been centred on survival only; whether or not he would be able to play golf again was at the forefront of his mind and while unconscious, he had been heard to shout to spectators to get away from the line of shot.

Once home he began to drill his body by means of 'laps' round his bedroom and occasionally he ventured from the house to be sought out by his wife who would discover him sitting by the roadside, his legs cramped.

By August Hogan was able to swing a club and the next month he was at Ganton Golf Club as the non-playing captain of the US Ryder Cup team. He had mellowed little and there was much press comment as he insisted that the clubfaces on some of the British team's irons were too deeply scored.

In December, he played his first full round of golf — from an electric cart —

but by the end of the year found himself able to play a full round at Colonial, Fort Worth. Immediately he entered the Los Angeles Open and when he arrived and played his first practice round it was only the fourth time since his accident that he had played a full round of golf. Still he had to wrap his leg in elastic bandage to assist circulation and in the evening he eased the cramps with hot baths. Yet he was proposing to play the normal four successive rounds. Hogan's scores were 73, 69, 69, 69 and he was in the clubhouse as the likely winner. Of those still on the course only Snead could equal him, needing to birdie each of the final two holes. Hogan was not amused — a play-off had not featured in his plans. Then the rains came and the play-off was delayed a week. Snead won but it mattered very little. The tournament had proved to Hogan that he could still play golf at the highest level. Had he failed badly, he might well have decided that his injuries and their after effects were too extreme for him to attempt to continue as a major golfer.

Thereafter, he was to limit his appearances in run-of-the-mill tournaments, as does Nicklaus today, and to concentrate almost exclusively on the major championships. Already a legend had been born and shortly Hollywood enshrined it in *Follow the Sun*, still the only film biography of a golfer.

In April Hogan finished fourth in the US Masters and the following month, tuning his game in the Greenbrier Invitational, equalled the all-time tournament record with 259 for seventy-two holes. Hogan dismissed the feat, saying that the course was a little short.

June came and with it the US Open at Merion Cricket Club and another challenge not merely to his nerve, but to his physical reserves. All British and US Opens at that time involved playing thirty-six holes on the final day: an Open was intended to be a test of stamina, both mental and physical, and it was a test only discontinued because of later TV demands.

Hogan began with a 72 and followed with 69, to stand two strokes away from the lead. In the final round scoring began to soar and Hogan was informed that he needed to play the last seven holes in just two over par to win. When he reached the 18th tee he had dropped three and now needed par on the 458 yard hole to tie. He drove well and slashed in a 2-iron to the green. Again it was a play-off, with Lloyd Mangrum and George Fazio. The result was Hogan 69, Mangrum 73, Fazio 75. Hogan's come-back was accomplished.

The 1951 Open was held at Oakland Hills and is still considered the most severe examination ever presented to a US Open field. Robert Trent Jones had been called in to toughen the course and had responded extravagantly. He had lengthened several of the holes and moved a multitude of bunkers up course so that the players could not sail their drives over them. Fairways were narrowed and the rough allowed to grow. All the competitors, including Hogan, were loud in protest.

After one round, Snead led Hogan by five strokes but then fell away while Hogan improved on his first round of 76 to 73. Now South African Bobby Locke had become the man to beat: he was a short hitter but one of the most accurate. As a putter he rates as one of the best of all time, rivalled only by Tom Watson, Billy Casper, Bob Charles and Walter Hagen.

Hogan began the last thirty-six holes with a surge, having birdies at three of the first five holes. Thereafter he fell away somewhat but still finished in 71, a score that put him two behind the leaders, Locke and Demaret.

The next time out Hogan played the first nine in level par and then embarked on the most commanding spell of golf he was to produce in a major championship. There was a flurry of birdies in what Hogan was later to consider the finest round of his major championship career. At the presentation ceremony his comment on the achievement was succinct: 'I am glad I brought this course, this monster, to its knees.'

The greatest achievement in golf history is usually considered to be Bob Jones's 'Grand Slam' of 1930 when he won both the professional and amateur championships of both Britain and the USA. Such a feat was not open to Hogan, a professional. His *annus mirabilis* was now, however, at hand.

He began with what he later considered his finest four consecutive rounds of golf in the US Masters: 70, 69, 66, 69. He won and set a championship record by five strokes.

He went on to Oakmont for the US Open. His first round of 67 gave him the lead and successive rounds of 72, 73, 71 meant that he led throughout; the first player to have done so since 1921. He had won the US Open four times in his last five starts, a sequence approached, but not equalled, only by Bob Jones in the 1920s. With Jones, Willie Anderson and Nicklaus, he is the only golfer to have won four times.

Friends had long urged him that greatness as a golfer must be proved on both sides of the Atlantic as Vardon, Jones, Hagen, Sarazen and Snead had done. If he entered the British Open at Carnoustie that year he would prove that he could adapt his game to links golf, which demands one ability not called for in America: judging the run of a ball up to the flag after pitching short of a green. The pattern in the USA is to fire in high shots full at the flag in the knowledge that on heavily watered greens of dense texture the ball will bite and quickly stop. At this time linksland greens in Britain were watered only to save them in drought conditions, though treatment is much different today. Hogan would also have to master the small ball, likely cold and the vagaries of strong and constantly shifting winds. No one told Hogan that greens were cut just once a week, flag positions not altered during the championship and goats used to crop the fairways. He was given advice about the continuing austerity of British food but decided to survive like the British did, even to tolerating a mutton diet, something no Texan considers fully fit for human consumption.

Hogan's distaste for the course was soon expressed (he offered to send for his lawn-mower from Texas to cut the greens) but his preparation was as meticulous as ever. He constantly practised on the course and paced it in reverse at dusk, learning the position of every hazard and the best areas of fairway to play for in order to have the best line of approach to greens. The local Scots appreciated his thoroughness and soon were calling him 'The Wee Ice Mon'.

Indeed Hogan's will was icy and relentless as his inevitable progress through the championship demonstrated. He began in low key with a 73 and then improved to 71. On the final day he again improved to 70 and in the afternoon set a new course record of 68. It was one of the comparatively rare occasions that a player has improved with each round, and he had improved by eight strokes on the previous Open total over Carnoustie. Hogan had proved his supremacy and the British press was unanimous that this was the greatest golfer yet seen.

He never again played in the British Open and, more strangely, this was his last win in a major championship. For the moment, though, he was at the summit and since then no player has won the Master, US Open and British Open in one calendar year. Even Nicklaus and Palmer have but once each threatened this achievement.

Hogan's decline can be put down to two main factors. He was into his 40s, a time when nearly every golfer is past his best, and in Hogan's case he had also to contend with the aftermath of the impact of a Cadillac engine and steering wheel. Then there was putting. Player and Nicklaus remain the sole exceptions to the rule that nerve on the greens fails from the constant wear and tear of having delicately to coast long putts up to the hole and resolutely thrust the short ones in.

There were dramas to come, however. Two years later Hogan was seated in the locker room at the Olympic Country Club in San Francisco waving away congratulations at having just won his fifth US Open. His scores seemed unassailable but a small town pro from Iowa , who had taken 87 in a practice round and whose highest achievement to that date had been to finish sixth in a run-of-the-mill tournament, still had a statistical chance. Jack Fleck had to birdie two of the last four holes to tie Hogan. He did just that and in the press tent afterwards stood bereft of speech, swaying on his feet.

So far the stuff of fairy tales. The next day the enchantment continued. Fleck came to the 18th tee in the next day's play-off one to the good at which point Hogan played the decisive stroke: he hooked into just about the deepest patch of rough on the whole course and it took him three more to regain the fairway.

The following year, Hogan needed to hole a short putt to earn a tie with Cary Middlecoff. It is said that he spent some considerable time at the edge of the green practising a variety of putting strokes before he stepped up to his ball and missed. Hogan had been trying to find a stroke, any stroke at all, that made him feel confident of a chance of pushing the ball into the hole.

Hogan had one more throw for the US Open left in him and that was at the age of 48. The 1960 at Cherry Hills in Colorado was arguably the most dramatic of all, containing such ingredients as Palmer's 65 dash in the last round to victory; Jack Nicklaus's near successful bid to be the first amateur to win since 1933; Mike Souchak's opening 68 and 67 that left him several strokes in the lead before he crumbled away; even the unlikely revival of Jack Fleck who, enchanted once more, birdied five of the first six holes in the last round; and there was the old hero, Hogan. After a weak opening round, he found the old precision and in one stretch hit 34 consecutive greens, a likely record for championship play. By the 15th hole he was tied for the lead with Palmer and Fleck. Hogan calculated, correctly, that a 4, 4, finish would do. On the 17th he was left with a short pitch over a lake that had to come down just past the hole and spin back towards it. He played the shot too well: his ball bit and then spun all the way back to the water's edge and that was that.

Hale
——— Irwin ———

Born Joplin, Missouri, USA, 1945

Hale Irwin is a very quiet fellow on a golf course; there is no punching of the air in triumph or exaggerated gestures of despair. The controlled neat swing reflects his personality. Such composure has no doubt often been put to the test in the fire of competition but I would guess never more so than in the final of the 1976 World Matchplay at Wentworth.

The match was closely contested throughout the 36 holes, and beyond, with Irwin narrowly in control throughout, having gone round the then par 73 course in 69 in the morning to David Graham's 70 and the pair continuing in the same vein after the break. On the 12th hole, Irwin seemed to have the match almost in his pocket when his ball lay 5 feet from the hole with the Australian some 25 feet away. Yet Graham holed that long one to set the pattern of what lay ahead.

On the 14th tee, Irwin stood 2 up with only four holes to play; by no means a certain victory margin but the odds would have been even more strongly in his favour, if bets were still being struck, after he sent in an almost perfect 4-iron the 180 yards to the flag to settle 2 yards from the hole. Even more so, once Graham sent his reply through the green. However, only a half for Irwin resulted for Graham chipped dead and Irwin missed his short putt.

There followed a par 5. Both the players hit drives that gave them open lines to the green. Graham's long iron was good but left him about 30 yards from the hole, while Irwin's was on line and pulled up only some dozen feet from the hole. Dormie 3? Not a bit of it. David Graham's putt was hit with just that perfection of pace which means that the ball will topple in if it catches the edge of the hole. Irwin missed and was now just one ahead with the testing finish of Wentworth that requires good placement of tee shots.

The initiative, after an eagle 3, was now with David Graham. On the short par 4 16th he took out his 3-wood for safety but came off the shot and his ball carved away to the right and into the crowd. Hale Irwin followed with a neatly struck 4-wood to a perfect position. Graham had the luck to find his ball in a lie and position that enabled him to hit for the green rather than chop back to the fairway. He finished some 7 yards away, while Irwin was a little nearer. The hole was halved.

The 17th, at 571 yards, is a formidable hole, not only because of length. There is out of bounds to the left, and none too far off the fairway, yet the tee shot must be aimed down the left for the player to have a chance of getting on in two: the ball almost always kicks from left to right. A drive down the middle will drift to the right and tall trees then block the fairway wood to the green. Graham's ball finished well down the middle; Irwin's was a few yards off the fairway to the right in rough trampled by the week's crowds. His shot to the green was blocked and he played a little left, his ball coming to rest almost 100 yards short. Graham's following wooden club was just short of the green and the odds heavily in his favour until Irwin's near perfect wedge approach pitched and held only 5 feet from the hole. Whether in reaction or not, from his position only 20 yards short of the green the Australian half thinned his little approach and was several yards past the hole. He followed, however, with a putt that seemed always to be missing on the left but which toppled in from that side. No doubt highly disappointed, Irwin still holed for his half and went to the last tee holding on to his one hole margin.

On this 502 par 5 which doglegs to the right, the tee shot again should not be to the right because of trees that block out the green. Graham drove down the middle and Irwin, being to the right, cut his second round the corner to only a few yards short, while Graham bunkered his 1-iron to the left front of the green.

Now came Hale Irwin's first culpable error. He failed to strike his chip cleanly and his ball pulled up some 5 yards short. Graham took his shot cleanly from the sand and the ball spun and stopped some 5 feet from the hole. Irwin then missed his putt, while Graham — almost inevitably by now -- holed his.

Extra holes, sudden death.

The 471 yard 1st hole at Wentworth is about the toughest on the course, a par 5 until remeasurement some years ago. It demands a long tee shot to be followed by a very long whack uphill to the green. With a drive and a 1-iron Graham was on the front while Irwin's 4-wood second was bunkered to the right of the green. From there, he played a fine recovery to 2½ feet. Both got their pars.

The 155 yard 2nd at Wentworth is no easy touch. A tall tree to the right has caught many tee shots over the years and otherwise length must be precisely judged. A ball pitching to the front of the green may run off again while a ball halfway up the putting surface faces a very tricky upslope when the pin is set to the rear, as it always is for championship play. Both then would attempt to hit the slope to the rear of the green and hope to run back towards the hole. Both hit 6-irons a touch too long but both came back onto the green.

It was Irwin to putt first from some 7 yards and he came up a few inches short. Graham holed from about 10 feet. Irwin gave him an effortful smile, a rather quick pat on the back and was gone.

He had lost three out of seven holes, and the match, while playing better than par golf with the only flaw just a little shot to the 18th that ought to have been close. On the greens, he had holed all the short ones but none of the near impossible long ones that Graham had coasted home so readily.

Back in the locker room it is said that his feelings were revealed as his golf bag was hurled across the room.

However, Hale Irwin could have been consoled by the thought that he had won the World Matchplay in the previous two years, a rare feat, and had received his first invitation as US Open champion. Three weeks before the 1974 event at Winged Foot he had dreamed he was the winner, quite a boost to the psyche of a golfer but one which is soon deflated by a couple of 6s on the card. We hear no tales of those with visions of victory who do not achieve it!

At the time, Irwin was in his seventh season on the US Tour but was by no means a big name. He had won only two tournaments, the Heritage Classic in both 1971 and 1973 and during this time had pushed himself into the top 20 money winners. Winged Foot suited his play for it is a difficult course, accuracy with tee shots, in particular, being essential.

Many US Tour courses more reward iron shots at the flag and sharp putting; the drives have space to fly erratically, length not accuracy being the more rewarded. Hale Irwin's winning score of 287 was one of the highest in the post-war period but single round scores in the high 70s and low 80s were very frequent. Irwin began with a 73 — one of the best scores against par of 70 — and when he followed with a 70 was tied for the lead with the formidable trio of Palmer, Floyd and Player. When he followed with a 71 to Player's 77 and Floyd's 78 this pair were out of it and Irwin was one behind a new leader, Tom Watson. This, though, was a Watson who had not yet learned how to survive the pressure of leading and had yet to win a US tournament. (He did so later the same month, the Western Open.) That 16 June at Mamaronek, however, he joined those who were finding it all too easy to go round in 79. Irwin produced nothing to stir the senses that final day. Of those fighting out the championship, he merely produced the steadiest golf. Jack Nicklaus had the day's lowest round with a 69 but began eleven strokes behind Irwin. The rest fell by the wayside as Irwin birdied only one hole but dropped few shots on an undemonstrative progress to a 287 total and victory by two strokes. He did it, towards the end, knowing that he had to produce, to win, a strong finish from Forrest Fezler and Lou Graham, playing ahead of him.

Being US Open champion is second to nothing as a tonic to the golfer's self-assurance. In the next few years, Irwin added more victories at home and overseas and was amongst the top group of money winners on the US Tour annually.

However, although he was a golfer of world status, his career needed the punctuation mark of another major championship. It is an oddity of golfing memory that those who win just one may be soon forgotten but a double victory is less perishable.

In 1979, Hale Irwin became only the fourteenth player to win the US Open twice. Again it was on a course — Inverness, Ohio — that brought forth high scoring from the field. Among qualifiers for the last two days, there were only 14 rounds throughout better than 70 out of 252 rounds played. Irwin had two of them, while his 67 was joint best and, basically, that was good enough to come near to ensuring victory.

He began with a 74 to find a host of players ahead of him. Twelve players had 70 or 71 (one of these, Lon Hinkle, was to follow with 77, 76, 81). A 68 in the second round, equalled only by one other player, brought him through the field, though he remained three strokes behind the leaders, Larry Nelson and Tom Purtzer. Irwin made even more of a move on the third day with a 67, again the day's joint lowest round. During it there came an unusually dramatic stroke from Hale Irwin. Just ahead of him, Tom Weiskopf was making a very strong surge indeed. Irwin was able to watch him, on the 523 yard 13th, hit his 4-iron second

Hale Irwin (right) greets Brian Barnes (visor).
Bernard Gallacher (centre)

close and hole the putt for an eagle. Irwin, some 220 yards from the green hit a 2-iron in to about a yard to complete a little spurt of birdie, birdie, eagle.

They both finished with 67s, leaving Irwin three strokes in the lead for the last day, a winning position but only if the nerve holds. Irwin's was severely tested and it showed. He later admitted he was 'choking' from the first tee onwards.

However, it was none too apparent to the turn and he increased his lead to six strokes with nine to play. Now that really is a winning position. He had enjoyed the luck that perhaps a winner deserves, hitting one drive into trees but bounding out and following with too strong an approach which hit the flag and came to rest only some 3 yards away.

Thereafter, he suffered a complaint well known to golfers at all levels: he tried to steer and control his wood shots rather than rely on the muscle memory of his swing to turn the ball from the right half of the fairway back to the middle. He lost the feel of 'releasing' the clubhead at the target and the result was a stream of off-line shots. He was several strokes in hand, however, even with just a couple of holes to go, only Player having produced much of a run in the last round, closing with a 68. That was good enough to bring Gary up to joint second with Jerry Pate. Irwin finished double bogey, bogey and was Open champion by two strokes, one of the least appropriate finishes of a champion in modern times.

Not long afterwards, he was to oppose his neat consistent play against the *bravura* of Severiano Ballesteros. After two rounds, Irwin led with 68, 68 against the Spaniard's 73, 65 and they matched each other with third round 75s but perhaps the spectacle of Ballesteros's cavalier tee shots and spectacular recovery play had diluted Irwin's resolve to be one of few to win both Opens the same year. He finished in 78, 6th place, to the Spaniard's 70.

Hale Irwin's major championship successes have come when his consistency of stroke is rewarded on threatening courses. He makes his living on the US Tour primarily however, in the regular week-by-week circuit. There, the reward for consistency is a steady flow of pay cheques and high-place finishes rather than the winner's enclosure.

Irwin exemplified this in 1978 when he set a record, $191,666, for the most money garnered by a non-winner, having thirteen times finished in the top 10. At the beginning of the 1980 season, he missed the 36-hole cut in the Crosby event, having survived on the previous 86 occasions, the best performance in recent years.

However, he is a tournament winner. To his Open Championships, he had added another twelve US tournaments by the end of 1982. Overseas, as well as the two World Matchplay Championships, he was Australian PGA champion in 1978, South African the following year, World Cup individual winner in 1979 and took the Japanese Bridgestone Classic in 1981. In 1983 he won Jack Nicklaus's Memorial Tournament.

Tony
——Jacklin——

Born Scunthorpe, Lincolnshire, England, 1944

When Tony Jacklin won the British PGA at Hillside in 1982 for his first win on the British mainland since 1973, this was regarded by the press as a return of the prodigal to the heights. For the remainder of the season he did relatively little; nor should too much have been expected of him. For some years, Tony Jacklin has been one of a group of very good European golfers who may be expected to win a tournament here and there. His play has not, however, justified the urge of so many to speculate at length about his chances in 'the Open starting on Thursday'. The simple enough reason is that he has not been a world class player since around 1973 or 1974 and has been eroded by the stress of playing tournament golf for nearly twenty years. The history of US and European tournament golf is spattered with the names of those who reached their own particular peak — and were heard little of again.

For example, who are Gary Groh, Pat Fitzsimons, Tom Jenkins, Larry Ziegler and Don Iverson? Or Jimmy Kinsella, Ross Whitehead, John Garner and Norman Wood? The first group won US Tour events in 1975; the second, European events in 1972. They are not failures because they have done relatively little since and neither is Tony Jacklin because he did not win more major championships after his Opens of 1969 and 1970: both, incidentally, further away in time.

Instead, he should be heralded as a British golfer who achieved, for a short space, as much as Henry Cotton in major championships. If we grant the pair equal status we have two British players whose deeds in great events have not been surpassed since the days of the Great Triumvirate before the First World War. Take in Europe as a whole, and there would be only Severiano Ballesteros to join them and perhaps rate higher.

Unlike these two, Jacklin's career followed a remarkably steady curve, both up and then down. He was an outstanding player by 1967 and then in both 1968 and 1969 won only one tournament. But how significant these two were. The Greater Jacksonville Open came to him in 1968, the first fully recognised event to be won in the USA by a British golfer since Ted Ray's Open win in 1920. His victory at Royal Lytham in the British Open of 1969 was the first by a British golfer since Max Faulkner's Portrush win in 1951. Perhaps 1970 was his best year, as his seven-stroke margin in taking the US Open was the greatest since Jim Barnes's nine lead in 1921 and he was the first British player to win since 1920. In the meantime, no British-based player had been worth even an honourable mention, the nearest approach being Phil Perkins's joint second place behind Gene Sarazen in 1932.

Tony Jacklin

At Hazeltine National, in Minnesota, Jacklin was confronted the first day of the US Open by a course which was very wet and therefore playing its full 7,151 yards. To compound the difficulties, there was a strong north-westerly wind. Jacklin came in with a 71, not normally a headline round, but this day he was the only man to break the par of 72 and found himself in a two-stroke lead. On day two the wind had dropped and better scoring was expected. (Nicklaus had taken 81, Player 80 and Palmer, with his low flight a good wind golfer, 79.) Jacklin went round in 70, a round that only Dave Hill, with 69, bettered. He was three strokes in the lead from Dave Hill.

The third day he produced another 70, one alarm coming on the 17th when his tee shot finished with trees blocking the route to the green. Jacklin lashed an 8-iron over, with both the height and carry to reach the green 160 yards away.

He began the last round with a four-shot lead on Hill, the next challenger a further three strokes away. Despite the lead, he had to conquer the temptation to play safe, which often enough leads to over-caution and sudden panic if shots begin to seep away. Jacklin did have a crisis: after six holes he was one under par but then went over on two successive holes. On the 9th, his birdie putt was far too strong and would have been several feet past but he had the luck to hit the back of the hole, his ball hopped in the air — and went in.

By now, Jacklin was in a trance-like state, a cocoon of concentration when only making the next shot exists, the world shut off. As he played the last hole he had a six-stroke lead, sent a 4-iron to the green and, for good measure, holed a long putt. He was the first Briton to hold the British and US Opens at the same time.

In America, Jacklin did not go on to build a formidable career. He had joined the US Tour in 1967, when he still had to consolidate his name in Britain, and for some time it had been fun. As the years passed, competing in a foreign land and incessant motel life lost appeal. He had one more tournament victory, the 1972 Greater Jacksonville Open, the last event won by a British player until Peter Oosterhuis's 1981 Canadian Open. In the years from Ted Ray's US Open win in 1920, there have been five wins in important US events, three of them going to Tony Jacklin. (The other, is Henry Cotton's win in the 1948 White Sulphur Springs Invitational, not a PGA-recognised event.)

But despite his success in America, where he won some $300,000, his performances in the British Open are the real barometer of his career. He first featured in 1967, coming in 5th, seven strokes behind Roberto de Vicenzo at Hoylake and the following year at Carnoustie was amongst the leaders until an 80 in the final round dropped him to 18th place, ten behind Player.

Then came his glory at Royal Lytham, his fellow protagonists Bob Charles, Peter Thomson, Roberto de Vicenzo, Christy O'Connor and Jack Nicklaus — all except O'Connor previous and recent winners of the championship.

Jacklin began with a 68 to excite British hopes, Bob Charles, champion in 1963, making the running with a 66. The New Zealander followed with a 69 to lead Jacklin's 36-hole total by three strokes. Also well up were O'Connor (71, 65 — one behind Charles); Thomson (71, 70); Wolstenholme and Moody (70, 71); and Casper (70, 70).

On the third day, Casper, Wolstenholme and Moody were gone. Charles and O'Connor fell behind with 75 and 74 respectively; Thomson held steady with another 70, while Vicenzo strode up the field with a 66. At the end of the day, after a 70, Jacklin held the lead. His score had been saved with some superlative bunker play (a very strong area of his game) towards the end of his round. On the 15th he got out to a foot from the hole, birdied the 16th after an immense drive and then hooked into a gulley behind bushes off the next tee. After his second shot he was still in the rough and then put his next into a greenside bunker and came out to just over a couple of feet and holed for a one over par 5. On the last he drove into a heavy lie in the right rough and with his second was bunkered on the right of the green, but came out to 3 feet to par the hole.

His 208 total put him two ahead of O'Connor and Charles, three better than

Vicenzo and Thomson; Nicklaus had made a move with a 68 but at five in arrears had far to go.

Jacklin and Charles were paired for the last day. By the 14th, Jacklin still had his two-stroke margin and on that hole increased it to three. Both dropped strokes on the 15th and parred the 16th, while Jacklin saw a shot of his lead go on the next when he took three putts after being short with his first from 11 yards. He went into the last with a two-stroke lead but if Charles should birdie . . . .

Jacklin hit a huge drive to carry the threatening bunkers on the 18th and hit his second to about 3 yards, with Charles a little further away, also in two. When Charles could not quite succeed with his longer putt Jacklin was champion.

The following year, as holder of both US and British Opens, he made a startling beginning to the defence of his British title at St Andrews, three weeks after he had won at Hazeltine National. On the 1st, he wedged to 4 or 5 yards and holed the putt and repeated the birdie on the next from about 5 foot. Two pars followed before he two-putted the 567 yard 5th for another birdie. On the 7th he hit a long drive onto a bunker lip but played a deft pitch and run from an uncomfortable stance to 4 feet and holed. The climax to the first half came on the 9th. He played a 1-iron from the tee at this 359 yard hole and followed with a 9-iron to the green which bounced once, bounced again and dropped into the hole for an eagle. Jacklin was out in 29, perhaps the best start made in a major championship by anyone, anywhere. He birdied the next, parred the 11th and his drive to the 312 yard 12th would have reached the green but was diverted by a scorer at the approaches. He 'only' parred the hole — failure after what had gone before — and then the rains descended on the parched course. On the 560 yard 14th he hit a good drive but came off his 4-wood second shot, perhaps distracted by a cry of 'Fore', and cut it into a bush. At that point the course was under water and play was suspended.

The next day, he bogeyed the hole and also the 16th and 17th, finishing in 67; an excellent score but not the marvel that had been in prospect. After two rounds, he was level with Nicklaus on 137, both one worse than Lee Trevino. After day three, Jacklin and Nicklaus were still level, joined by Doug Sanders, leaving Trevino with a two stroke lead.

On the final day, winds gusted up to 60mph and many of the last day qualifiers scored in the high 70s, Trevino with 77 amongst them and Jacklin also, with a 76 and 5th place behind the play-off between Nicklaus and Sanders.

The following year at Royal Birkdale Jacklin was once more in the thick of it, producing rounds of 69, 70, 70, 71 for third place, two behind champion Trevino and one behind 'Mr Lu' from Taiwan. He was not overly disappointed because he did not feel he had played well.

Tragedy was to follow in 1972 at Muirfield, perhaps twice. He began 69, 72 to Trevino's 71, 70, while a highly motivated Nicklaus (he had won both the Masters and US Open that season) was after the Grand Slam and had begun 70, 72.

The third day, Jacklin played finely for his 67, the high point being an eagle on the 558 yard 5th hole. He established a lead over Trevino early on. But Trevino's finish was breath-taking and must have taken the wind from Jacklin's sails. He finished with five consecutive birdies but more remarkable than the card scores was the manner of their accomplishment. On the 14th, he holed from 5 yards; on the 15th from twice that distance and on the 188 yard 16th was bunkered, thinned his explosion shot but struck the flag on the second bounce and down and in went his ball; he reached the par 5 17th in two and two-putted for another; on the last, he sent his second shot through the green but holed a long chip shot. Where Jacklin might have held a comfortable lead at the end of play, he was a stroke behind.

The final day was closely contested by Trevino and Jacklin, though Nicklaus became a major factor from six strokes behind. He birdied six of the first eleven holes and at one point had edged into the lead. After Jacklin birdied the 14th, there was a three-way tie. Nicklaus then dropped a shot on the 16th and failed to birdie the 17th, finishing with a magnificent 66 that should not have been quite good enough to beat either Trevino or Jacklin.

As Mary Tudor had her Calais, Jacklin has his 17th at Muirfield, a hole which some argue changed the whole course of his career. He drove long and straight while Trevino was bunkered and still behind Jacklin's drive after his recovery. Trevino then hit a 3-wood short of the green and into long grass, while Jacklin hit his second to within a short pitch of the green. Trevino had hit his fourth shot through the back. He would have to struggle for a 6. Jacklin pitched up a little short of the flag while Trevino, recognising defeat (he had just said: 'That's it. I've thrown it all away.') carelessly selected a chipping club, gave a glance at the hole — and ran his ball in for a 5.

Jacklin had now to hole his putt to take the lead. He putted firmly — too firmly — and was about 3 feet past. When he missed the return the championship was Trevino's, unless he faltered in the last. He didn't. Jackline dropped another shot to finish third, behind Nicklaus.

Each year from 1967 onwards, Jacklin had contended for the Open. Indeed, if we stretch credulity, he could have won them all. But Muirfield in 1972 was the end for him as far as major championships are concerned. He has never since featured, other than momentarily.

In the years that followed, Jacklin was considered by most to be the best striker of a golf ball in Britain and many on both sides of the Atlantic considered him the most reliable long driver that there was. As recently as 1982, he was only a dozen yards shorter in European Tour averages than the leader, Greg Norman. He despaired increasingly of his putting and his wedge and short iron play suffered from the pressure of feeling he had to get such shots close to the hole for his putter was going to lose, not save, strokes.

There are many who have argued that success spoiled Tony Jacklin. Wealth poured down upon him, bringing a Rolls-Royce and a country mansion in the Cotswolds, and the lad from Scunthorpe was well-satisfied, not having that supreme appetite to be the greatest golfer in the world. Others claimed that the demands on his time from his manager Mark McCormack for money-making engagements left him tired and with insufficient time to practise. Perhaps, but the Palmers, Players and Nicklauses thrived on the same diet.

My own feeling is that few golfers, except the very greatest, stay at the top for long. With seven or eight years as a very superior golfer indeed, Tony Jacklin showed himself more of a master than any British player since the Great Triumvirate, with the sole exception of Henry Cotton.

Mark James

Born Manchester, England, 1953

A few years ago I wrote a golf book and wanted to include in it a photograph or two of untried professionals I thought might become major players. I think I settled on Ballesteros, Jerry Pate and Mark James.

Of course, there was never much doubt of Ballesteros from the moment he burst upon the golfing consciousness at Royal Birkdale, and Pate's 1976 US Open victory soon proved no flash in the pan. Mark James, though, remains an enigma.

I drove up to St Andrews from County Durham a couple of days before the start of the 1978 Open to take a close look at certain players. The time for close looks is during practice days rather than when play begins in earnest and the multitudes gather. I was feeling that slight glow of self-righteousness that comes when you have got up at 5 in the morning when work has not forced you to. This was dispelled quite quickly by the sight of Mark James leaving the 18th green, having already completed his first practice round by 9 o'clock ...

During that day, I saw him several times more. There were other practice round sightings, with James — fairly unusually — always marching alone, except for his caddie, and expressionless. The main purpose of a practice round is to learn the course, to find out the best placement of a tee shot so that the golfer has the best line, for him, into the green that suits the flight of shot that you would prefer to play. It is best done unsociably on your own.

James was not content with these exertions alone. He put in spells on the practice ground, working to get the feel of certain kinds of shot he would need at St Andrews, particularly running shots or, the reverse, as high as possible with maximum stop worked on the ball. He also watched certain other golfers.

As dusk neared, and I was thinking that it really was time to eat, James was still there. By now he was out on the course without clubs, leaning on walls and fences to see how others approached the playing of certain holes.

Perhaps the fairy tale ending of this recollection ought to be that James went out and won that Open. Alas, after looking through all my notes on that championship I find no mention of his name. (For the record, Jack Nicklaus won by two strokes, with Crenshaw, New Zealand's Simon Owen — enjoying a brief taste of glory — Ray Floyd and Tom Kite tied for second place.)

Nevertheless, by 1983 Mark James has shown a taste for the big occasion. In 1976 he was in his first year on the professional circuits and in the Open at Royal Birkdale he produced a 66 in the last round, a score equalled only by Johnny Miller, the champion that year. It pulled him through the field to joint 5th place to tie for the best British position.

Overall, in his first year he finished 15th in the European money list and had reminded observers of the golf scene that it is possible for the truly talented amateur to make the transition to the professional ranks without a few years of despair.

James had a short, but outstanding amateur career. At Woodhall Spa in 1974 he won the English Amateur by 6 and 5 in the final and the following year at Hoylake faced the American Vinnie Giles in the final but was eclipsed 8 and 7. He had come from a very good Walker Cup at St Andrews. He played in the top foursome with Richard Eyles on the first morning, overcoming the strong American pairing of Jerry Pate and Dick Siderowf by one hole. In the afternoon, after the other three foursomes had been lost, he played top in the singles and beat Jerry Pate 2 and 1, a man who was to be the next year's US Open champion. On the second day, again with Eyles, another strong American pairing was dismissed by 5 and 3, the widest British margin of the whole match. The only blemish on his record came that afternoon when he lost heavily to Gary Koch.

Nevertheless, James's was the best British performance, his three points being a substantial proportion of the British grand total of $8\frac{1}{2}$ against the $15\frac{1}{2}$ of the Americans.

Mark James

In 1979, James went to the Lytham Open having won the Welsh Classic about a month before, his second career win on the European Tour to add to another in Zambia. He began with a near-disastrous 76 but then fired rounds of 69, 69. At that stage he was three behind leader Hale Irwin but only one behind the eventual winner, Severiano Ballesteros. This was his first real taste of being within reach of an Open Championship win. On the final day, he easily overhauled Hale Irwin's 78 with his own 73 and finished fourth, again as the leading British player.

He was even more in the limelight in 1981 at Royal St Georges. After a 72, 70, 68 start he found himself paired with Bill Rogers for the final round and centre stage but five strokes behind the American, enjoying easily his finest season which saw him finish as undoubtedly the player of the year. Early in the round the American faltered, however. James made up a little ground and could have closed the gap completely with more luck with his putter. He struck a few good ones from medium range but always they failed to drop. Eventually, the American played finely and James himself faltered in mid-round. Nevertheless, he was again leading British player, tied third with Ray Floyd behind Langer and, of course, Bill Rogers.

Over that final Open round, James had found himself opposed to one of the world's best putters and this is a department of his game that causes James some despair. He regards himself as a relatively poor putter, a not uncommon feeling amongst players. After all, so many putts present the apparently simple problem of hitting a ball a short distance dead straight but the trick of it is elusive and James more than most seems to feel that he cannot solve it. It is therefore surprising that when the European Tour began to keep statistics for driving length and accuracy, putting and the rest in 1982 James came out of it remarkably well. Nick Faldo registered as the best putter, averaging 28.5 a round. Then there was a big gap to Bob Charles at 29.3 and Mark James, surprisingly, came only half a stroke worse than this, signing in at joint 7th at 29.8 per round; figures that actually put him in much the same class as maestros of the putting surface.

In the long game, James is equally a perfectionist, seldom indeed satisfied with his striking and always in the search of the perfect shot. Accordingly, he is usually disappointed: even the greatest manipulators of a golf ball on a good day will not usually admit to more than two or three perfect shots in a round of golf. This disappointment accounts for the fact that James is seldom indeed to be seen with jolly visage. His normal expression while contemplating the progress of his ball through the air ranges between disgust (for a good shot) and despair (for an average one). If the ball has actually sailed deep into the undergrowth, however, you can scarcely tell from the James expression for there can hardly be anything left in his emotional range without resort to suicide.

I make these remarks not in any real spirit of criticism. Golf is a demanding pursuit. There is little to grin about after a shot that falls short of the ideal. To me, Mark James's dedication to mastery means that he is far more likely to achieve his targets than those satisfied with less.

Aged thirty in the autumn of 1983, James has for eight years been amongst the very top group of British players and has been in the Ryder Cup team three times (all the years, in fact, that he was eligible). In general play, his best year was 1979, at third in the Order of Merit, while he has always been a consistent money winner and at the end of 1982 had eight tournament wins to his credit (more than Nick Faldo). The full promise, however, has yet to be fulfilled.

His swing is not for purists. It lacks the possibility of elegance through being short. Where Cotton has preached the advantages of the three-quarter swing over the decades, James has gone a stage further, often apparently not getting the clubhead much above shoulder height. But from that position he can generate as much power as all but the Greg Normans of modern golf. His stance also has phases of being distinctly unorthodox as he tests the efficacy of this and that theory so that he has played from as open a position as Lee Trevino at times.

Bobby
Jones

Born Atlanta, Georgia, USA, 1902

'Of all the great athletes, Jones came closest to what we call a great man.'

'As a young man he was able to stand up to just about the best that life can offer, which isn't easy, and later he stood up with equal grace to just about the worst.'

'In all the years of contact with the famous ones of sport I have found only one that would stand up in every way as a gentleman as well as a celebrity, a fine, decent, human being as well as a newsprint personage, and who never once . . . has let me down in my estimate of him. That one is Robert Tyre Jones, Jr, the golf player from Atlanta, Georgia.'

The first two quotations are evaluations by Herbert Warren Wind and the last is by Paul Gallico. Each emphasises that Jones was more than a great golf player, more than incomparably the greatest sportsman of his age, so for a while I am going to talk about Jones' life during the period of about 23 years, from his retirement from competitive golf to his death.

By the autumn of 1930 Jones had completed a planned project that just one golfer since, Jack Nicklaus, might have attempted with some chance of success. Only Nicklaus as a young amateur had the capability to win the Amateur and Open championships of Britain and America in a single year. Jones, competing infrequently in Britain, made his one real attempt in 1930 and successively won the British Amateur Championship at St Andrews, the Open at Hoylake, the US Open at Interlachen and the US Amateur at Merion. Since then, this has come to be known as either the Grand Slam or the Impregnable Quadrilateral. As an amateur, he could not play in the US PGA and had yet to develop the US Masters. If they had been available to him, an 'Impregnable Sextuplet' might well have resulted.

Jones was very much an amateur and part-time at that; in the two years 1928 and 1929, for instance, he competed in only five tournaments. Apart from Jones himself, no amateur has won the US Open since 1933; no amateur has won the British Open since 1897. In fact, once a fair body of men on both sides of the Atlantic had taken to golf to earn themselves a living, it became almost inconceivable for an amateur to win the US or British Open, yet Jones was expected to win every time he entered. Today, partly as a result of the US collegiate golf system, amateurs play highly competitive golf for almost the whole year, yet few have challenged any major championship or professional tournament.

It does not seem that Jones ever considered playing golf as a professional but when he announced his retirement he had certain money-making projects in mind. One was for a series of instructional films, made in Hollywood. Many stars of the day were only too happy to give their services free as guinea pigs, probably simply in order that they could play against Jones. The films were highly successful.

During his career, Jones had built up a matched set of clubs by feel alone and had insisted on hand-forged heads made in Scotland for his irons. At the time, US-made heads were rather thin and elongated. Jones entered into an agreement with Spaldings to help design a set which would get the best out of the Scottish format and, of course, incorporate the steel shafts that Jones himself had been denied in his career. The resultant clubs, which came out in 1932, were the first matched set and included features such as the flanged sole, which have since become standard on nearly all irons. So successful were they that production continued until 1973, two years after Jones's death.

At about the same time, there came the project which has assured Jones of another kind of immortality. Clifford Roberts came to Jones and suggested that he collaborate on founding a great golf course. Alister Mackenzie was hired as architect and Jones worked closely with him, hitting hundreds of shots to help Mackenzie determine where tees, greens and bunkers should be sited. The course came to reflect Jones's belief that it should be suited to expert and duffer alike. Therefore, fairways are broad, bunkers number only between forty and fifty, while the greens are large and undulating and water must be carried in many shots to the green. The duffer is reassured by the open prospect from the tee; the fairway bunkers are often out of reach; pin positions on the greens are normally undemanding; and the carries over water are often only a short pitch after two shots have been played to a par 5. When a tournament is on, though, all this is reversed so that, for example, the duffer's short pitch becomes a long and bold second shot to open up birdie chances. The name of the course? Augusta National, now the most well-known course in the world and perhaps the best, if you deny the claims of linksland golf and the likes of Muirfield, St Andrews, Turnberry, Royal St George's.

To augment the prestige of the new course a substantial tournament was needed and Roberts and Jones had the idea of inviting players that he had known in his competitive days. On 22 March 1934 began the Augusta National Annual Invitational Tournament. Roberts had wanted to call it 'The Masters' but Jones vetoed the name as being too grandiose; however, a few years later this name had caught on.

In the first year, crowds came to watch, expecting Jones to beat the best of the new generation as he had beaten previous competitors. This was his first competitive appearance since the 1930 US Amateur, and he finished 13th, suddenly a prey to a disease new to him — the yips. When putting he described the sensation of having the ball rapidly disappear as his blade approached it. Ironically, this was to be his best performance in the event.

In 1947, he completed two rounds and then announced that he would have to withdraw, as he had a minor problem of soreness in the neck and shoulders. 'I'll see you on the first tee next year, boys,' he said. Jones had played his last competitive round of golf. Five years later he had played his last friendly game and by that time leg irons meant that the lazy majesty of his swing was gone. The soreness had been a first symptom and was rapidly followed by double vision, weakness of both legs and the right arm and loss of feeling. The soreness had progressed to pain. There were two operations from which much was hoped, but they produced nothing. Eventually it was established that Jones was suffering a rare congenital disease of the spine. It is inoperable, incurable and is called syringomyelia. It would kill Jones surely and slowly.

By the early 1950s, Jones would occasionally burn himself when he let a cigarette burn down too far, as he could not feel the heat. Progressively his muscles weakened so that by 1964 he could move only in a wheelchair. Later he could not strike a match and by 1968 had lost the use of his arms completely. His feet and ankles were swollen to four times their normal size, his bones were distorted and his hands were claws. On 18 December 1971 he died.

There had been achievements during these years of constant pain and decline. After his 1926 victory in the British Open Jones had published *Down the Fairway*, written in collaboration with O. B. Keeler, a journalist from Atlanta who had followed just about every tournament Jones played in. It is a minor classic. After his retirement, Jones wrote a golf instruction column for several years and later distilled it into *Bobby Jones on Golf*, one of the most thought-provoking books on how to play the game. Later still appeared an autobiography of his playing career, *Golf is My Game*. This corpus of just three books establishes Jones as being at least in the top dozen of those who have written about golf. Of course the knowledge and insight were there but he was also a stylist with a gift for the memorable phrase.

His association with the Masters that had begun before the championship's 1934 commencement continued until a couple of years before his death and not a few who attended annually regarded, not the event itself, but the chance to meet and talk with Jones as the high-spot. Towards the end, he was involved in one incident that remains the most famous disqualification of all: that of Roberto de Vicenzo in 1967. The details are discussed elsewhere but Jones had to make the final decision. Vicenzo had signed a card which said that he had taken 4 on the 71st hole of the tournament yet thousands on the course and millions on TV had seen him take 3. Tommy Aaron, his marker, had merely written down the wrong number and Roberto, thinking of the 5 he had scored at the last, which should have been a 4, had signed the card without proper examination.

Jones decided that the rules of golf cannot be bent and Vicenzo did not play off against Bob Goalby but was second.

Bobby Jones weighed 5 pounds at birth and was for several years a weakly child, able to digest little more than egg white and black-eyed peas, but by the age of five he was able to follow well behind his father on the East Lake course at Atlanta. There exists a photograph from that time that shows Jones had a remarkably similar swing to that of his prime years. By the age of eleven he had scored an 80 and by the age of 14 he was coming to be regarded as the most promising golfer in America. Already his drives were reaching to 250 yards and he had won the Georgia Amateur after a 70 in the afternoon round. He was

Bobby Jones

allowed to go to Merion Cricket Club for the US Amateur and won his first two matches before being knocked out by a former champion. But already the 14-year-old was a sensation, so much so that his Boswell, O. B. Keeler, was later to refer to the 'seven lean years' before Jones took the US Open in 1923 but in those 'lean' years Jones had not reached the age of 21. In 1919 he reached the US Amateur final and the next year played for the first time in the US Open, finishing 8th, then 5th the following year and joint 2nd the year after that. The 'lean' years were nearly over. Though not having won a major championship during them, Jones had come to be recognised by observers as the most precocious genius at the game that had yet appeared.

In 1922 he gave a mature performance in the US Open, but was pipped at the post by a youth 18 days older than he. Gene Sarazen had begun his last round four shots to the bad to Jones but came in with a 68. He remains the youngest winner, at 20 and a few months, of a major championship since World War I. The following year, with three holes to go, Jones had the Open within his grasp. He then proceeded to hit out of bounds, bogied the next hole and took a 6 on the last hole, a par 4. 'I didn't finish like a champion,' Jones commented. 'I finished like a yellow dog.' A comfortable win by three or four strokes had declined to an

18-hole play-off with Bobby Cruickshank. Jones doubted that he had the nerve to win a major championship. Perhaps the next day would provide the answer.

After seventeen holes the two players were level. Jones's drive lay on a bare sandy patch. He was some 190 yards from the flag and the green was fronted by water. Cruickshank would not be able to get home with his second shot so Jones had a very simple choice to make: to knock his ball short of the lagoon or risk everything. It is said that Jones did not hesitate. He took out a 1-iron and lashed his ball to 6ft.

From the age of 20 to his retirement eight years later, this is Jones's US Open record:

1922   tied 2nd
1923   tied 1st, won play-off
1924   2nd
1925   tied 1st, lost play-off
1926   1st
1927   tied 11th
1928   tied 1st, lost play-off
1929   tied 1st, won play-off
1930   1st

Four people have won the US Open four times: Willie Anderson, Ben Hogan and Jack Nicklaus. We shall discount Anderson's achievements between 1901 and 1905: golf was in its infancy in the USA. Nicklaus had more than twenty-three entries up to 1981 to achieve his four wins: he began at 18 and won for the fourth time when he was 12 years older than Jones was at his retirement. In modern times, then, only Hogan grasped the US Open as firmly as Jones, with four wins in five appearances between 1948 and 1953, yet he played sixteen times between 1940 and 1961, the years when he had a realistic chance to win.

It is only on his US Open record that we can measure Jones against his sole rival for supremacy in the history of golf, for this was the one Open event in which he competed annually. The story of his campaigns for the British Open is significant also, however. Here Nicklaus's record is: played 20, won three, 2nd seven times, while between 1963 and 1980 he just *once* finished worse than 6th, unparalleled consistency in a major championship. Hogan's record has perfect symmetry: played once, won once.

Jones first entry came when he was 19. After two rounds, he lay on 151 then in the third round went to the turn in 46, dropped two shots on the 10th (a hole now named after him) and took five to reach the next green. Jones then tore up his card. It was as the supreme golfer of his time that Jones next appeared at Royal Lytham in 1926, having failed to win the British Amateur and deciding to stay on to see if he could manage the Open instead. On the 17th hole in the last round there occurred one of the famous swings in golf. Al Watrous drove straight and put his second shot on the green. Jones hooked off the tee into sand. If a splash out of sand is just about the easiest shot in golf to play a long and accurate shot from it is arguably the most difficult. There is a plaque at Lytham today commemorating that from a sandy lie Jones hit a 4-iron about 170 yards, carrying greenside bunkers and a few minutes later was Open champion.

The following year, St Andrews saw Jones's least famous but supreme performance in any major championship. At the end of his career Jones felt that he had never dominated a major championship throughout, that he had always faltered at some point, especially when the thing seemed won and he had momentarily lost concentration. But in 1927 he led off with a 68, which equalled the course record, and a four-stroke lead on his closest pursuer but perhaps the quality of his round is better demonstrated by the fact that the golfers holding 4th place had gone round in 76. Scoring was higher in those days and the par was 73. The next day, Jones was one under par and Bernard Darwin was moved to report in the *Times* that Jones was already the winner unless 'he bombards continuously the stationmaster's garden'. Jones did not. He added a 73 and a final 72. With 285 he had beaten the Open record and the second place man by six; and was eleven shots better than the previous winning score at St Andrews. He was carried shoulder high from the last green, holding aloft his putter, Calamity Jane, to protect it from harm.

Jones's next appearance in the Open was at Hoylake in 1930, his Grand Slam year. He was not playing well but by now he had the knack of scoring adequately when his swing was out of tune. In the third round he dropped a frightening eight strokes to par on the first three holes, an experience that brought the best out of him so that he still managed to finish in 74. Then in the final round he was just off the 8th green in 2, yet there was a 7 to write on his card as he went to the next tee. He struggled in with a 75 and won by two.

Jones's record in the Open was, therefore, unparalleled. As a mature player he entered just three times and each time he won. His most likely rival as the greatest golfer of the 1920s, Walter Hagen, never won a British or American Open if Jones was in the field and only once did he finish in a higher position.

Jones's victories in amateur championships do not command quite the awe of his achievements against the best in the world. He regarded the British Amateur as the hardest tournament of them all to win, but the truth of the matter is that Jones competed only three times and won in 1930, the Grand Slam year. In 18-hole matches, someone may be fast away from the blocks and home before he can be caught. Seven times Jones reached the final of the US Amateur, in which he competed first as a 14-year-old in 1916 and every year it was held thereafter. Five times he was champion.

In 1930, he was under extreme pressure. The dream of the Grand Slam was almost fulfilled with the two British titles and the US Open already his. Interest was frantic. One newspaper is said to have despatched a team of sixteen writers and photographers to cover Jones's progress. Some 4,000 to 5,000 turned out to watch even Jones's *practice* rounds. Takings for the championship were $55,319, not an enormous sum yet, despite inflation, this was three times the take of thirty-five years later. Then there were the Marines. To protect the great man, fifty Marines in full-dress uniform were assigned to keep well-wishers at arms' length.

To complete the Slam, Jones would have to win two 18-hole matches while the quarters, semis and the final itself were to be over thirty-six holes. His first round opponent was C. Ross Somerville, six times Canadian Amateur champion and four times runner-up. In 1932 he would also win the US Amateur. Somerville went to the turn in level par but Jones was there in 32 and four up. In the afternoon, against less testing opposition Jones was no less than ten strokes worse, but in the lead. The 18-hole matches that made him uneasy were now out of the way.

He took his quarter final by 6 and 5 and demolished Jesse Sweetser, the 1922 champion, by 9 and 8. The final on 27 September 1930 was watched by a crowd of an estimated 12,000 that swelled to nearly 20,000 by the end, which came on the 11th green, with Jones the champion by 8 and 7. The wonder of the age had accomplished the feat of the century. To Jones it meant, he was later to write, 'the cessation of worry'.

What was it that enabled Jones to be a golfer dominant enough to have won seven of the fifteen Opens for which he entered and twenty-three of fifty-two tournaments? Technically, he was almost perfect, though Sarazen remarked that he would have had to shorten his backswing if he had wished to be a day-to-day professional tournament player and Henry Cotton has written that there was a suspicion of looseness at the top of the swing. These strictures apart, just about every observer of the day felt that Jones's basic swing was both mechanically and poetically perfect. It embodied some features that would not be standard today, as a result of using hickory rather than steel shafts. Jones played with his feet unusually close together, which helped to free his hips in the backswing, and with his hips he made a turn of about 90 degrees, just about double the present norm. He wanted a turn away from the ball that was as free and rhythmic as possible and the acceleration down again to be slow and unforced.

As a driver, Jones was long for the era but nowhere near as long as improved balls and steel shafts have made today's long hitters. At fourteen, he was said to be able to drive 250 yards and later that distance would have represented a good average for him (in his famous 66 at Sunningdale, not a notably long course, he needed a wood or 2-iron to reach ten greens). He tried to hit the ball straight and preferred to work a gentle draw on the ball. His reputation stood highest in two departments: long, straight iron play and putting with an exceptionally light putter. Here he had superb touch, which made him one of the best approach putters ever and his holing out of the short ones was good. His weakest area, as for Palmer throughout his career, and the young Nicklaus, was with the pitching clubs. Modern players concentrate more of their practice on these shots than any other but there is no evidence that Jones devoted special attention to them; indeed he did not practice intensely and sometimes did not touch a club for months. Then he would put in a few hours practice, enter a tournament to tune up and shortly after collect another national championship trophy.

As with all superb golfers, it was will and nerve that enabled Jones to win, despite the fact that he always suffered extreme tension when he played and lost pounds in weight for this reason during a championship. Bernard Darwin wrote than Jones 'stands for ever as the greatest encourager of the highly strung player who is bent on conquering himself'. A temperamental weakness that Jones himself acknowledged in retrospect was that he was prone to a wild long shot or loose pitch when in a commanding lead but, as his lead evaporated, he would then rouse himself once more to superlative play. All this, and also according to Harry Vardon, he was 'the finest judge of distance I have ever seen'.

Tom
—— Kite ——

Born Austin, Texas, USA, 1949

When Tom Kite first played the US Tour, it was to be very much in the shadow of Ben Crenshaw, who began his own professional career by immediately winning a tournament and being regarded as the most exciting prospect from the amateur ranks since Jack Nicklaus.

For Kite, it was a similar experience to those of his amateur days; though he had tied with Crenshaw in 1972 for the National Collegiate Championship, an event that on the American scene ranks only below the US Amateur. In that event, Kite had been runner-up behind Lanny Wadkins for the 1970 title. Again, as a professional, it was Wadkins rather than Kite who made headline news: he won over $100,000 in his first year and topped $200,000 the next, 1973. No one paid young Tom Kite much attention. Wadkins, however, showed himself to be highly inconsistent from year to year. Not so Tom Kite. A look at his annual money winnings shows they resemble the books of a small company which is doing very nicely:

	US $	Money list place
1973:	54,270	56
1974:	82,055	26
1975:	87,045	18
1976:	116,180	21
1977:	125,204	14
1978:	161,370	11
1979:	166,878	17
1980:	152,490	20
1981:	375,699	1
1982:	341,081	3

Consistency is the name of Tom Kite's game. In 1973, his first full season, for example, he only three times in 35 entries failed to survive the cut-off made in Tour events after 36 holes have been played. Yet his highest placing was no better than a fifth place in the Ohio Kings Island Open, eleven strokes behind winner Jack Nicklaus.

His second season showed the same tendencies — but more so. He missed just one cut but increased his number of finishes in the top ten from two to eight. In 1975 showed the same almost inexorable consistency, spiced a little by closer

Tom Kite

approaches to a first tournament win. He was second in the Los Angeles Open and third in the Crosby and was this time nine times in the top 10.

So the years passed up to 1980 with increasing income (partly the result of rising prize funds). In 1976 and 1978 he tasted victory, taking the oddly named IVB-Bicentennial Golf Classic as his first win, followed by the BC Open. He also made occasional visits to Britain and played very consistently in the 1978 British Open at St Andrews, with rounds of 72, 69, 72, 70. He finished tied for second place with Ray Floyd, Simon Owen and Ben Crenshaw; two strokes behind the champion, Jack Nicklaus. But the day-by-day leaders were Aoki; Crenshaw, Aoki and Ballesteros; Watson and Oosterhuis. Never in the lead at any point, Tom Kite remained as anonymous as ever.

In 1980, he was one of a strong American contingent at Walton Heath for the European Open. Over the first three rounds he never led and on the last day produced only a 75, the second worst score amongst the top 14 finishers.

Did Tom finish about 10th? No; he became European Open champion. He had finished 71, 75 against Lon Hinkle's 74, 77 and his good golf over the first three rounds gave him the edge in consistency over the rest of the field.

Kite's *annus mirabilis* followed. He went into the year still with his two US Tour wins and the European Open only, and added only the Inverrary Classic to his total. How then did he accumulate $375,000? Simply by becoming even more consistent in his performances. There was, however, a story to do with his clubs.

Kite is only about 5ft 8in and strong rather than powerful. It stands to reason that he is not amongst the longest hitters, sometimes having difficulty in reaching the long par 4s and par 5s in the two strokes that are essential. The par 5s are the holes on which all US Tour players expect to record birdies and indeed are very often playing their second shots with irons. Kite cannot reach the 5s when conditions are unfavourable: into even a medium breeze or if the hole is uphill, for example. Much the same can apply to long par 4s. Frequently, then, he has to use a wedge for the extra shot. Kite is an excellent player with a wedge, the most specialist club in the bag after the driver and putter for most professionals; they may frequently change sets of clubs but once the right wedge is found it remains while others pass on. Before the 14-club only rule came in, such a player as Lawson Little or Walter Hagen carried well over 20. The extra number was largely made up of more pitching clubs.

Kite decided to sacrifice variety of choice in his long irons for an extra wedge so that he had two for the longer shots to give different flight characteristics. Of course, he also had the sand iron for short high shots, but the sand wedge, because of its heavy weight, is difficult to control for full-swing shots. (Most club golfers use it only from sand.)

Armed with his extra pitching wedge, Kite achieved spectacular success over the two seasons 1981-2. It can only be said, not very excitingly, that he became more consistent. His victory total increased only by one each year, the Inverrrary Classic already mentioned and the 1982 Bay Hill Classic, where he beat Jack Nicklaus and the South African Denis Watson in a play-off.

The year of 1981 best illustrates the enhanced consistency. He entered 26 US tournaments and won money in each, an almost unprecedented achievement, and finished in the top 10 no fewer than 21 times: the most consistent performance since Byron Nelson's great spell at the end of World War II, with no rivals from an earlier period.

In spite of this he had only one victory and three second place finishes. There is obviously a pertinent question to be asked about Tom Kite. If the man is capable of playing to a very high standard almost all the time, why does that consistency so seldom carry him through to first place? Well over $1½ million garnered on the US Tour brings him to 11th place at the end of 1982 amongst all-time money winners. I doubt if he would make the all-time top 100 as a tournament winner with a US total of five at mid-1983.

I don't have the answer and neither, as far as I've heard, does Tom Kite.

Tony
—— *Lema* ——

Born Oakland, California, USA, 1934

It has often been said that it is impossible for an overseas player to turn up for an Open Championship, have a look at a links course and then go out and win the Open. First there must be a learning experience. The player must accustom himself to hitting a drive into the middle of a fairway only to find his ball in hollow, downslope or sidehill lies. This can be disappointing enough, for all players really prefer to have their feet on the same level as the ball; worse still if the drive has pitched on the fairway and then, on bone-hard ground, has ricochetted sideways into bunker or rough. He must also learn that high-flying iron shots, however exactly they may be targetted on the flag, may land on an 'unfair' hard undulation of green and, instead of nestling by the hole, skip through the back of the green or, as bad, pull up sharply and then roll off and away.

The high flight so favoured by most Americans is also at the mercy of the winds which are seldom stilled on British links courses. Walter Hagen, as a result of seeing his high pitch shots almost curve back to him during the 1920 Deal Open, certainly went away a wiser man and learned to play the low-flighted pitch and run — and returned to win.

Jones too had a disastrous first experience in 1921, tearing up his card, and Nicklaus 41 years later arrived as US Open title holder and finished 29 strokes behind Arnold Palmer. In 1923, Gene Sarazen failed to play in the championship proper, having taken 85 in a qualifying round.

All in all, it was felt that a player needed time to learn how to play links golf before he could hope to win an Open Championship. That opinion perhaps ought to have died out after Hogan came, saw and conquered in 1953. But Hogan was a thorough and icily determined man. It had been put to him that he really ought to win the British Open to complete his record, so he came over in plenty of time to Carnoustie and learnt how to deal with those differences before the championship began.

Not so Tony Lema. In the midst of a flood of success in America, he arrived at St Andrews for the 1964 Open with no time to learn the course. He had to rely on his caddie, 'Tip' Anderson, to give him the exact line for his drives — St Andrews is a course with many semi-blind teeshots and bunkers invisible until you find your ball at the bottom of one.

The general public might well think that a golfer should be well able to knock a golf ball with his driver where he is told but all golfers know that a blind tee

Tony Lema with the 1964 Open Trophy

shot is always intimidating. It is useful to know in some detail which border of the fairway is the most horrific with regard to pot bunkers, gorse, bare ground, enveloping long grass and the like. It can be almost impossible for the ordinary golfer to hit straight. Many professionals have similar difficulties. They can, however, usually rely on themselves to hit it *not* to the right or *not* to the left, if that is where maximum disaster threatens. Basically, they have a safe drive to call on, one which may be short or certainly not hit with carefree swing but can be relied on to curve predictably.

The prolific and sometimes random bunkering at St Andrews, however, calls for more than this. Tip Anderson would have been telling Tony Lema on, say, the 3rd to keep it 'just the weeniest bit right of yon bunker', on the 6th 'straight on the hangars' or at the 14th 'on the church spire to the right'. Lema had to hit it straight, obviously not really knowing where he'd be if a wild slice or quick hook crept in.

He did hit straight, and got through the first round in 73. Relatively familiar with the course, he improved to 68 in the second round. This was good enough to put him in the lead and all the players who were to finish eventually with good placings were well behind. Nicklaus, for instance, started 76, 74, Vicenzo 76, 72, Harold Henning 78, 73, and Gary Player 78, 71. The holder, Bob Charles, began with a 79.

Lema followed on the final morning with what on paper looks an impeccable 68, but was not. He began 4, 5, 4, 5, 5, 4 against par of 4, 4, 4, 4, 5, 4. This sounds none too disastrous but of course it all depends on the context. The context was that Jack Nicklaus was doing one of his 'going for everything' acts when well down the field. Nicklaus had begun the day nine strokes behind Lema. Over this stretch, with a sequence of birdies, he pulled himself up to within a stroke of Tony Lema. Lema responded superbly to the danger and his score from that point on was 3, 3, 3, 3, 3, 4, 4, 4, 3, 3. He was, therefore, six under par for the last twelve holes. To all intents and purposes his championship was safe. Though Nicklaus followed his third round 66 with a 68, Lema's last day scores of 68, 70 brought him home by five strokes in 279, one outside the best score in an Open at St Andrews of 278, set by Kel Nagle in 1960 and still not bettered in 1983.

This victory made Lema one of the Big Four of the day — Nicklaus, Palmer, Player and himself — and there were many that felt he had moved ahead of Player as well.

Lema's life in golf was very much a rags-to-riches story. He was born the son of a labourer of Portuguese descent who died when Tony was three, leaving a widow to bring up four children in a poor industrial area. Lema picked up money when he could and drifted into being a caddie, this time also picking up a passion for the game of golf. After service in the Korean War, he became an assistant professional and eventually went on the US Tour, having found a sponsor. Lema spent more money than he earned, but did win an event in 1957. He then went into a slump, earning a very few thousand dollars for some seasons. Although he was so natural and rhythmic a swinger and a putter blessed with smooth action and touch, he was less good at keeping going after bad luck or a bad shot. However, in 1961, he became a winner again and in 1962 took three tournaments, in one of these presenting the press with as much champagne as they could drink. This earned him the nickname 'Champagne' Tony Lema. In 1963 he rose to fourth on the US money list and maintained that position the following year, winning four times in the USA in 1964. In 1965, he became only the third player at that time to reach $100,000 in one season — Palmer and Nicklaus were the others to have surpassed this target — and was second on the money list.

In 1966, however, his name was not well up the list though he won a tournament. In July, he and his wife were killed in a private light plane crash. A career was left behind which had not been finally shaped. Tony might well have gone on to achievements that would have ranked him with the great golfers, perhaps with half-a-dozen major championships in his record. He had only some four years as one of the top players and then, suddenly, after the 1966 US PGA Championship, it was all over.

Gene
——— *Littler* ———

Born San Diego, California, USA, 1930

Money, apart from major championship wins, has come to be the measure of American golfers and the rest of the world follows suit. By the beginning of the 1980s, Gene Littler stood 9th in all-time money winners in a professional career of 26 years. His $1½ million will be rapidly dwarfed in the coming years and Gene will sink down the table as inflation and prize money continue to rise. Less ephemeral is that he was 10th amongst the list of US Tour winners ahead of such illustrious names as Lee Trevino, Gary Player, Tom Watson, Julius Boros and Johnny Miller. To put the thing in perspective at the end of 1979, Snead, for example, had won 84, Nicklaus 66, Littler 29, Trevino 22 and Watson 16.

Yet Littler throughout his career has remained a shadowy figure, always away from the spotlights that have followed such as Hogan, Palmer and Nicklaus. Indeed Littler himself has ruefully said that the TV cameras long had the habit of switching to another player if he hove in sight and that his name has been missed off the leader board towards the climax of tournaments. He also laughs at the suggestion that winning a US Open is worth $1 million. It certainly did for a Trevino, Miller or Palmer but not for Gene Littler and even less so for Orville Moody.

One reason is the lack of drama in his golf, the quiet of his personality, which contrasts with the passion of Palmer's play, the once frightening power of Jack Nicklaus and the spectator appeal of Trevino.

'Gene the Machine' early became Littler's nickname on tour. It reflected somewhat his lack of appeal, but to his fellow professionals applied much more to his golf swing. Gene Sarazen had been early in recognising Littler's ability and once remarked: 'Here's a kid with a perfect swing like Sam Snead's — only better.'

Like Jones, and Snead himself, Littler was largely self-taught, learning mainly from watching local players whose style appealed to him. The result was that the club went smoothly back, then came an imperceptible transition to the downswing and away went the ball, not vast distances but quite far enough. His particular mastery was of the short irons, where his feel for the shots gave him an advantage over the powerful hitters. In his own game, for instance, Nicklaus for long recognised that he was better at the power shots and the most delicate — putting and chipping. He found most room for development in the kind of shot that is hit crisply but without force, the area from, say, 130 yards in. It is perhaps significant that as Nicklaus's brutal power has lessened with the passing of the

Gene Littler

years, his feel for the short irons has increased as he has more and more swung the club rather than hit with it.

Littler played in the Walker Cup in 1953 (one of fewer than a dozen to have played in both this and the Ryder Cup) and in the same year won the US Amateur Championship. The following year, still as an amateur, he won the San Diego Open, one of a handful of non-professionals to have won such a tournament since the days of Bob Jones. Perhaps being deprived of the winner's cheque decided him to turn professional, which he did the same year, amongst other achievements, finishing 2nd in the US Open.

The following season Littler won five tour events, including the Tournament of Champions, which he also took in 1956 and 1957, a record sequence. This was the peak of his career, according to Littler himself, a rare time for a golfer when the game seems easy and all the shots fly sweetly from the middle of the clubhead.

At the end of this period, Littler went into a decline which he found hard to deal with. A 'natural', he had never thought deeply about the mechanics of the golf swing. He had a 'strong' grip, showing three to four knuckles of the left hand at address and the clubface was shut at the top. As the off days grew more frequent, so did abrupt hooks. First he tried to compensate by swinging flat, for he was extremely reluctant to change a grip so ingrained. Eventually he was persuaded to change his grip and found the pattern of shot — a slight draw — that persists to this day.

In 1959 he had his best season with five wins and was 2nd money winner but he had yet to win a major championship. This came in 1961 at Oakland Hills, the course that ten years previously Ben Hogan had called a 'monster'. Though there had been changes in the meantime, it is worth mention that his score was six strokes lower than when Ben brought the monster to its knees.

Being Open Champion does not seem to have increased Gene's appetite for glory. Even by this time he had become a golfer who sees the game primarily as the pursuit which earns him a living: in Gene's case a most substantial one. Year after year he finished comfortably in the money list. If he happened to do exceptionally well early in the season, he knew what to do: go back to the family in La Jolla, California, and give full rein to his hobby of buying and rebuilding vintage and classic cars. At the Littler home, a modern American automobile would be seen in the driveway; garage protection was preserved for such delights as a 1920s Rolls Silver Ghost roadster, 1914 Model T Ford, a 1963 Jaguar, a 1929 Rolls Ascot phaeton and a 1931 Model A Ford. In 1969 they must have been at their most seductive. He won $100,000 early in the season and the question was soon 'Where's Gene gone?'

So Littler continued on his consistent, undramatic way. His consistency best illustrated by the fact that he qualified for the US Ryder Cup team every year since he first became qualified (about 1959) to 1975.

His record in the major championships continued below the level expected of him. He won 'almost' a major, the 1965 Canadian Open, and finished in a tie with Billy Casper for the 1970 US Masters, losing the 18-hole play-off 74-69.

When Masters week returned two years later, Gene had been operated on for cancer of the lymph glands below his left arm. The trouble had been caught early and the prognosis was good but as regards golf, Gene was left-side orientated and the operation had weakened or removed important muscles on this side. As he gradually came to be able to swing a club again he found that he had lost only negligible length on his tee shots; his problem was lack of power from the rough. Where once he would have been able to force a mid-iron out, from the same lie he had to be content to wedge back to the fairway. But Littler is amongst Tour players, one of the most consistently in the fairway, reflected in the fact that he always finishes well up in the averages kept of those players who stray over par the least often.

After the operation, he was back in tournament golf by the autumn and doing well enough for it to be clear that his career was by no means over. He tied for 7th place in the Pacific Masters, a tournament he was later to win in successive years. In 1975 he won this and also three US tournaments.

Littler is not boastful about his game and indeed refers wistfully to the early years when he found the golf swing so easy. To the spectator it is still as smooth as ever but Littler himself does not like what happens to the ball. He refers to himself as always 'shanking' it along the fairway and 'thinning' it onto the greens. The most boastful thing he will permit himself to say is yes, he does 'keep the ball in play'.

By 1977, Littler still had just one Major Championship to his credit — the US Open of 16 years before. He had just taken six weeks holiday from the US Tour when the US PGA Championship opened at Pebble Beach, a course on the Pacific coast testing enough for Jack Nicklaus to have taken 290 in *winning* the US Open there five years previously.

Littler opened with a 67 and followed up with a 69. When he had a 70 the following day, the championship was almost in his grasp; even more so when he went to the turn in his final round in 35, which gave him a five stroke advantage on his nearest pursuer.

Then the machine broke down. He dropped shots at each of holes 12 to 15 and Lanny Wadkins, six strokes to the bad as the final round began, caught him with a final 70 to Littler's 76 (41 on the back nine).

The play-off was sudden death and after his collapse, no one gave Gene a chance of pulling his coals out of the fire. On the first play-off hole, Wadkins had to hole a 20 foot put for a half — and did so. The next was again halved and then Littler's nerve cracked again: he stubbed a chip shot and it was all over. Gene Littler did not become the oldest man to win a major championship, at 47.

This was almost certainly his last chance and he is also unlikely to increase his 29 Tour wins. Yet in 1981 there was obviously plenty of life left. In the Vintage Invitational, an event for the over 50s in the relatively new Seniors Tour he won by nine strokes with finishing rounds of 65, 64, the two lowest rounds by any competitor. On that Tour he is one of the leading handful of players and still capable of strong performances on the full Tour, as he showed in the 1983 Los Angeles Open, being tied for the lead after three rounds of 67, 69, 66.

Bobby — *Locke* —

Born Germiston, South Africa, 1917

Of all the truly great golfers, Arthur D'Arcy Locke was the most unlikely looking fellow of the lot. At least in modern times, most of them have hit the ball with some savagery and have been athletic in both swing and appearance. Not at all so the mature Locke. He had the portly appearance and stately progress down the fairways of world golf that reminded people of an archbishop rather than a champion golfer and in the peak years of his early 30s he looked distinctly middle-aged. Yet quite a few rate him highest of all in the post-World War II era and most would at least concede him a place in the top half dozen.

He first came to the fore as a seventeen-year old (having won the South African Boys Championship a few years before) when in 1935 he won the South African and Transvaal Amateurs and the South African and Natal Opens. He repeated that performances in state championships the following year and sailed for Britain to test himself against a higher level of competition. In his first British Open, with scores of 75, 73, 72, 74 at Hoylake, he was leading amateur and 8th overall.

During that season, he discovered and worked on a feature of his game that was later to be central to his success. A short hitter, Locke believed that the grip on a golf club and the swing should above all be gentle and relaxed; that any attempt to introduce a hit into the stroke diverted the clubhead, through tension, from its proper path. He arrived in Britain fading the ball and averaging only about 200 yards with his tee shots. How, without compromising his certainty about how a club should be swung, could he achieve the extra 50 yards that he saw was necessary?

The answer, he decided, was to draw the ball, though that is an understatement: he was eventually to produce a looping banana-shaped hook, aiming far out to the right on his tee shots and swinging the ball back to the fairway. Even with his short irons, where it is far more difficult to produce fade and draw because of the loft of the club, he continued to aim right of the green and with a high, gentle flight the ball swung back towards the target.

Back in South Africa he worked on his game and before he turned professional early in 1938 he added to his record the South African Amateur and Open (by an eleven-stroke margin) and five more state Open or Amateur titles. In Britain that year, he won his first major title, the Irish Open, against a full professional field. He did it in unlikely fashion, beginning with an 80 at Portmarnock and being nine strokes behind Henry Cotton at the halfway point, then having birdies at each of the last four holes to win. He finished in the top 10 of the Open and later again won the South African Open and also the New Zealand title.

Again in South Africa, he won the Transvaal Open over a course measuring more than 7,000 yards with rounds of 66, 69, 66, 64 for 265. His 26-stroke margin of victory may be a record for a professional tournament and certainly betters Jerry Pate's 21 stroke margin in a recent Colombian Open that seems to be accepted as a record today. He added his fourth South African Open title and in Britain beat Reg Whitcombe, 1938 Open champion, in a 72-hole challenge match and then added the scalp of the 1939 champion, Dick Burton, over the same distance. He won the Dutch Open and back in South Africa in 1940 took his third successive South African Matchplay title and his fourth Open in a row. His dominance over other South African golfers was complete. He then joined the South African Air Force and did not touch a golf club for 2½ years, piloting a hundred Liberator missions in the Mediterranean theatre.

The Locke who returned from war was the 14 stone figure that was to become so familiar, rather than the 10 stoner who had departed. His golf was unaffected and he cleaned up as usual in South Africa in 1946 and for the first time was seen at his best in Britain. He was second to Snead in the Open but won three tournaments and took the Vardon Trophy for the season's best stroke average with 71.2. He also made the very significant move of inviting Sam Snead to come to South Africa for a series of exhibition matches with him. Snead accepted and won two of them to Locke's twelve. Snead's confidence was affected badly enough for him to have a couple of bad years on the US Tour. Locke felt that if he could trounce Snead, who with Hogan and Nelson was the best current American player, it might be worth having a go at US tournaments.

So, in April, he turned up for the Masters. On the practice ground 'the old guy who hits everything with a duck hook' was a curiosity and some thought he had 'the worst swing ever'. Odd it certainly was, as the clubhead at the top of the backswing did not point towards the target, but looped well right. They also thought his backswing was far too long, his clubshafts too whippy and his wrists too floppy. His rounds of 74, 74, 71, 70 for 14th place caused some surprise for this was respectable scoring in a first American event. They had not noticed Locke's putting as yet, though it was fresh in Sam Snead's mind. He had noticed that Locke in their matches in South Africa had paid little or no attention to where the pin was set on courses strange to him. He was just concerned to knock his ball to the green and then completely outputted Sam.

Locke's putting method was by then well established. His first principle, like many great putters, was to grip the club extremely loosely. 'So that it nearly drops from your hands', said Locke. He then aligned the ball opposite his toe (which is further forward than normal) and adopted a very closed stance, the right foot withdrawn, and the feet nearly touching. He then addressed the ball off the toe but hit it in the middle except for short putts, which he liked to strike from near the heel. He used an old hickory-shafted implement with a rusty head, which he used to take to bed with him to prevent it from being stolen. The most essential element in good putting, he felt, was simply to strike the ball well so that distance was consistent.

After the Masters, Locke went off to the Carolinas Open which he won, winning again at Houston; in a further tournament he was third. Next, in the

Bobby Locke

Philadelphia *Inquirer* tournament he found Ben Hogan in top form. His start was 65, 69; he managed a swing of seven strokes in the third round and eventually won by four strokes. This was the win that made America sit up and take notice. Who was this African from the bush that could give the great Hogan a five stroke lead and then cruise away from him? Not long after, Locke was voted the 'best driver': it had been realised that though he might not hit the ball far, he hit it far enough and was seldom to be seen seeking it in the long grass. In the US Open he came close to winning, but he needed to par the last nine to tie with Snead and Lew Worsham, and eventually finished third.

Locke continued piling up the money and was paid the then enormous sum of $5,000 to appear in George S. May's Tam o' Shanter, a tournament which attracted more attention and was worth far more money than the three major US championships. Locke needed only to play the last five holes in two over par to win, but dropped shots and eventually was in a 36-hole play-off with Ed 'Porky' Oliver. He won comfortably and, with $7,000, had won easily the highest prize then available in golf.

By the time Locke left America he had won seven tournaments and, playing only a part of the Tour, was second to Jimmy Demaret on the year's money list.

The following year, he did a little less well: he won three times and had ten other top five finishes, including fourth in the US Open. His outstanding achievement was to win the Chicago Victory Open by sixteen strokes, a margin that is still easily a US Tour record. In 1949 he was in America again and won two events but in that year his outstanding achievement was in Britain: he won his first Open. At Sandwich, he tied with the record score of 283, despite one round being played in high winds. He was level with Harry Bradshaw, who is popularly supposed to have lost because he had to hit his shot out of broken glass during the second round and dropped one shot. In the 36 hole play-off, Locke won by a convincing twelve strokes. (They had proper play-offs for major championships in those days, not the almost sheer chance of sudden death.)

At about this time Locke was banned from the US Tour. The reason given was that he missed two tournaments in which he ought to have played. Gene Sarazen thought it 'the most disgraceful action' he had heard of from any golf organisation — in this case the US PGA. The ban was lifted the following year but, though Locke continued to compete occasionally in the USA, he thereafter preferred to concentrate on Britain. He enjoyed playing before a British audience and had proved all he cared to on the US Tour. He won thirteen events in South Africa and Britain. At Troon in the British Open he set a new record mark at 279 with rounds of 69, 72, 70, 68 and beat Roberto de Vicenzo by two strokes. He also won the Vardon Trophy and in a visit to America took the Tam o' Shanter. He had needed to birdie four of the last five holes to tie Lloyd Mangrum, did so, and then took the play-off over 18 holes with 69 to Mangrum's 73.

In 1951, he won six South African events and was third in the US Open, an event he entered because, he said, he wanted to win 'for the British Empire'. His third Open win followed at Royal Lytham, as Peter Thomson (by now his main rival) finished a stroke behind. After Hogan's 1953 win, Thomson had the better of the rivalry for the following three years, winning each time with Locke second in 1954. He continued to be a formidable player, however, taking ten events in 1954. Four of these were in Europe, where he was again Vardon Trophy holder, as in 1952 and 1953.

In 1955 and 1956, his star seemed to be on the wane, though he was still adding to his tournament victories and took the 1955 Australian Open. In 1957, Thomson was favourite to win the Open for the fourth consecutive time but Locke, nearing forty, produced one of his finest performances at St Andrews. With 279, he equalled his Open record and came home three strokes ahead of Peter Thomson for his fourth victory, a sequence since World War II equalled by Tom Watson and beaten by Thomson's five.

This was perhaps the final climax of Bobby Locke's career. He never featured strongly in the Open again, but added a few more wins in South Africa to his record. As Gary Player emerged, Locke stepped out of the limelight. As a pair in 1956 and 1960 they came second for South Africa behind American pairs in the Canada (World) Cup. Locke's last win came in the 1960 East Rand Open in South Africa and his last achievement in Britain was to come second in the Dunlop Masters the same year.

Soon, the Locke trademarks of loose-fitting plus fours, white shoes and white cap were seen less frequently, though he continued to make sentimental journeys to the British Open. He had won 49 professional events in South Africa, including the Matchplay seven times and the Open nine times; 22 in Europe, including four British Opens and an estimated seventeen in America, including beating Julius Boros for an unofficial 'world title' when they were respectively US and British Open champions.

Sandy
── Lyle ──

Born Shrewsbury, Shropshire, England, 1958

There used to be a time, especially in the years after World War II, when British Ryder Cup players consistently found themselves outplayed from the tee by the Americans. Basically, they were still using the kind of swing which derived from the days of hickory-shafted clubs. There was a difference in playing techniques. British players tended to push the clubhead into the ball and lift up at, or just after, the point of impact. Americans, absorbing the lesson of the success of Byron Nelson, in particular, had adopted a swing more suited to the evolution of the steel shaft and the big ball. They pulled the clubhead into the ball, drove through the ball with the legs and kept the clubhead low along the target line for far longer than their British counterparts.

It was not until the arrival of Tony Jacklin that at last there was a British player who showed he could use modern methods as effectively as the best Americans. Another such may prove to be Sandy Lyle, a golfer better endowed physically than Jacklin and with no superior in world golf.

For long it was the standard complaint that British golfers lacked power. Post-war rationing was an early reason given and, when that wouldn't do any more, the theory was advanced that the climate was against British players. An average American player spent his developing years playing on golf courses in sunshine while the Britons were muffled up to the neck in sweaters and windcheaters for more than half the year and were little better off when summer came.

It followed that Americans learned to swing freely from an early age, while to play in shirt sleeves in Britain was a comparative rarity. The British swings that emerged were supposed to give evidence of their origins in cold, wind and rain. (Later, the same people have been silent on the question of how Bjorn Borg could arise from Swedish tennis darkness or Lendl and Navratilova from Czechoslovakia.)

Possibly Lyle's short backswing does derive in part from the constrictions of winter golfing attire but he generates enormous power from a basically hands and arms swing. His precision of striking is rated as highly as anyone's. Lyle's sheer length is best illustrated, perhaps, by the fact that he reckons to hit a 1-iron about 280 yards, a distance that Nicklaus in his long-hitting days did not command. Neither, quite, does Ballesteros, whom Nicklaus has judged to be the longest hitter with irons that he has seen.

Greg Norman is currently rated the longest straight driver in the world but is not actually longer from the tee, though more reliable. Lyle, indeed, has shown a

Sandy Lyle

tendency to caution in his short career and leaves his driver in the bag except when he considers length really necessary. For the rest, he relies on the 1-iron or less powerful clubs. With his 1-iron, he is still further down the fairway than nearly all with their drivers, so he concedes nothing to the opposition but does lessen his own chances of dominating by hitting far shorter clubs into the greens.

Lyle, the son of a professional, was early recognised as an outstanding prospect and was in the England Boys team at fourteen. By the age of seventeen he was a full amateur international, had become the youngest winner of the English Open Strokeplay title and had represented Great Britain.

At nineteen, he last competed as an amateur, won four important titles and played in the Walker Cup team.

His career as a professional has been smooth. He qualified in first place for the European Tour and went off to Nigeria and won the Open. He had a quiet first season in Europe to be 49th on the money list, but since then has been remarkably consistent in finishing high in tournaments, although less so at winning. The consistency has kept him in the top 3 of the money list each year from 1979 onwards, twice in first position: 1-1-3-2. This can be compared with Norman's 17-2-4-1 (though the Australian has made far fewer tournament entries), Jacklin's 9-42-13-20, Langer's 56-9-1-6, Faldo's 21-4-2-4 or Ballesteros's 2-3-7-10 (again far fewer entries).

By the end of 1982, Sandy had won nine tournaments, including the 1979 European Open, in which he finished with a 65, having birdied five of the first six holes, when already in the lead, and won by a highly convincing seven strokes. The following year, he was leading individual in the now much debased World Cup (debased, because so many players decline to represent their country in the event).

For some time, he has been arguably the best British prospect in the Open Championship. His best effort has been at Troon in 1982 when, after three rounds, he led the eventual champion, Watson, by a stroke but eventually finished three strokes behind him in 8th place.

In Britain, he has not quite commanded the attention that his play would seem to deserve. He lacks spectator appeal, his play lacking emotional intensity. To watch Sandy Lyle play is to experience the sight of a young man strolling around a golf course, seemingly uninvolved in any drama there may be. The feeling is enhanced by the fact that he makes golf appear a rather simple matter of quickly setting up for the shot and then giving the ball a whack. On the greens, too, there are no agonisings before the stroke and acquiescence if a putt fails to drop.

It actually looks as if he doesn't much care one way or the other yet almost certainly this is the mask he has chosen to conceal the feelings that others allow to show. The fact that he is Open champion will have to provide glamour.

Graham
—— Marsh ——

Born Kalgoorlie, Australia, 1944

Seldom, if ever, have two brothers excelled on the world stage at two sports as have Rodney and Graham Marsh. The first is one of the great wicketkeepers of cricket history, and a record holder; and Graham might also have shone as a cricketer. He represented his state, Western Australia, as a batsman at the Under-15 level but fractured his arm badly. He then took to golf to strengthen the affected limb — and was hooked.

Marsh went on to qualify in and to teach mathematics, and to play golf as an amateur. In 1967 he won the Western Australia Amateur and was runner-up for the national title. At that point the guru of the Australian golf scene, Norman von Nida, advised the reluctant schoolteacher to chance his arm and turn professional. Having an alternative profession to fall back on, Marsh took the risk. By the end of 1982, he had won close to $2 million worldwide and become known in most countries of the world where golf is played.

Exceptionally, he has prospered most in Japan, a country of very high golfing standards and by no means ignored by international players. However, while most arrive as members of, for example, a group of top US Tour players or as individual combatants, and in either case play just a tournament or two, Graham Marsh has tended to centre his year on the Japan circuit.

It has rewarded him richly. His first victory there came in 1972 in the Dunlop International, while in 1982 he birdied the first play-off hole to take the Mitsubishi Galant. In between he has added to his haul almost every year and now approaches a total of twenty victories, having taken four events in 1974 and three in both 1976 and 1977.

Marsh has been almost equally successful on the little publicised Asian Circuit, which has probably increased interest in golf in more countries than any other professional circus. He began by winning the 1971 Indian Open and was number 1 money winner on the Asian Circuit in both 1972 and 1973.

Peter Thomson was very influential in pursuading Marsh to put so much of his golfing efforts into Far East golf. Thomson never took to the style of golf in America and his published comments show him to be none too fond of Americans themselves. He felt that, if the USA was indeed the centre of the golf world, something ought to be done about elevating the rest of the world. He can hardly complain about the effectiveness of Graham Marsh's efforts.

In Europe, Marsh is the man who usually appears late in the season, plays a few tournament rounds and departs soon after having won a lot of money, often by consistent high finishes rather than outright wins, though he now has ten European career wins.

Consistency is indeed a key feature of Marsh's play. He does nothing badly and has a very full range of shots indeed, all performed with a welcome absence of flamboyant gestures: the air punched as the long putt sinks, extravagant despair as a ball runs off into a bunker. Marsh is more a journeyman performer, giving something of the impression of a man doing the day's work with honest competence, yet the man is in fact a virtuoso.

Although Marsh has campaigned for the most part outside the USA, professional pride did demand he succeed there and he gave it a try for a few years, though he has now tapered his tournament entries away to nothing. 1977 was comfortably his best year. He was named Rookie of the Year (at the age of 33!) and took more than $100,000 home with him. He also won his sole US event, the Sea Pines Heritage Classic. He won by a stroke from Tom Watson with scores of 65, 72, 67,

Graham Marsh (right);
Tommy Horton (left)

69. Yet he played by no means the full season. That year he won also in the Philippines, Japan, France and England. In this, his best season, he is estimated to have won close on $300,000 worldwide and one of his successes was in his closest approach to a major championship. Marsh had reached the final of the World Matchplay in 1973 and was level with Gary Player after 36 holes, his only superior as a world traveller. Thereafter, Player saved himself with a series of the precision bunker shots of which he is a master and eventually won on the 40th. But in 1977 there was a different final opponent for Marsh — Ray Floyd. Marsh disposed of him by 5 and 3, having earlier beaten Hubert Green 5 and 4, Manuel Pinero 2 and 1, and Hale Irwin, finalist the three previous years, by 7 and 6.

However, Marsh undoubtedly needs a full major championship on his record to raise him beyond dispute to the ranks of great players. I suppose his nearest approach came in the Carnoustie Open of 1975. Then he finished in 6th place but was only two strokes worse than Jack Newton and Tom Watson's play-off score.

Oddly, he has also been relatively ineffective in Australia. His first win did not come until the 1976 Western Australia Open, hardly a major event, and he did not win again until 1982 when he took the South Australian Open and the Australian Masters, the latter an event of fast-rising prestige.

Cary
Middlecoff

Born Halls, Tennessee, USA, 1921

The 1981 US amateur champion, Nathaniel Crosby (son of Bing), was not considered to be a golfer capable of winning this championship because of an extreme oddity in his swing. He came, until 1983, to a dead halt at the top of his backswing. Observers felt that such a pause destroys all possibility of rhythm.

They must have forgotten the illustrious career of Cary Middlecoff, a very successful golfer indeed during the 1950s and a winner of three major championships and thirty-seven US Tour events during that period; a formidable total that ranks him only below Snead, Nicklaus, Hogan, Palmer, Nelson and Casper. Middlecoff not only came to a perceptible pause at the top but remained poised there waiting to strike for, he says, 'over a second'. A second may sound quite a short period of time but readers might like to contrast this with their own average good swing and admit that all too often they fail even to complete the backswing in their anxiety to get the perilous job of hitting the ball over with.

For what reason did Middlecoff pause? Precisely to avoid the common error of both major and minor golfers: failing to complete the backswing. There is also the problem of managing the transition between finishing the first act of the swing and beginning the movement back into the ball.

With Middlecoff's action, both problems were eliminated. Indeed, with so long a pause, he could afford, if the backswing felt 'wrong', to halt the whole process and go back to the address position, and try again.

Most writers on the golf swing, whether correctly or not, have spent far more time discussing what should happen between taking aim and the top of the backswing than what should happen in the split second occupied by the swing down into the ball. This last process, by many of them, is considered the inevitable result, good or ill, of what has gone before. Middlecoff's method ensured, or almost so, that his backswing could hardly be far wrong.

Despite the success of this unusual feature of his swing, Middlecoff himself considered it only an individuality of his own playing style and did not advocate its use by other golfers. He felt merely that it suited him. In his excellent book, *The Golf Swing*, published in 1975, he stresses that the backswing can contain a variety of oddities such as the Gay Brewer double loop, taking the club away on the outside in Miller Barber fashion, the Nicklaus flying right elbow, the Nelson sway or the Vardon lift. Middlecoff felt, however, that all good golfers become essentially the same as they approach the moment of impact.

Middlecoff's pause was very much in keeping with his extremely deliberate

Cary Middlecoff

overall approach to the game. He is given some credit for the slow pace of tournament, indeed all, play today. He took a considerable time to align himself at the target, something that until then was usually accomplished quite briskly, and had the more general reputation of being the slowest US player. In 1957, when he tied with Dick Mayer for the US Open, the latter took a camping stool out with him for the 18-hole play-off. Mayer wanted to get the weight off his feet while Middlecoff went about his laborious business. Or perhaps it was a ploy to unsettle the previous year's champion, to disturb his rhythm and cause him to play faster. If the latter, it may well have been successful, for Mayer won in some comfort with 72 to Middlecoff's 79.

Born in Tennessee, Cary Middlecoff also grew up in that state and established a very good record as an amateur, winning the Memphis Amateur at the age of seventeen and being state champion in 1940. He repeated the latter victory in each of the following three years. In 1945, he had outstanding amateur success when he won the North and South Open against a professional field and the following year was chosen for the Walker Cup, but withdrew because he had decided to turn professional.

For Middlecoff, this decision should not have caused much financial worry for he had by then qualified as a dentist, a sound enough career to fall back on. Middlecoff never practiced dentistry. He won a tournament in his first year and was soon the most prolific money winner in US golf. From 1949 to 1956 he was always amongst the top ten money winners and was second in the money list for four of those years. Three times during this period he had five or more wins in a season. These results in today's terms would have brought in $500,000 in a good year, though the most Middlecoff won in a season was less than $40,000.

For posterity, however, major championship performances count for far more than money and tournament winnings. Here, 'Doc' Middlecoff quickly featured, coming second in the 1948 US Masters. The following year, at Medinah, he became US Open champion, beating Sam Snead and Clayton Heafner by a stroke, with Bobby Locke a couple of strokes further away. That year he won another six events. There was no doubt that a new star had arrived.

As the years passed, Middlecoff piled up money winnings in tournament golf and by the end of 1954 had taken his total to 28, but had not added another major championship. It came in 1955 in the US Masters, an event in which Middlecoff had consistently finished well up the field, but had not come close to winning since his 1948 second place. In 1955, he began with a sound 72. It put him amongst the leading group who were left well in the wake of Jack Burke's 67. Middlecoff went out on the second day and got to the turn in 31, at that time a record. He finished in 65, eleven strokes better than Jack Burke (champion, incidentally, the following year) could manage. More important, perhaps, the round gave Middlecoff a four-stroke lead on the man to watch, Ben Hogan. During the round, he holed what is sometimes claimed to be the record length of putt, one of a measured 86 feet on the 13th green. Record or not, it did nothing to harm Middlecoff's reputation as a great putter. He has not gone down in golfing lore as one of the names to stand with Locke, Casper, Charles, Hagen, Watson (and a few others) as one of the all-time greats, but amongst his contemporaries his reputation was high indeed.

Middlecoff finished the championship in 72, 70 to finish seven in front of Ben Hogan, at the time a record margin for a Masters champion.

In 1956, Hogan was again the victim, this time in the US Open, which he was desperately anxious to win for a record fifth time. At Oak Hill, Middlecoff produced the remarkably consistent scoring of 71, 70, 70, 70 to win by a stroke from Hogan and Julius Boros, Hogan missing a short putt late on to tie.

During Middlecoff's career, American entries for the British Open were a rarity (Hogan made just one, successful, attempt, Snead did not defend after his 1946 victory) and Middlecoff was not an exception. He came over for the 1957 St Andrews Open, however, and scored steadily, being in contention for a while before finishing 14th, ten strokes behind winner Bobby Locke. The US PGA, a matchplay event during Middlecoff's career, also escaped him, though he reached the 1955 final and went down to Doug Ford.

After his play-off defeat in the 1957 US Open, Middlecoff's best years were behind him and at that point they were indeed good years for he was the biggest money winner of his day. After 1957, he won two more events on the US Tour and his finest late performance came in the 1959 US Masters, in which he was second, beaten by a stroke by Art Wall's spectacular closing 66.

The cause of his downfall in his late thirties was the all-too-common one of the putting twitch. Perhaps, also, his laborious playing methods took more out of the nerves than a brisker approach: the slow weighing up of each shot and meticulous alignment before swinging allowed ample time for tensions to build up.

Johnny ———— *Miller* ————

Born San Francisco, California, USA, 1947

One round of golf took John Laurence Miller to a place in golf history. It was a 63 accomplished in the afternoon of 17 June 1973 at Oakmont Country Club on the final day of the US Open. He began in fairly carefree mood for he was too far behind the leaders to have a chance of winning. After three rounds, Arnold Palmer, John Schlee, Jerry Heard and Julius Boros were tied at 210 and there was a total of twenty players with better scores than Miller, who lay six strokes behind the leaders on 216.

There have been great final rounds in golf to bring a player from behind to win — Palmer's 65 in 1960 or Gene Sarazen's 66 in 1932 are examples — but even rounds with this kind of scoring would not have been good enough on that day. Miller needed a great round of golf, or the collapse of his rivals, to win.

He began by hitting a 3-iron in to less than a couple of yards and holing the putt; and followed on the next with a pitching club to about a foot. On the 3rd, a soaring 5-iron bit and held but was some 8 yards from the hole. Down went the putt. Miller was back to even par for the championship after his 76 in the previous round and improved matters on the 549 yard 4th hole. Here he hit long and straight, cut his fairway wood shot but compensated by sending his sand iron absolutely dead. The leaders were beginning their final round with the knowledge that Miller had as good as caught them.

He parred the next three and then made his first mistake, missing a short putt on the 8th green to drop a shot to par. However, he made the anticipated birdie on the par-5 9th hole when he hit the green with a long iron second shot and safely holed out with two putts to be out in 32. Good though this scoring was, par on the return journey would be nowhere near good enough.

Miller's pace hotted up. He birdied each of the 11th, 12th and 13th holes, his iron play by now looking infallible, every shot boring in on the flag. On the 14th, he had another chance of a birdie from a dozen or so feet but failed; but on the next another medium iron plummeted down near the flag and he was eight under for the round. For the first time he was a quite likely winner, but still having to hold what he had, while a 68 from those who had begun in the lead would push Miller out of the limelight. Miller held his game together, missing a birdie chance on the 17th when he wedged to about 3 yards but could not hole the putt. On the last, a par 4 of 465 yards, he unleashed one of his longest drives and had only a medium iron to the green. His putt clipped the hole and stayed out.

It was a 63, at the time the lowest score ever recorded in a major championship, and still the lowest winning round. It may long remain so. Miller's scoring had not depended overmuch on his putter. He had holed only one really long one — and that not a monster — which had been balanced by a three-putt. The keys to his score had been excellence through the green; better iron play has never been seen.

For the record, Miller totalled 279, with rounds of 71, 69, 76, 63 and was followed one stroke behind by the now forgotten John Schlee with 280 after a final 70. Then came the bigger names of Weiskopf, Palmer, Trevino and Nicklaus, the latter being one of only three other players to break 70 with a 68. There are some who have claimed that Oakmont, with holding greens that day, was playing easily. Certainly the scoring of the rest does not bear this out.

Miller has produced another great run from behind in one of the most stirring contests in golf history. This was the three way battle for the 1975 US Masters.

After two rounds, Nicklaus opened a five stroke gap on Tom Watson, Arnold Palmer and Billy Casper with his 68, 67 start but then stumbled a little in the third to a 73, which left him a stroke behind Tom Weiskopf, who had a 66. Miller had opened 75, 71, which put him no fewer than eleven behind Nicklaus and near to missing the cut, which was on 148. His third round made him a factor. He began with a par, birdied the next six and reached the turn in an Augusta record of 30, finishing in 65, one off the Masters record.

The final day, Miller and Weiskopf were off last; just ahead of them were Nicklaus and Watson, the latter a young hopeful with a reputation for collapsing when in good positions. He did so this day, sending two iron shots into the water fronting the short 16th.

Miller continued his chase of the leaders. Starting four behind Weiskopf and three behind Nicklaus he had five birdies during the first half and went to the turn in 32 to Nicklaus's 35 and Weiskopf's 34. The eleven stroke deficit after two rounds on Nicklaus was wiped out; Weiskopf led by two.

The issue was settled on the 16th. Nicklaus's iron shot was heavy and so well short of the hole, though it cleared the water comfortably enough. He then struck one of the finest — and luckiest — putts to win a major championship, a curving left to right uphiller of around 15 yards. When he parred the last two, Miller had to birdie them both to catch him. He came close, sinking one of several feet on the 17th and then having one of about 5 yards on the next to draw level. Ideally, Miller would no doubt have liked a straight uphill putt to tie but what he had was a downhiller with right to left borrow. He missed and one of the great chases of championship history was over. Miller had a final 66 to be joint second with Weiskopf but that crucial one stroke behind Nicklaus. He had caught his man but Nicklaus had holed the most unlikely of putts to pull ahead once more.

Having recounted these two great surges from far behind, I must now admit that Miller considers himself 'a great front-runner'. By this he means that he relishes a lead and, once there, is not inhibited as so many are by fears of losing. He is your man for opening a small gap on the field and then pulling further away as round follows round. In this he is the reverse of Nicklaus, who on average thinks he plays his best golf when there is a deficit to be made up and a startling last round becomes a necessity.

Johnny Miller

This flair of Johnny Miller's was seen most notably in his greatest period, which most would agree fell in the time between his 1973 US Open win and the 1975 Masters. Take, for example, his performances in the first tournament of the 1975 season, the Phoenix Open. There, he began with a 67 to tie for the lead and followed with a 61 to be six ahead. By the end of it all the second place man was fourteen strokes behind, the biggest margin in US Tour history after Locke's sixteen stroke victory in the 1948 Chicago Victory event. The following week at Tucson, he began with a 66 and followed with 69, 67 to lead by three. In his final round he was eight under par after twelve holes but finished with another 61 'only', for a nine stroke win.

That fortnight saw arguably the most irrestistible golf that has yet been played. Eventually, however, there was to come one of the most complete falls from grace known to the game.

Whatever happened to Johnny Miller? He won the 1976 British Open at Royal Birkdale, and took two US tournaments. The following year he was down to 48th on the US Tour money list and in 1978 an unthinkable 111th. The reasons for the decline are complex and not conclusively known to anyone. Was it, for instance, money? With his tournament winnings compounded by endorsement contracts ($1 million a year from just one clothing contract) he was well fixed for life. He could afford to sit back and relax as many of us would do. Miller himself has said that he had to start the season well. By the time the Masters arrived in April he was usually bored with golf. He could pour out birdie after birdie in individual tournaments but, like Gene Littler, thought of home and family if money and glory came early in the year. Even in his greatest year on the US Tour, 1974, when he won eight tournaments, it was in only 21 tournament entries out of about 40 available on the Tour.

Of the great players, only Nicklaus has been apt to play less often than that. But the reason here is a simple one: he has come to be stirred by only the major championships, knowing that he cannot key himself up more than a few times in any one year, and wants to be recognised by posterity as the greatest golfer who ever lived. There is little morally praiseworthy in that; small blame to Johnny Miller if he did not have that ambition and merely played, for a couple of years, at least as well as the few who have aimed at the ultimate peaks of golf.

More surprising than Miller's decline is the fact that he was eventually able to climb back a long way towards the top. By 1978, his swing had become hurried — almost something to be got over and done with — the ball was too far forward and he was aiming right and trying to draw the ball back rather than the previously successful straight hitting or slight fade. Worse, he was pushing his hands into the ball rather than the pull on the club with the left hand that had brought him, and many others, success. In 1979 there were possible signs of a revival on the US Tour. He still finished well down the money list in 76th place but had at least come close to a tournament win when he tied Tom Watson for the Hall of Fame Classic and lost the play-off. Then, in the autumn, he won the Lancome tournament in France.

The following year he climbed to 30th place on the money list and won his first US event since 1976. His progress continued in 1981 and 1982 with three more wins. A kind of glory returned when he won a freak event, the Sun City $1 Million Challenge, at the turn of 1981-2. For Miller, it meant a cheque for $500,000, far and away a record first prize, after a tense play-off with Severiano Ballesteros that went on and on and on for nine holes before the Spaniard three-putted in the dusk. More important than the money, perhaps, was the fact that Miller was at last back on the world stage.

Young Tom Morris

Born St Andrews, Fife, Scotland, 1851

If Severiano Ballesteros were to die tomorrow, you would have an identical situation to that created by Tom Morris Junior a century and more ago. Although there are doubters, unconvinced by two Masters, an Open and a hatful of more run-of-the-mill tournaments and national championships, today's consensus is that the young man from Pedrena is the most charismatic champion since the young Palmer or the middle-aged Walter Hagen. For Young Tom Morris died at roughly the age Severiano has now reached and when Jack Nicklaus had only began to scratch at the surface of fulfilling his ambition of being recognised as the greatest golfer who has ever lived.

Tom Morris, son of an Open Champion, was a golfing genius by the age of 13, when at Perth he won a £5 match — obviously a fair sum for the time when Open Championship winners were stepping up to receive a like sum — and three years later he was at Carnoustie, tieing and in the play-off defeating most of the leading lights of the time. In the same year, he failed in the Open Championship, however, coming only 4th. Total dominance lay just ahead.

In the Open of 1868 he won £6 and was champion by a couple of shots over Bob Andrew, who, though never a winner, had finished high most years since the event had begun in 1860. He was five ahead of the reknowned Willie Park. He had also, at the age of seventeen, beaten the scoring record by five strokes.

The following year, his father Old Tom Morris, must have sharpened his game, for he finished eight ahead of the man in 3rd place but three behind his son, who had beaten his own championship record by another three.

Yet Young Tom Morris's finest hour was yet to come. At Prestwick in 1870 he left the 5th place man 25 strokes behind, and that was a man who was later to win three consecutively, while the joint seconds were twelve to the bad, a margin never again approached. The Open Championship record had also been lowered from Young Tom's other records by a further five strokes. His total of 149 remained the record until the event was played over 72 holes from 1892 onwards.

All Young Tom's wins were recorded at Prestwick over a 12-hole course played three times and this is what the card, had there been one, would have looked like:

1	578 yards	3	167	5	440	7	144	9	395	11	132
2	385	4	448	6	314	8	166	10	213	12	417

It is extremely difficult to allocate a par to the Prestwick of well over a century ago. To some extent, par derives from the thought that a golfer ought to be able to knock the ball into the hole on putting greens in a couple of tries and there is also a notion of how far the ordinary golfer ought to be able to hit a golf ball. All greens in Tom Morris's days were accorded little close attention. There is some evidence — not conclusive — that they were occasionally cut. They were also the part of the course from which the golfer teed up and struck his next shot. Thus far, it is clear enough that Morris was putting on surfaces that would have provoked today's tournament professionals to reach quickly for an airline schedule and their most forthright invective.

Golf of the time was also basically a cross country pursuit: you started at one point and finished, after numerous happenings en route, at another. Fairways did not at all march inexorably from tee to green. Rather it was much more a matter that some parts of the course were better to alight on than others. Where these parts were depended on how nature had arranged matters. Then there was the object to be struck: the gutta percha ball. Sandy Herd in 1902 struck just one shot with a rubber-wound ball and, much though he had previously scorned the thing in theory, found that he'd hit a longer drive than ever before. He used it in the Open.

Young Tom had no such option open to him. Gutta percha it had to be and how far could he have expected to knock it? There is no evidence that he was excessively long off the tee, in which case 240 yards would have been the absolute of ambition, so a little under 200 yards is Tom's likely distance.

Considering what today's designers demand of us, the par of Prestwick around 1870 looks like: 6, 5, 3, 5, 4, 3, 3, 5, 4, 3, 5, a total of 51. To achieve that, with good striking, you would have to arrive at closely cut, smooth greens, whereas the truth of the matter was that a winter green of today, cut without forethought on a much-divotted patch of fairway, would be far better.

Tom's 1870 victory meant that he had won the championship belt originally donated as the prize, by having won three championships consecutively. No championship was therefore played in 1871. By 1872, the claret jug so well known today had been presented and Young Tom won it, to extend his sequence to four, a feat never again performed, while only Peter Thomson has taken three in a row, during the 1950s.

That was almost the end of Young Tom. He did not win in the following two years, though he was a close second in 1874. Soon after this, he was dead.

Little has come down to us about the features of his play. We know, however, that he hit hard enough for his shafts sometimes to break in mid swing. He may also have been the first player who aimed successfully to stop his ball near the hole. Others were content to avoid trouble and get their balls on the green. On those laughably rough greens, he was also rated very highly as a putter, nerve and not giving way to disappointment probably being more useful qualities than deft touch.

His grave at St Andrews remains visited by many on a pilgrimage to the home of golf, St Andrews.

Byron Nelson

Born Fort Worth, Texas, USA, 1912

Golf equipment used to have a profound influence on the development of one's game. Today, it does not. The golfer who buys a glittering set of new irons with an attractive motif on the back or a new driver with a titanium shaft and then paces the 1st tee, eager to see what new manner of man he has become, is doomed to disappointment. He may play no worse and will very likely soon be saying to you that he's 'not quite used to them yet'. In a week or so, though, he will be playing, with these irons, just about the same standard of golf as he was with the old lot. The driver is always a different matter. One will either be highly delighted or will no longer dare to touch the thing.

The truth of the matter is that modern clubs are usually good and claims to have found a magic formula remain unproven. (The possible exception is, however, the Karsten Ping putter. That really has made mishit putts get rather nearer the hole than they otherwise might have done.)

There have been three stages in the development of golf equipment that have had a clear effect. The first was the change from the feathery ball to gutty; the second the introduction of the Haskell ball in 1902; and the third the replacement of hickory shafts by steel from 1930 onwards.

When the new balls appeared, a good player merely found that he could hit further. The Haskell in particular made the long shots of golf far easier and the chipping and putting a little less so because of the much increased liveliness of the ball. Steel shafts were a different matter and golfers who had grown up with hickory used the swing that they had evolved in their youths with steel too. Byron Nelson was the man who showed that a different swing had become possible. That swing is basic to all good players, even though the look of the thing is as different as Littler from Trevino or Nicklaus from Palmer.

Hickory shafts, could not be used for extended practice sessions on full shots. Henry Cotton, for instance, a player who was born to hickory and matured in the age of steel used to have his tournament set and others that he practised with: it didn't matter if he broke the shafts of those. This was not, though, the most significant difference; that lay in the torsion of the hickory shaft. It is expected and indeed required that the steel shaft should flex. It is most undesirable for the clubhead to twist open during a full swing. This would happen, and the more powerful the swing the more did the face open. This meant that in general, players did not dare hit full out and even at reduced power they had to have the knack of closing the clubface with their hands at just the right moment when in the impact zone. Small surprise that a 70 in the morning might become an 85 after lunch. Manipulating with the hands was therefore essential, whereas today informed talk is far more likely to centre on topics such as the importance of clearing the hips or driving through with the legs, matters which received little attention before the coming of steel shafts. Using hickory, adjustment with the hands at impact was essential but in recent times emphasis has been on the use of the lower body.

In the swing of Byron Nelson, we can see most of the elements of modern techniques fully and maturely demonstrated. He took the club back 'in one piece' (that is, nothing seemed to dominate the backswing at the beginning: hands, arms, hips, shoulders and legs all began moving at the same time and remained together). Although there was a very full shoulder turn, hip movement was restricted, in marked contrast to Jones's 90 degree turn. On the downswing, the legs appeared to lead the drive into the ball and both legs remained in motion through impact, again in marked contrast to the then usual teaching that a golfer should hit against a firm left side.

What was the result of these technique changes in competitive golf? 'The finest golfer I have ever seen', said Tommy Armour, thus ranking him above, for instance, Jones and Hagen, while Jones himself admitted 'I never came close to the golf Nelson shoots.'

Nelson was brought up in the same town as Ben Hogan and as boys they both worked as caddies at the same club. Give or take a few months they were the same age and turned professional at much the same time. Though both became the dominant golfers of that period, their careers in manhood were very different. Ben Hogan's career is told elsewhere so I will not labour the point; but that Nelson won his first major nearly a decade before Hogan and had *retired* before Hogan became a world name, indicates the contrast.

Nelson's first major championship victory was in the 1937 Masters, where in the final round he achieved one of the most remarkable swings seen in that event: he gained six shots on the leader, Ralph Guldahl, in two holes. Guldahl played them in 5, 6, Nelson in 2, 3. He won the event by two strokes, after he had broken the record in the first round with a 66, which ranks with the great rounds of golf of all time, statistically more perfect than Jones's Sunningdale round of 66 when qualifying for the 1926 Open. Nelson was on each par 3 in one stroke and all the 4s and 5s in two strokes. He single-putted only twice. In his other Masters victory he achieved a comparable swing to the one he had managed over Guldahl. Nelson and Hogan met in an 18-hole play-off after Hogan had made up eight strokes on Nelson, the early leader, over the last two rounds. After five holes in the play-off Hogan had a lead of three and then played the next eleven holes in one under par, good enough scoring, yet Nelson had meanwhile gained five strokes and was in the lead, which he held to the end, winning by 69 to 70.

In the US Open he twice tied; first after the four rounds with Lloyd Mangrum and Vic Ghezzi in 1946. All three had 72s in the first play-off round and had to go out again. Mangrum again had a 72 to win, with Nelson and Ghezzi one shot worse.

On the other occasion, Nelson did better. This time after four rounds he had tied with Densmore Shute and Craig Wood. After the first play-off round, Shute

Byron Nelson, with his pupil, Tom Watson (left)

was eliminated but Nelson and Wood were tied with 68s. Nelson then, at the 4th hole, hit a full 1-iron into the hole for an eagle, which accounts for his eventual three-stroke margin over Wood.

Nelson's record in the matchplay US PGA was even more impressive. He reached the final in three successive years — (1939-41) — and between 1939 and 1945 reached the final five years out of six. He won twice, in 1940 and 1945, the years which saw some of his best golf. In one round, after thirty-two holes, Mike Turnesa was seven under par and stood one up on Nelson, who then scored birdie, birdie, eagle and won the game. At the end of the final, Nelson had in all played 204 holes and was no less than 37 under par.

This was indeed Nelson's *annus mirabilis*, the year when he was virtually invincible and if the Masters and US Open had been played during the war years it is difficult to see who would have beaten him.

As a haemophiliac, Nelson had been rejected for military service. For a couple of years after Pearl Harbor to play professional golf was considered in some way unpatriotic: by 1944, this was no longer the climate of opinion and the players were competing for war bonds rather than straight cash, which seemed to lessen the frivolity of golf in wartime. In that year Nelson had seven wins, a very rare occurrence on the US tour — or anywhere else for that matter.

The dates 11 March 1945 and 4 August 1945 are more significant: between them Byron Nelson became the golfing wonder of the age. On 4 August, he won the Canadian Open; on 11 March he had won the Miami Fourball. In between he had won every tournament in which he competed, which meant that he had won eleven tournaments in a row. The next best achievement is a sequence of four. Altogether that year he won eighteen PGA-recognised tournaments, almost double the number of any other player before or since.

Nelson collected a little over $63,000 in war bonds but if he had been playing for the vastly higher purses current today his take would have been well over £1½ million, or about three times as much as Tom Watson's best pay year!

The next year he won five times and in 1947 took the first two tournaments and then announced his retirement in favour of ranching. His sudden departure was much like Bobby Jones's. Jones had won all there was to win and so had Nelson. In the latter's case, though he was reputed to have nerves of ice, perhaps he knew better and his retirement has in fact been put down to stomach tension. The man who seemed able to win as he liked was as much prey to fears as anyone else and less conscious than some of his eventual place in golf history.

In later years, possibly because Nelson's 1945 achievements are still entirely without parallel, many have cast doubts on his mastery that year. It has been said that many of the best players were not on the US circuit that year though the truth is that most of them were; that courses in a nation at war were ill-kept and so preferred lies were sometimes allowed; that rough was cut short so that fewer balls were lost in club play; that the courses were short. All these things are true to an extent but they can only go a very little way indeed to explain why Byron Nelson that year was some 320 strokes under par; that he once played nineteen consecutive rounds under 70; that in a tournament in Seattle he tied both the low score for a PGA tournament with a 62 and the four round low with 259; that his stroke average over 120 rounds played was 68.33, which is nearly a stroke a round lower than anyone has recorded on the US circuit, either before or since.

Nelson's achievements that year are only matched, and then in an entirely different context, by Jones's Grand Slam of 1930. Certainly, if he had kept his appetite for competitive play, he must have improved on his record of five wins in major championships and his 54 US tour wins, which today rank him only below Snead, Nicklaus, Hogan and Palmer.

Jack Nicklaus

Born Columbus, Ohio, USA, 1940

In this book I have avoided trying to set golfers in their place in history but the name of Nicklaus has cumulatively become so towering that some discussion is perhaps almost inevitable. Many would now assert that Nicklaus has long succeeded the aim with which he started out as a young man — to be the greatest golfer of all time. It is interesting to see how this claim stands up under comparison with his rivals.

First it must be seen who those rivals are and then how their abilities and achievements compare. As rivals, I would put forward the names of Young Tom Morris, Harry Vardon, Walter Hagen, Bobby Jones, Henry Cotton, Byron Nelson, Sam Snead, Ben Hogan, Gary Player, Arnold Palmer and, particularly after his 1982 Open successes, Tom Watson.

Some of these have to be dismissed almost immediately on grounds of lack of evidence. Tom Morris won four Open Championships and then died. We can only speculate on what he might have gone on to accomplish. Even so, it would have been in an age before the objective evidence of the camera and at a time when golf was not established even in Britain as a whole, let alone become the international game it is now, until long after his death. Reluctantly, I must concede that the same applies to Vardon, though to a much lesser degree. In his case, he was recognised as the best player in the world, closely followed by James Braid and J. H. Taylor, but again until after World War I, when Vardon was nearing fifty, it was a small golf world. Cotton, the dominant player in Europe for approaching twenty years, must also be dismissed. Apart from two trips to America early and late in his career, he did not attempt to pit himself against the best golfers of the other half of the golf world. Byron Nelson has to go also. Although he had a phenomenally successful record on the US Tour, especially in the two seasons before his retirement, he competed very little outside the USA and overall his career was too short. This latter point is, I feel, important: our greatest of all golfers must either show his greatness over a long period of time or be dominant to an even greater extent over a shorter length of time. Snead has to go for a very different reason: his major championship record, lacking a US Open, though with seven other major championships, is too far short of the Nicklaus achievement. Instead we may allow him to be the best swinger of a golf club ever, the most prolific of all US tournament winners, with 84, and, at 71 in April 1983 and still able to play par golf, incomparably the longest lasting of golfers.

Even Arnold Palmer will have to go at this point. A player of almost the same era as Nicklaus, he is clearly inferior as a major championship winner, with eight to seventeen in four events: US Amateur and Open, Masters and British Open. In each of these, Nicklaus has more wins, and also has 69 US Tour wins at the end of 1982 to Palmer's 61.

On much the same basis, Player must now go. He has won each of the major championships (the US Masters and British Open three times each) but his total is nine and in none of these events has he bettered the Nicklaus record. At 121, however, he has more worldwide victories, though overseas Nicklaus has for many years limited his appearances to such major events as the British and Australian Opens. He can, however, claim to have a better matchplay record with his four wins to Nicklaus's one in the World Matchplay at Wentworth, two of these involving heavy defeats of Nicklaus in the final. If judgement were to be based on a height and weight basis, Player also has a very strong claim to be considered the best pound for pound golfer ever.

We are now left with Hagen, Jones, Hogan and Watson. Walter Hagen ranks third, with eleven championships, in the all-time list. He has more British Open wins than Nicklaus, with four, and his five wins in the US PGA put him level with Nicklaus. His four in a row in 1924-7 is not bettered by anyone in any event. His US Open record is much inferior, with two wins, and as he did not compete as an amateur he had no opportunity to parallel Nicklaus's two successes in the US Amateur. There remains the Masters, devised by Bobby Jones and Clifford Roberts and first played in 1934, a few years after Hagen's career had declined with the passing years.

So far, a case of Hagen versus Nicklaus remains unproven but there remains another yardstick. Jones accumulated thirteen major championships while Hagen was compiling his eleven. Hagen was not eligible for Jones's amateur championships; Jones could not play in the US PGA. In the US Open, Hagen did not win with Jones in the field and the like happened in the British Open.

We are now left with a great foursome: Nicklaus, Watson, Jones and Hogan. This we ought to reduce to three. Watson has been the pre-eminent major championship performer of the last several years but has so far totalled 'only' seven before his 33rd birthday. To the same date, Nicklaus had eleven wins and nine even if we discard his US Amateur victories. Watson's record is, however, superior in the British Open, with four wins in eight entries to Nicklaus's three in some twenty years. Any case for Watson must rest on what he achieves in the remainder of the 1980s and whether or not Nicklaus can further raise his own total.

So there remain three players, each of which was dominant in his own era and considered with little doubt the best player in the world. That is all a golfer can do: be the best of his day. Jones and Hogan in conversation once agreed on this but I suspect Nicklaus would not and this may well be the prime reason for his relentless endeavour to build the greatest record of anyone in the major championships. This he has certainly done but we may wonder how Jones would have fared had he continued, rather than retired at the age of 28. Or Hogan, probably more dedicated in his pursuit of perfect striking than either of them, had he not been so injured in his 1949 car smash. Though it preceded his greatest major championship years, the after effects made him less fit when he

Jack Nicklaus wins the 1980 US Open

reached Nicklaus's present age.

So we are left with three players, each dominant during his best years. One, Jones, was early a great golfer and retired young. Another, Hogan, was into his middle thirties before he refined his playing abilities to the extent that he could be a major championship winner and Nicklaus, a genius in youth as Jones and with a far longer career.

Hogan has always been an inspiring example to all golfers of what can be achieved through perseverance: no other great player has been so long an also ran as Hogan. It is also difficult to see a rival in sight for the ability to play the kind of shot required, and then be so free from errors. He is inferior to the other two only in the length of time he took to reach the top.

Jones was, of course, a player of a different age, competing on courses far less well manicured than today or in Hogan's time and with far inferior balls and clubs. He certainly has the best record, as recounted elsewhere, in terms of competitions entered and won.

Nicklaus, on the other hand, has been a great player at a time when the general level of professional play has been increasingly high. If we look at the early results on the 1983 US Tour, we find that it seems to be becoming necessary for a player to throw in a freak round in the very low 60s to go with others all below 70.

In the end, it is not possible to make a clear choice amongst the three. Each was superior to the other in certain ways; each was the favourite for every championship he entered in his best years. It is perhaps time to concentrate on the career of Nicklaus alone. This career falls into various phases, some clear-cut, some not. The first is his play as an amateur.

At the age of twelve, Nicklaus first broke 80 and at sixteen won the Ohio Open. At nineteen, he was US Amateur champion. The following year, 1960, he was individual winner in the World Amateur Team Championship, completing four rounds at Merion in 269, figures in which some saw a superiority to Hogan, who had won his Open there in 287, though with the course set up more severely. The same year, Nicklaus set an amateur record for the US Open with his 282 total and finished second to Arnold Palmer. In 1961, he took the US Amateur for the second time and had already shown himself to be the greatest amateur since Bobby Jones. At that point he turned professional, though I believe he had ambitions to equal Jones's performances as an unpaid player.

In his first season he added the US Open, beating Palmer in a play-off to do so. The following year he won both the US Masters and PGA and added two more Masters in 1965-6. In 1966, he won the British Open at Muirfield in a legendary performance during which he almost entirely abandoned the use of woods for his tee shots because of the length of the rough and running fairways. Thus he accepted the loss of his superiority in length over the rest of the field and won through on precision as much as anything else. By 1966, then, he had joined Sarazen, Hogan and Player in having won each of the major championships. The following year he added his second US Open, pushing Palmer well into second place with his closing 65.

These half-a-dozen professional years saw a different Nicklaus from the player who later evolved. He was thought of as the most powerful player in the world (though he was not) and normally carried out brutal frontal assaults on golf courses, a massive drive followed by a far shorter iron into the greens than his fellow competitors were using. He was not seen as a great shot-maker at this time but as a player highly reliant on power. His natural arrogance and belief in himself had the rather odd effect of making him a cautious player. Nicklaus knew that he was the best and did not want to risk the mistakes that might let the less gifted in. Thus his strategy was frequently to play the first three rounds as safely as possible, lagging putts, playing irons from the tee and taking safe lines into the greens. His lowest round was often his last as he tried to come from behind.

After 1967 there was a lull in Nicklaus's accumulation of major championships, On the US Tour, after three years out of four as leading money winner in 1964-7, he fell out of that position for 1968-70. It began to be thought that his best days might be passed, that his desire to win might have declined or that he had burned himself out.

He came to the British Open in 1970 having recently finished no better than 51st in the US Open, his worst finish since missing the cut in 1963. His victory at St Andrews rekindled his will to win. The Nicklaus of the 1970s was a more formidable proposition than the youthful storm-trooper. He had always been a good putter but was more suspect in the touch shots from 40 yards in. Nicklaus specially improved his bunker play but was never to be in the highest class either from sand or for short approaches where the shot had to be manufactured. However, he practised these aspects intensively and markedly improved. It could now be said that the reason for Nicklaus's success was that though he was not best at anything he had no serious weaknesses to the same extent that Jones was uneasy with a niblick, Palmer with a wedge or, late in his career, Hogan with a putter.

Perhaps his best years were 1971-5. In that period he had 26 wins on the US Tour, including the PGA three times, the Masters twice and the US Open once. He had completed the feat of winning all major championships at least twice each and passed Jones's record of thirteen major championship victories when he won the 1973 US PGA.

Since then, it has perhaps been slightly downhill, though such a judgement would hardly stand up if Nicklaus were to have a great year in the 1983-6 period, something not at all impossible. His physical powers are still formidable and his nerve unimpaired.

Nevertheless, as I write in 1983, he had not finished higher than 12th in the US money list since 1978, the year he took the British Open for the third time to become the only man who has won each of the four major titles three times or more.

However, it is common knowledge that Nicklaus has for long regarded normal tournament play as competitive practice for the major championships and in fact he has won just one of these in the period 1979-82. But Nicklaus used to win other events even when his sights were set on the majors.

There have been several challengers to Nicklaus as the world's best current golfer, all eventually dismissed. First there was Arnold Palmer, to be followed by Gary Player. Then Jacklin, Weiskopf and, especially, Johnny Miller seemed to be establishing themselves as challengers before dropping by the wayside. Over all

Nicklaus's career the only period in which he has not been the undisputed number one has been the several years since the emergence of Tom Watson. A comparison of their performances since 1975, the year Watson won his first major championship, the British Open, may be of interest. Since that time the scores go (to the end of 1982):

Major championships: Watson 7, Nicklaus 5
Other US wins: Watson 24, Nicklaus 12
US money: Watson $2,622,666, Nicklaus $1,748,446
US money list average
annual placing: Watson 3.75, Nicklaus 15.125

The figures appear to show that Nicklaus is clearly below Watson in highly relevant categories, although they begin two seasons before Tom reached his peak. If Nicklaus has cut back his tournament appearances, so has Watson. (In 1981 Nicklaus played 16 US tournaments, Watson 21. In 1982 Nicklaus played 52 tournament rounds, Watson 78 while other leading players were putting in around 100 rounds, 118 being the US Tour maximum that year.)

However, whatever the state of the argument for the last several years, Watson has far to go to equal Nicklaus's overall achievements: too far, most would assume.

The outstanding arena for Nicklaus's performances over the years has been the British Open. He first appeared in 1962 and was joint 34th. From there, in the period 1963 to 1980, joint 12th was his worst finish. Every other year he was no worse than 6th and thirteen times he was third or better, by far the most impressive display of consistency in the event ever produced. He won in 1966, 1970 and 1978.

He was less consistent in the US Open. Here, from 1960 to 1982, he was seventeen times in the top 10 finishers and in the top 4 eleven times. Four times he has won. The story is similar for the Masters. He has five victories, been four times second and seventeen times in the top 8. The US PGA he has also won five times, been second or third six times and has 13 placings of fourth or better.

In this host of major championships, he has only five times failed to survive the 36-hole cut in a total of 90 entries. He even surmounted the hurdle in the 1981 British Open when, after beginning with his worst ever round of 83, he followed with a 66 to ensure safety. In national news reporting, the 83 attracted more attention than leadership after the first round!

On the US Tour, Nicklaus went into 1983 with 69 wins, 50 second place finishes and almost $4 million in money earnings, while his world-wide money winnings approached $5 million. He had, incidentally, won the Australian Open six times, one of the only overseas events other than the British Open in which he has competed at all regularly.

Obviously Nicklaus's sheer ability in all departments of the game has contributed substantially to his success, though it is doubtful if he has as wide a range of talents as Sam Snead. What has made Nicklaus doubly formidable is his nerve, which is enhanced at times of crisis rather than, as with so many lesser mortals, tending to crack. A golf writer once asked him why he did not just go out and win everything by twenty strokes. He replied that he could produce his best only under pressure, something seen the many times when Nicklaus has gone into the last round strokes behind and has then played at his finest.

Perhaps he was most under pressure after his 1979 season when he won nothing for the first time ever and sank to 71st on the US money list. His response was to take lessons on his short game during the close season and emerge to take the US Open and US PGA.

Jack Nicklaus

Norman
Von Nida

Born Sydney, Australia, 1914

If Jim Ferrier can be said to have been the first great Australian golfer, then von Nida was undoubtedly the second. The physical contrast between two golfers can seldom have been more marked. Jim Ferrier was over 6 foot 3½ inches while von Nida was nearly a foot shorter and much lighter. They were nearly exact contemporaries but chose different paths to the top.

Von Nida, of German/Irish ancestry, came to golf by being a caddie in Brisbane and was inspired by the early experience of carrying for Walter Hagen during his 1929 exhibition tour of Australia as British Open champion. For a while after, von Nida practised on the same course, trying as a fifteen-year-old to emulate the strokeplay of the American, whom he was later to beat in an exhibition match.

Von Nida's first success was to be a caddie champion of the area but by the age of eighteen he was amateur champion of Queensland. Where Ferrier was able to continue as an amateur for a good many years, von Nida could not and after his first major success quickly turned professional as a club assistant. He soon found that this was a dangerous occupation. In a trick-shot exhibition, the boss's version of the William Tell trick was to hit a golf ball off von Nida's knee. He failed. J. R. Quarton fainted when he saw the consequences for the knee, which was in plaster for some months.

Von Nida never returned to that job, being offered a full professional's job for a retainer of no less than £2 a week. He soon shook off the effects of the blow and, though so small, was extremely strong. Von Nida himself credited work on the roads and splitting sheep heads in an abattoir as the source of his wiry arms and hands, both so essential to a golfer.

His was not, however, to be a story of gradual improvement in tournament play. There weren't any and even after World War II when names such as the Ampol and McWilliams Wines tournaments began to appear no Australian could hope to make a fortune until recent times on the Australian circuit.

Von Nida continued to develop his game and in 1935 won the Queensland Open, beating Jim Ferrier into second place. The following year, he took the first New South Wales Open and the same year defeated Gene Sarazen, that year's Australian Open winner, in a challenge match. Such challenge matches were indeed the main source of his earnings from golf ability. Again and again he would pit himself against well-to-do amateurs for sums of money they could comfortably afford to lose while von Nida could not. But the one thing above all that distinguishes a successful golfer from others is not the knack of striking a golf ball well but nerve. Von Nida made a living.

In Australian golf in the years leading up to the war he won the Queensland Open three more times and another New South Wales title. He did not secure either the Australian Open or PGA, but was runner-up to Jim Ferrier in both 1938 and 1939 for the Open. In his first venture overseas he won the Philippine Open of 1938 and repeated this the following year.

When war came he had no international reputation and he was no better than one player amongst the top group of a very parochial Australian scene. A memorable challenge match came in 1941 before Service life swallowed him up. It was against Teddy Naismith, 1939 Australian matchplay champion, over 72 holes. On the first day, von Nida shot 68, 69 to be fifteen up and, having put up most of the money himself, his life savings looked utterly safe. The next morning, von Nida cut his hand while shaving and went into the Forces a poorer man.

When he came out, what should have been his best years had passed him by with no fortune won. Von Nida sailed for England and arrived with £17 in his pocket for the 1946 season. He should have won his first event but did not, although he took the *News Chronicle* tournament shortly after. At the end of the season he was joint second amongst money winners behind Bobby Locke, having amassed £1,330. His aim, however, had been the Open. He led the qualifiers but came in joint 4th, Sam Snead being the winner. Von Nida derived most satisfaction from the way he had played the famous (or infamous) Road Hole at St Andrews. Then a 466 yards par 5, it has since become a 4, possibly the hardest anywhere in the world, demanding a tee shot to cross the out-of-bounds on the right if the second shot into the narrow green is not to be impossible. Von Nida holed it in two 3s and two 4s during the championship.

He went home with more confidence in himself and won both the New South Wales and Australian PGAs, the latter being his first major Australian title. It was the first time Eric Cremin was to lose a final, since having won in 1937-8, and he was still losing them in 1962, for the seventh time!

During his next campaign in Britain, all von Nida's qualities were at their finest. His small stature meant that he was not a long hitter, and did not expect to reach par 5s in two. He was, however, an extremely straight hitter, having much earlier decided that to try to play with a drawn or faded shape of shot was not for him. Having grown up on courses with punitive rough, he missed few fairways. He was also a short game master. His pitching was excellent and the acknowledged maestro of bunker play, Gary Player, later rated von Nida highest of all in this department. On the greens, he was variable and was eventually to suffer the yips. But not in 1947.

His second entry was in the Brand Lochryn at Moor Park and at the end he had to cover the last four holes in two under par to beat Max Faulkner, and did so. He followed with the Dunlop Southport by five strokes, a second place to Dai Rees, a losing play-off to Henry Cotton and a defeat of Flory van Donck in a matchplay final. He had finished in first position in four of six tournaments. There followed the Open at Hoylake and after the two qualifying rounds von Nida was the best by two. In the championship proper he began 74, 76 to be seven behind the leaders but a 71 brought him level with Henry Cotton, Arthur Lees and Fred Daly.

It was, however, the Inshman Daly's year and von Nida finished joint fifth.

In the next event he won the North British, his 271 total equalling the record for a British tournament at that time. In one nine hole stretch he three-putted four times yet still went to the turn in 33. In the remainder of the season, he won once more and lost two play-offs, one for the Dunlop Masters. By the end of the season he had won the Vardon Trophy with a record stroke average of 71.25 and had record money winnings of over £3,000.

In 1948, he was again in good form and won five events during the season, starting the Open as clear favourite but finishing joint third, six behind Henry Cotton at Muirfield.

Thereafter, he was not again so major a force in British golf and while competing in America had little success; but he had his best years in Australia. He won the Open for the first

Norman Von Nida

time in 1950, beating the emerging star, Peter Thomson, by a stroke. The following year he was second to Thomson but came back again in 1952 with what was then a record total of 278. He retained the title the following year, Thomson again being second, and was runner-up in both 1954 and 1955. By 1951, he had four PGA matchplay titles and was runner-up in 1960.

However, his peak years were the few from 1946 to 1953. Thereafter he added a New South Wales title in 1954 and, finally, the Queensland Open of 1961. More than many, von Nida found tournament play a strain, especially with the overseas travel imposed on an Australian, and more than anything else his putting went. He also seemed to feel that a golfer was finished once he reached forty and believing it, was.

In later years, he was free with both advice and coaching to emerging Australian stars and there is scarcely one he did not help: Thomson, Crampton, Devlin, Graham and Norman amongst them.

Greg
Norman

Born Mount Isa, Queensland, Australia, 1955

Standing 6 feet 1 inch and weighing an athletic 13 stones and a bit, Greg Norman gives the golf ball just about the most savage clout in modern golf. On the 1982 European Tour, for example, he averaged about 281 yards from the tee, and not always with his driver. Like all present professionals with power to call on, he often resorts to an iron for safety to be short of threatening fairway bunkers or, equally, when a fairway is closely tree-lined. Norman himself reckons that he can hit up to 350 yards, especially if he's angry after having just come off a green where a short putt failed to drop.

He is often rated the longest straight driver in the world. This is not to say that he always hits the ball as if along a ruled line but that he is straight enough to use the driver when other long hitters might consider it too risky. It might be fair to say also that Norman is the world's longest hitter who is also a very good golfer. There are many long hitters around with a very limited game. They can hit the full shots well, and perhaps be excellent putters too, but fail when judgement, touch and rhythm are called for on half shots and from the approaches to greens.

Norman himself has often been criticised in this respect. It has been pointed out that he appears to be happier when hitting every shot full out and less than deft when finesse is called for. However, he has spent a lot of practice time on the little pitches, run-ups and putting and has looked much more secure in the last season or two.

He is a golfer with the attitude of the young Nicklaus: it is much easier to score well if you can overpower a course. The key to this is the long drive, carrying bunkers positioned to catch errant drives of the length more normal mortals reach. If the ball finishes in the rough, the long driver also has the strength and clubhead speed to force his ball not only out but also onto the greens. Nicklaus, as he lost some of the early power, worked hard on expanding his range of strokes and there are signs that Norman will too.

But for the moment the power is still very much there. It is obtained from his height — ideal for the modern power golfer — and the fact that he takes the club back on a wide arc, with a very full shoulder turn. So far so good but any of us who are 6 feet 1 inch and not arthritic could do that. Greg Norman was born with the ability to accelerate a golf club, though he enhanced this by practice. That is something most of us cannot do beyond innate limits, anymore than we leap Olympic distances or throw a cricket ball on low trajectory from long boundaries full into the wicket-keeper's gloves.

Greg Norman

Norman discovered these gifts fairly late and did not try golf until he was seventeen. He used to caddie occasionally for his mother, a three-handicap player, and decided that if she was so good, perhaps he might be also. Greg's first handicap was 27 but in a couple of years he was down to scratch. By 1956, he was a professional and playing in his first tournaments. The normal route to success as a tournament golfer is via a long process: learning how to compete, to deal with pressure, to score reasonably when playing badly, to produce outstanding shots when they are needed and few bad ones. Yet Norman won his fourth tournament, the West Lakes Classic in Adelaide. After opening rounds of 64, 67, 66 he was able to cruise to a comfortable five-stroke win.

It was obvious that a new star had arrived.

In 1977 he played in Europe and won his first event there, the Martini, having a

66 in the last round. This was to be a tournament that he performed particularly well in, winning again in 1979 and 1981.

By 1980, he was a major player in Europe, finishing second to Sandy Lyle in the Order of Merit and beating him in the final of the World Matchplay on the last hole. Earlier he had produced- startling scoring in the French Open, winning (with scores of 67, 66, 68, 67) by ten strokes. With a round to go no one was in reach of Norman and he then cruised further away.

He is a good front runner. Given a good lead, he does not play defensively but even more boldly. In the Scandinavian Enterprises Open at Helsingborg in Sweden, he began with one of the worst scores of the whole field, a 76, but came back with 66, 70. With a round to go he was still behind. The USA's Mike Krantz, for instance had 69, 68, 69 to lead Norman by six strokes but then faded to 77. Norman had the best round of the tournament, a 64, and beat Mark James by three and Severiano Ballesteros by four.

He also enhanced his prestige in Australia that year, becoming Australian Open champion. He had finished second in 1979 and was to have the same placing, behind Bill Rogers, in 1981. That year, he became Australian Masters champion instead and also won the Dunlop Masters, the longest established sponsored British tournament and ranking only behind the Open in Europe. At Woburn, he began 72, 68 to be two strokes behind but then produced a 66 to lead. A final 67 saw him home by four from Graham Marsh.

He produced an even better performance in this event in 1982. He began 68, 69 and closed with a pair of 65s. With an hour or two to go, the tournament was over unless Greg broke a leg. He finished at seventeen under par and with an eight stroke victory. His length from the tee was demonstrated by his hitting a green at 371 yards. He did not use his driver but a 3-wood!

Towards the end of the 1982 season, in which he finished as leading money winner on the European Tour, Norman announced that he would in future concentrate on the US rather than Europe. He has possibly been sensible to give himself the feeling that he is a superior golfer before fully undertaking the US Tour. Failures there have been many, while others have taken years before becoming tournament winners or even making a good living from high finishes.

So far, Norman has not won in America, though he has competed there frequently, and he may have been over-rated: he has not yet won a major championship, as has his near contemporary, Ballesteros. There has been much money on him in the British Open but he has not finished high. His best major championship performance came in the 1981 Masters, the first year he had qualified for an invitation. Norman began 69, 70 and was amongst the leaders at that stage and tied with the eventual winner, Tom Watson. Norman continued tidily enough with a pair of 72s for fourth place, one behind Nicklaus and Miller and three behind Watson. It seemed to be the general opinion that Norman would be assisted into the traditional green blazer of the champion before many years had passed.

So, without a major championship to his name, there remains a question mark against Norman and he has also still to prove himself in the hardest school, the US Tour. The next few years should show how far he can follow the man from whose books he learned the game — Jack Nicklaus.

Peter
Oosterhuis

Born London, England, 1948

With the European golf world at his feet and the living easy, Peter Oosterhuis did what no other British player has ever done: accepted fully the challenge of the US Tour.

Of course golfers in plenty in the distant past have sought fame and fortune in America. Willy Anderson, Jim Barnes, Tommy Armour and Light-Horse Harry Cooper are examples. They did not, however, give up successful careers in the British Isles but emigrated as unknowns and built up careers in America.

Another group, which includes Peter Townsend, Tony Jacklin and, today, Nick Faldo have campaigned on the US Tour but, except perhaps for Jacklin, have always seen Europe as their main sphere. Their ideas would be adjusted only if they enjoyed great success in America.

Not so Oosterhuis. He tested the waters in the USA, nearly won the 1974 Monsanto Open, had tied for third after leading the 1973 Masters and decided that he had the nerve and skill to pit himself against the Americans and other world stars, and made the total psychological commitment of settling there, rather than buying a return ticket.

What did he leave behind him in Europe?

Peter Oosterhuis did not have an official handicap when he entered the Surrey Junior Championship at the age of fourteen, but with rounds of 79, 71 he came out the winner and was awarded a handicap of five. At the age of 18 he won his first important senior event, the Berkshire Trophy and was British Boys champion. He then played in both the Walker Cup and World Team Championship teams (he was low individual) before turning professional in 1968.

It is an irony that at the time his weakness was in the vital short approach shots from around 50 yards down — the ones that demand variety of flight, exact judgement of distance and, above all, feel.

In his first professional season he finished 17th in the Order of Merit and moved up to 7th the following year. His apprenticeship was over and thereafter Oosterhuis dominated the European Tour while he remained in Europe and there is no reason to suppose that he would not have continued to do so for his occasional trips across the Atlantic have produced some excellent results.

In 1971 he moved to the top of the Order of Merit and remained there until his departure for the US at the end of the 1974 season. His consistency was remarkable and is best seen in the fact that he won, for four years in a row, the Vardon Trophy for the season's best stroke average, an unprecedented feat. It is interesting to see how Peter's stroke average reflected his superiority during his last European season, 1974. Only a handful of players were below 73 a round, while two, Dale Hayes, of the backswing quicker than the eye can see and Neil Coles, still good enough to win his 27th tournament when nearly 49 in 1982, returned averages of 71.47 and 71.73 respectively. Oosterhuis's return was 70.76, which can also be compared with that of Tony Jacklin, who had then not fallen far below his best, of 72.48. Oosterhuis won approaching twice as much money as anyone else.

Of course, golf is not primarily about stroke averages, or even money earned, but tournaments won. At this point he had won nine major European events and seven others, most of these in South Africa. He had also finished second in the 1974 Open to Gary Player.

At the end of the year, having qualified at the US Tour school, he gave up the near certainty of continuing British-based success because he wanted to be a great golfer and to him that meant becoming one of the best players in America.

Peter Oosterhuis

Oosterhuis reached the age of 35 in 1983 and it now looks likely that the verdict of golf history will be that he failed though a few, very few, golfers have enjoyed their best years at around the age of forty.

He began well enough, at 34th place on the money list and a second place finish but did not improve on that in the seasons that followed, even declining to 65th, 93rd and 105th in 1978-80. Yet on those rare appearances in Britain, mainly confined to the Open Championship, his game appeared as strong as ever. He had a chance to win in both 1978 and 1982, leading with nine holes to go in 1978 but eventually finishing three strokes behind Jack Nicklaus. In 1982, though never in apparent contention, he finished joint second, with the South African Nick Price, only a stroke behind Tom Watson.

He also had a remarkable record in the Ryder Cup, for several years perhaps the best ever established by a British player. From 1971 to 1977 in singles he beat successively Littler, Palmer (twice), halved with Trevino and beat Miller, Snead and McGee. Yet in 1983 he will not even be eligible for the Great Britain and Europe team. It has been decided that only the top twelve players on the

European money list will be chosen. Oosterhuis could be US Masters, Open and PGA champion, add a few more, and still not qualify. In a similar piece of idiocy, Severiano Ballesteros was not chosen for the 1981 team though on that occasion the latest adjustment of PGA rules did leave spaces he could have filled. So, it seems that henceforward a Ryder Cup place is to be a reward for honest soldiers of the European Tour.

In 1981 and 1982, Oosterhuis's results at last improved in America. He had not won a tournament since beating Miller for the 1974 Italian Open, when the Canadian Open came his way. Oosterhuis had rounds of 69, 69, 72, 70. At the halfway stage he lay four strokes behind a man who had shot a 62, Leonard Thompson, but the eventual contest was amongst those who scored steadily in each of the four rounds. Oosterhuis came in a stroke ahead of Nicklaus, Lietzke and North. The $76,500 he won for his victory was around $16,000 more than he had previously won in a whole year on the US Tour.

The irony is that Oosterhuis's abilities are almost certainly better suited to European golf than the US pattern. Most US Tour courses suit the man who can hit the ball high and far and who likes to know that his iron shots into the greens are going to bounce predictably. Oosterhuis himself claims to prefer knowing how the ball is going to behave and says that he would rapidly lose his swing in British links and winds, and his temper when balls dart sideways into the rough from drives or run through greens.

With hindsight, it is easy to see the decision he ought to have made nearly ten years ago: he ought to have continued to base himself upon the European Tour but regard himself as a world player competing in South Africa, Australia and the US. With continuing tournament successes under the belt it is easier to stroll onto centre stage and perform well in the various continents. As it is, he remains an also-ran in America and out of sight, out of mind, in Europe; all the result of a decision that was courageous but wrong.

Oosterhuis's abilities have prospered despite the fact that he is 6 feet 5 inches tall. It used to be said that a golfer should be rather under medium height and square of build, and these criteria seem only to have modified with the experience of recent years. It does help to be able to stand upright and relaxed and then not too far away from the ball. Oosterhuis fully becomes one of our masters of golf when he begins to crouch for the short shots and then he becomes one of the superior players that golf has known at getting the ball near the hole and putting. From his kind of height, the exacting coordinations of golf in the full swing have never long been mastered by anyone, Peter Oosterhuis included.

Arnold Palmer

Born Latrobe, Pennsylvania, USA, 1929

In the history of golf many players have been respected, some even revered. There would be few to argue, however, that anyone in his prime has generated more excitement, or been more the object of adulation, than Arnold Daniel Palmer. Almost alone, he made golf into a mass spectator sport in America, while in Britain from his first entry in the Open Championship in 1960 he was the main force in elevating the event to its former status as the world's premier event.

What was it about the man which made this happen? Why did 'Arnie's Army' come to follow him rather than other successful players? Some of the factors are intangible and as a whole the phenomenon is none too easy to analyse. Some things, however, are clear enough.

In the first place, he made even the swinging of a golf club a dramatic event. He was not a simple rhythmic swinger but made the achievement of hitting a golf ball hard look more like a boxer delivering a round-house right hook than a matter of effortless acceleration. Indeed, an American golf writer described the sight of Arnold Palmer mounting even the teeing area as being comparable to a boxer clambering into the ring. Palmer was a very powerful man (and still is to a lesser extent) particularly in the forearms, and prone to hook. He overcame this tendency by going through the ball very forcefully with his right hand, maintaining the movement into the full follow-through. The momentum had the effect of making him off balance at the end of the swing and, as a result, Palmer's hitting a golf ball was an apparently perilous enterprise.

Writing of him at his peak in the early 1960s, Henry Cotton observed that Palmer sometimes finished 'on his knees', had 'little style' and rarely finished two consecutive swings in the same position. To the common man Palmer was playing the same kind of game as they were, without the rhythmic, easy uncoiling of a Littler, Snead or Weiskopf. He finished in the rough no more than anyone else but it certainly seemed that he did, and, once there, whatever the lie of the ball, was seldom content with a steady wedge shot back to the fairway. Rather, the turf and branches would fly and the ball explode out towards the green.

For many years now, Palmer has been a hesitant performer once on the green. He still has good days, but they have for long been rare. More usually he seems tentative, not expecting to hole anything other than the very short ones and content to steer the ball near the hole rather than into it.

It was far different in his great days. Then, Palmer was thought of as one of the great putters of golf history, on a par with Locke, Hagen and Jones. But while they

Arnold Palmer, Troon, 1962

were exceptionally gifted with touch, especially masterly at judging length of run on a green, Palmer's forte was boldness and confidence. Once in real striking distance he went for the hole and was seldom short. He always 'gave the hole a chance' and if his ball ran a few feet past was not disturbed, feeling that he could knock the return in.

As Palmer matured, which for a golfer frequently means to grow older and worn by the stresses of competitive play, most good judges felt that his swing improved. He also set himself to hit a higher ball with the advantages this brought to iron shots holding the green and woods pitching on fairways and stopping quickly rather than rolling away into rough and bunker. He was never likely to become anything approaching a stylist, but became a consistent driver and hit far fewer outright bad shots with any club. Of the great players, he remained perhaps the least accurate with a wedge. Once rated the best putter on the US Tour, he has still to develop a twitch, but has not been better than a moderate putter for many a long year.

Palmer first became a national name in the US in 1954, when he won the US Amateur against Robert Sweeny in an extremely close-fought final that went past the 36th. He turned professional shortly afterwards and suffered no learning pains on the US Tour. He won his first event, the Canadian Open, in 1955 and two others the following year, while in 1957 he had four victories and had joined the ranks of players to be reckoned with. From that year until the 1972 season he was never out of the top ten US money winners, was first four times in 1958-63 and in the leading three on five other occasions. He was the first man to win over $100,000 in a season. Today, of course, this is a feat barely worthy of notice. More than thirty pass such amounts annually, with inflation and the far higher amounts on offer in real terms.

He passed the milestone of his first major championship in 1958 at Augusta, Georgia, when he won the Masters by a stroke from Doug Ford and Fred Hawkins. The Masters, indeed, was to be the event that saw the best of Arnold Palmer. The next year he was third, beaten by a last round 66 from Art Wall and his own 74. In 1960, he led the tournament throughout but with two holes to play found himself a stroke behind Ken Venturi. The last two holes at Augusta National do not offer easy birdies, but Palmer had 3s on both to edge in by a stroke.

This feat entrenched the legend that Palmer was a great last round player and it was to remain with him. Oddly, his great contemporary, Jack Nicklaus, has a statistically far better record in this respect. It was, however, to Palmer that the cry used to go up: 'Charge, Arnie, charge!'

In 1961, he was joint second, a stroke behind Gary Player, beaten because Player got down in two from a greenside bunker on the last hole, while Palmer took a highly unlikely four strokes.

The year of 1962 saw Palmer and Player again involved, this time joined in a play-off by Dow Finsterwald. Palmer had begun 70, 66, 69 to lead the South African by four and Finsterwald by two but there was no Palmer charge this time. He had a 75. For the play-off the next day, however, there emphatically was: after nine holes, Gary Player had established a three-stroke lead over Palmer, going to the turn in a two under par 34, with Palmer one over. Palmer's last nine 31 was not a record but the only better score in history has been 30. He won by three strokes from Player, with Finsterwald well out of it on 77.

In 1963, Nicklaus won his first Masters, with Palmer five strokes away in joint ninth place, his worst finish since 1956. In 1964 he gave his most brilliant Augusta performance. With Ballesteros, Nicklaus and Player, he is the only winner to have broken 70 in three rounds. His scores were 69, 68, 69, 70, and brought him home six strokes ahead of Jack Nicklaus and Dave Marr as the first man to win the championship four times. That was his last victory, though he was to continue to feature in the event for some time. In 1965 he was second, fourth in 1966 and 1967, but never in real contention again.

In the US Open, Palmer featured for a longer period of time, despite winning just once (though he's still trying). That win was also significant in the building-up of the legend of the last-round Palmer charge. In 1960, that Open had seemed to be in the pocket of Mike Souchak, a formidable tournament winner who never won a major championship. Souchak had begun 68, 67 at Cherry Hills to lead Arnold Palmer by seven strokes. Going into the final round he was still six ahead. Palmer's scores at that point had been 72, 71, 72. He remarked that a 65 could perhaps see him home. Perhaps, but it was by no means likely, for it was scoring that no one in the field had approached, except for Souchak's 67. Nor was it approached again in the next Cherry Hills Open in 1978.

Palmer drove the first green, a par 4, and his resultant birdie there seemed to inspire him, for he had been three over par for the hole in the previous rounds. He then birdied the next three holes as well and had caught the field when he birdied two more shortly afterwards. He reached the turn in 30, a US Open scoring record and parred his way home for the 65. It brought him victory by two strokes from a young new name, amateur Jack Nicklaus, who had led Palmer by four into the last round.

Palmer continued to feature strongly in the US Open for many years. In 1962 he tied with Jack Nicklaus but lost the 18-hole play-off and tied again the following year, this time losing to Julius Boros. In 1964, he contended forcefully with a 68, 69 start but faded considerably to finish well behind Ken Venturi. His worst experience in golf lay two years ahead at the Olympic Country Club in California.

After three rounds, which included a 66, he lay three strokes ahead of Billy Casper, with whom he was paired for the last round. Palmer opened up with two birdies and reached the turn in 32. This left Casper seven strokes adrift of Arnold. On the 10th tee Casper remarked that he would 'really have to go some' to get second place. Palmer, fatally, began to think of the US Open record. If he could play the last nine in 36 strokes he would beat Ben Hogan's 1948 mark of 276. The prospect receded when he immediately dropped a shot but got that back with a birdie on the 12th. With four holes to go, the record was still in reach and Casper still no threat, five strokes behind. Palmer then was bunkered on the 150 yard 15th and took three to get down. Casper was on with his tee shot and when he sank his putt was suddenly back in contention — but only just, at three behind. Spectators could not have thought so. The 16th at Olympic measures over 600 yards and Casper's gesture after his birdie was to play an iron off the tee for safety. Palmer now met disaster. His drive hit a tree and dropped into deep rough. He then attempted too long an iron. After two shots he was still in the rough and only a little over 250 yards from the tee. His eventual 6 was not, in the circumstances, too bad.

Meanwhile, Casper had made a move of his own. Going undramatically up the middle of the fairway he had dropped his third shot on the green and holed the putt. Palmer was now only a stroke ahead. One more hole and they were level. Casper had made up the five strokes in three holes. They both parred the last hole, Palmer with great difficulty after he had put his tee shot into thick rough.

Ever since, it has been commanding leader's nightmare in a major champion-ship that he should 'do a Palmer'.

However, there was still the play-off to come the following day. Palmer seemed unabashed by his previous mistakes and went to the turn in 33 to lead by two strokes. Casper then birdied the 12th, while Palmer missed a short putt and the pair were level. On the next, Casper holed a second long putt and went into a lead that was not threatened. He won by four strokes, despite three-putting twice on the closing holes.

This was certainly the last US Open that Palmer 'ought' to have won but he was nearly champion again the following year at Baltusrol. There, he went into the last round tied with Jack Nicklaus and had a 69, one of the lowest scores of the day, but was eclipsed by Nicklaus's 65.

Thereafter, he was 6th in 1969, 3rd in 1972, 4th in 1973 and, finally, 5th in 1974. He featured at times in other years but achieved no high placings.

If the US Open saw the most sustained performances in major championships from Arnold Palmer, arguably the British saw his best. This came in the short period 1960-2. When he arrived at St Andrews in 1960 it was as the newly crowned US Open champion. His entry marked the revival of interest, which was to grow rapidly, from important American golfers in the event, leading to the British Open being now the most international of the majors. Palmer began 70, 71 in the Centenary Open. Remarkably, this left him seven behind Roberto de Vicenzo and five behind Kel Nagle. Vicenzo faltered thereafter; Nagle did not and, though Palmer finished strongly with a 68, the Australian was champion by a stroke.

Palmer was back at Royal Birkdale the following year, a championship that saw some bad weather, particularly on the second day (both the men who finished joint third, O'Connor and Coles, had 77s). Palmer came through that day with a 73, to trail Dai Ree's 36-hole total by one, but with a 69 in the morning took the lead on the last day and with a 72 in the afternoon held off Dai Rees to win by a stroke.

His finest performance in a British Open and arguably any major champion-ship came at Troon in 1962. Gathered there was the best field of American golfers since before the war and included Snead, 1961 US Open champion Gene Littler, the new US Open holder, Locke, Jack Nicklaus and such winners of the near future as Bob Charles, Gary Player and Peter Thomson (already four times champion). The course that year seemed to favour the shorter hitters. The fairways were hard after drought and Palmer's length might get him into trouble rather than be much of an advantage.

Thomson, whose golf was ideally suited to running conditions, led the first day, with a 70, Palmer and Nagle close behind on 71. Nicklaus was out of it with an 80 which had included a 10 on one hole. After two rounds, and Palmer's 69 to Nagle's 71, the championship was developing into a repeat of the Centenary.

On the final day, Palmer dropped two shots in the first four holes and was back to level with Kel Nagle. He then produced some of the best golf of his lifetime and for the remainder of his round was seven under level 4s for a 67 and a five stroke lead on Nagle at lunchtime.

In the afternoon he went to the turn in 33 and the title was his, eventually with a 69. His 276 total was a new Open record, his margin of six over Nagle the biggest since Hagen in 1929 while the man in third place was no fewer than thirteen strokes behind. The man who was soon to take Palmer's place as the perennial ante-post betting favourite, Jack Nicklaus, was 29 behind.

To me, this was his finest hour and, an oddity of golf history. He was never again better than 7th, positions he achieved at Muirfield in 1972 and Turnberry in 1977, the last result pointing to an oddity of a different kind in Palmer's career.

The fairly sudden decline of Arnold Palmer from the ranks of major champion-ship contenders aroused much comment as to causes, most analyses tending to the decision that a decline in both putting ability and boldness of through-the-green play were the prime reasons. Less discussed is how well Palmer has continued to play into what can no longer be called early middle age.

The reason for this is clear: the man loves to play golf. Well, don't they all, you might ask. The answer would be 'No'. Many regard golf no more enthusiastically than going off to a hum-drum job. Tournament play is acute strain even to a man playing very well and despair to those who are not. But Palmer loves to play and loves to compete, activities by no means synonymous. When past fifty, he was reluctant to play the US Senior Tour, believing that he might still win on the main Tour, where his last win came in 1973. To some extent this faith is justified. He won in Canada a couple of year or so ago and even led the British Open in 1982 at most under par for a while on the first day. As a 53-year-old at the beginning of the 1983 US Tour season he began the Los Angeles Open in startling fashion with 66, 69, 68 to be only one off the lead. Had he managed to win, it would have perhaps been the most popular victory since Ben Hogan came back to tie the same tournament after his crippling car accident. By a quirk of fate, after three rounds, one of the four ahead of him (at the age of 52) was Gene Littler, another subject of this book. At one time Palmer got into the lead in the final round but faded just a little to a 72. In the hectic competition of the Tour this brought him down to 10th place.

So Palmer had to be content with his career total of 61 Tour and nineteen foreign wins, the former 4th on the US all-time list. Money-winnings have long ceased to really matter to Palmer but, despite the vast increases in prize money which to some extent came after Palmer's best years, at the end of 1982 he still ranked as high as 6th in all-time US winnings and is one of only a dozen players to have won over $2 million worldwide.

Gary
Player

Born Johannesburg, South Africa, 1935

It is an undoubted advantage for the professional golfer to have been born in either the United States or Europe. At least his tournament travelling will tend to be hundreds rather than thousands of miles. Even in these days of rapid intercontinental travel a player such as, say, Watson in the US, or Lyle in Britain, sees competing outside his home Tour as the exception rather than the rule. The schedule is exhausting enough anyway, without the additional strain of jet travel around the world.

So the number of international golfers (those who live in one country but play most of their competitive golf elsewhere) is small. Some players have chosen to base themselves in a new country — Graham, Crampton and Devlin are examples that come to mind — but very few have chosen world travel as their norm. Of this group in recent times Greg Norman, Graham Marsh and Gary Player are prime examples. There is no doubt at all that Player is the greatest travelling performer of all.

He started young, coming over to Britain in 1955 and doing none too well. At that age he sought advice about his swing and technique, as he was always to do. One British professional told him to forget professional golf and go home and get an honest job.

Player disregarded this but he did take note that most seemed to think his grip was a hooker's and this was modified. He had always been committed to practising hard, which is one reason for his becoming the best sand shot expert that the world has yet seen. He came back the following year and won the Dunlop tournament.

Most South Africans at that time would have been content to pit themselves annually against the best in Britain, but Gary's ambitions were always aimed at the heights of golf. By 1957 he was playing in America and won not much, but enough, money to feel that he was good enough to continue. The following year he surmounted the great hurdle of winning a US tournament, the Kentucky Derby Open. Three years later, he was leading money winner, the only time an overseas based player has done this. He was also Masters champion, and was feeling a little lucky. He had played finely for three rounds in 69, 68, 69 but had stumbled during his final round and after 72 strokes was bunkered beside the last green. He got down in two. A few minutes later, Palmer was in the same bunker and took four to get down and lost by one.

This was not Gary's first major championship victory. That had come when he was twenty-four at Muirfield in 1959. It was a closely fought event but Player had come through with the strongest last round, a 68, to win by two strokes, yet he finished in despair, having dropped two strokes on the last hole and thinking he had thrown victory away. But the leaders did not go out last at that time and all was well in the end. Except for Ray Floyd's last hole in the 1982 US PGA, it is difficult to recall another occasion when a winner has finished by dropping two shots on the last hole.

With this victory, he had succeeded Locke as the leading South African golfer and, early in the 1960s, was accepted as a member of the 'Big Three', with Palmer and Nicklaus. He laboured under the disadvantage of being a small man at 5ft 7in, and in consequence lacked length from the tee. Golfers have sought different remedies for this. His fellow-countryman Locke decided to learn to hook every shot; Cotton, a short, accurate player early in his career, for a time followed the same course but settled on developing strength in his hands, first by constant exercise and later by hitting and stopping the club and hitting car tyres; Tommy Horton uses carbon fibre shafts.

Player went for increased physical strength and rapidly became reknowned for the strenuous exercise schedule he subjected himself to. He also concentrated on developing a wide swing arc so that the result equalled that of much taller men. In the end, no one of comparable class has given a stronger impression of hitting full out with every ounce he possesses. Nevertheless, it has been his play from the medium irons down to the putt that most would think has brought him his success. When Player is not hitting the power shots, he becomes a different man, superbly poised through the ball and crisp in striking. When just off the green, he has a great variety of shot to call on; all the way from the high, soft sand wedge to the run-up. His bunker excellence may have been exaggerated, if only slightly, because of the excellence of his putting over the years. Undoubtedly he is superb at getting down in two from sand but it may be that his holing out has made a great contribution to that. For most of his career, Player has used a short backswing and putted with a firm jab at the ball, rather than the smoother motion almost all others have favoured.

In 1962, he took his third major championship, this time the US PGA. After 72, 67, 69, he led into the last round and with a closing 70 held off fine finishing 67s from Bob Goalby and Jack Nicklaus. He had now only to win the US Open to complete a modern version of the Grand Slam — winning all four major championships. In 1958, Tommy Bolt's year, he had come quite close, finishing second but four behind Bolt. He did not feature strongly again until 1965 at Bellerive, Missouri. Player scored steadily throughout with 70, 70, 71, 71 and the almost unimaginable happened when he tied, not with an American but the Australian 1960 British Open champion, Kel Nagle. Player took the play-off by 71 to 74. It was the first victory by an overseas golfer since Englishman Ted Ray's 1920 achievement and the first time an American or British player had not come in as champion.

Gary Player then embarked in pursuit of further glories and the aim of a second Grand Slam. Later in that season, though, on 15 October to be precise, on the West Course at Wentworth, there came a confrontation that was, almost on its own, to cause Gary Player to be regarded as the best matchplayer in the world.

The opponent was Tony Lema, who was killed the following year in a plane crash. He had won the 1964 British Open and wished to be regarded as a member of the Big Three at Player's expense; as if in emphasis of this, the sporting goods firm of Slazenger had recently dropped their endorsement contract with Player and signed up Tony Lema worldwide.

The 36-hole match began quietly with three pars apiece, but Player drew first blood by firing in a 4-iron second on the 497 yard (note that all holes are given at 1965 yardage) 4th hole to some 5 yards and then holing the putt. He held that lead to the turn to be out in 34 to Lema's 35. On the 10th (192 yards) Player struck a splendid iron shot to some 8ft while Lema hit trees and came down in rough ground. He scrambled his ball onto the green but was still 6 or 7 yards from the hole. Nevertheless he holed that long one and Player failed to do so. Player may have felt that little harm had been done, but he didn't know what lay immediately ahead. For the remainder of the morning, all was disaster for Player. He made errors while Lema

Gary Player

birdied five holes out of seven. At the end, Player had to get down a 5 yard putt to avoid going into lunch seven down

He had not in the least given up, however, and after eating went directly to the practice ground to try to find out why he was getting a hook on the tail end of his drives. He thought he had found the answer. Alas, on the first hole, he hit a duck hook into the trees to go seven down!

There were soon signs of recovery as he took the next two holes to be only five behind. The 4th was halved and Player won the 192 yard 5th with a birdie 2. Four down was a bad but not completely impossible position with thirteen holes to go. Another disaster then occurred: on the 347 yard 6th, Lema safely got his 4; Player went firmly with his birdie putt and slid 2ft past, then missed the return.

At about this time Player overheard a spectator say that the match was all over. Player later wrote that from this point he felt 'supercharged', probably a reference to that rare state experienced by a golfer when he feels he can do anything and concentration seems total.

The next three holes were halved, Player having to get a 5 yard putt down on the 9th to avoid going six behind. Nonetheless, five down with nine to play meant that Lema really had only to hit three or four moderate shots into greens and the resultant halves would bring him home without alarms.

Lema missed the 10th green again and this time did not get down in two more. Four down. On the 408 yard 11th Player drove down the middle and his iron stopped some 5ft away. He scored a birdie and was three down.

The next was halved and Player had all the better of play on the 437 yard 13th. He drove down the middle of the fairway, while Lema, feeling perhaps that he could possibly be caught, hooked under the pressure into the trees. He could only play out, making little more than 40 yards ground. Player hit a 5-iron to 10ft. With his third, Lema only reached the front of the green but from there improbably holed a putt of at least 8 yards. Instead of having an easy two-putt for the hole, Player now had to hole out to have any realistic chance of catching Lema. He did, and was two down.

The next two holes were halved. On the 380 yard 16th, golfers tend to drive off with a 3-wood or an iron, as length is not essential but accuracy is. Player, however, noticed that Lema had selected a 3-wood so decided to use a driver himself. A good one would put increased pressure on Tony Lema. Striving for length, Lema hooked and eventually had to play 3 from the tee. One down.

On the very testing 17th, 555 yards, both were short in two strokes, Player by less than 20 yards, Lema 90 yards back. He pitched to 10ft, Player to a little less and both holed their putts. (It is remarkable that though Lema hit a few erratic shots through the green, his holing out remained apparently nerveless.)

The last, 495 yards, saw good drives from both of them but, with his second, Lema hit a low hook. It was not in trouble but he had failed to reach the green and was some 50 yards short. Player hit a 4-wood, that narrowly missed trees, to 10ft. Lema's pitch came up well short of the hole after biting quickly and Player levelled the match after two-putting. So to sudden death.

Quickly, it was all over. The 1st was rated at 476 yards and Player found the green with his second shot while Lema did not, hooking into a greenside bunker. Player had covered the last nineteen holes in 70 and gone from seven down to one up in the space of eighteen holes. Shortly after, he passed out and came to find himself crying and trembling. He was later to say of the match 'It contains my whole life story.'

The next day, Player overcame what might have been inevitable reaction and took his first World Matchplay Championship, beating the 1965 British Open champion, Peter Thomson, by 3 and 2.

Over the years, he took it four more times, his victims in the finals being Jack Nicklaus, Bob Charles, Jack Nicklaus again and Graham Marsh.

However, the World Matchplay is not a major championship and cannot be so while it remains an invitation event in which the year's major championship winners do not always compete (Nicklaus and Watson particularly).

Player's next major championship came at Carnoustie in 1968. The scoring this time was variable by all the contenders. Casper, for instance, led Player by five strokes after two rounds but finished with a 78. Player started with a 74, Nicklaus a 76 and, going into the last round, Player was two behind Casper, level with Bob Charles and two ahead of Nicklaus. It was a dour struggle settled by the relative collapse of Charles (76) and Casper, while an eagle from Player late on settled the issue with Nicklaus, who had threatened to catch up.

Player won no more major championships for some years and as he left his mid-thirties it seemed his best years were past.

In 1972, however, he returned to take the US PGA at Oakland Hills and one of his best years followed in 1974. In the US Masters, he followed rounds of 71, 71 with a 66 and went into the last round one behind Dave Stockton. With nine holes to go several players were battling it out and Player eventually made the championship his when he hit a 'shot of the year' to within inches with a 9-iron over trees on the 17th. When he parred the last he had won by two strokes over Tom Weiskopf and Dave Stockton.

Some three months later, he took his third British Open at Royal Lytham during the first year the big ball had to be used by the whole field. In strong winds he began commandingly 69, 68 to open up a five-stroke lead on Bobby Cole and Peter Oosterhuis. He then faltered a little to a 75 in the continuing wind and Nicklaus drew to within four shots, with Oosterhuis three away. Player went steadily the final day after a good start and came home four ahead of Oosterhuis and five on Nicklaus. In what was overall his best year, he also won three times in South Africa, the Australian Open, a US Tour event and broke 60 with a 59 during his Brazilian Open win.

Since then, Player has won just one more major championship, the 1978 Masters, the most legendary of his 121 tournament victories. He began 72, 72, to be five strokes behind leaders Lee Trevino and Rod Funseth, the latter making a rare appearance in the spotlight. The next day, Hubert Green produced a 65, which put him seven ahead of Player and three ahead of Funseth and Tom Watson. These four eventually were to contest the finish.

Player went to the turn in 34, making three birdies but also dropping a shot. His wife had persuaded him to try to stroke his putts rather than use his customary jabbing action. He had played well as regards striking through the green but gained nothing on the putting surface. All suddenly changed, as Player made three pars and six birdies on the run in, seven on the last ten holes. He was home in 30 for a round of 64, both numbers equalling Augusta records for the Masters. Coming up the last, however, the other three all had good chances of reaching a play-off. Watson missed the green with his second and could not get down in two, Funseth failed for a birdie, while Green came closest of all. He hit a magnificent approach shot and then missed a putt of no more than 3ft by a remarkably wide margin.

Player went on to produce perhaps his last great spell of golf, coming from seven behind Severiano Ballesteros in the Tournament of Champions to win the following week. Finally, still in April, he began the Houston Open 64, 67, 70 to be three behind Andy Bean but overtook him in the final round. Fewer than a dozen players have won three US Tour events consecutively. Player then came within reach of making it four in a row when he was tied for the lead after three rounds in the New Orleans Open, but he eventually finished 5th.

At this time, Player was 42 and has since achieved little on the US Tour, though he came second in the 1979 US Open. He has continued to do well in South Africa and Australia and is said to be looking forward immensely to competing on the US Senior Tour when he reaches the age of fifty.

Dai
Rees

Born Barry, Wales, 1913

Since Harry Vardon wrote his books early in this century the golf grip has gradually become standardised amongst good players. The left hand is placed on the shaft and the right hand below it with the little finger riding over the forefinger of the left hand. The main variation then is how 'strong' or weak the alignment of the hand is, a rule of thumb being the weaker the grip, the better the player.

When Harry was setting forth the arguments for this grip, his opinion was that its great advantage was that it married the two hands and helped them act as one, the right not overpowering the left so much in the hitting area.

Vardon, however, had huge hands and perhaps took little account of those with short fingers and some players (Nicklaus is the outstanding modern example) use the interlocking grip. Though similar to Vardon's it involves the difference that the little finger of the right hand fits between forefinger and middle finger of the left and the two then 'lock' together. For most people, this grip makes the two hands feel even more as one and the little finger does perform a function rather than merely rest on another. Unfortunately, to most it feels most unnatural and, though many follow Nicklaus's advice about many matters, his grip they leave severely alone.

There remain other possibilities. Harry Bradshaw, for instance, overlapped two fingers (or was it three?) and the Whitcombe brothers of 1930s British golf allowed a thumb to dangle in space.

A select few, who include Art Wall, a Masters winner, Bob Rosburg and Dai Rees used what has come to be known as the baseball grip. The name is unfortunate. It implies a brute-force approach to the game whereas all that happens is that the little finger is allowed to help to hold the club. A better name might be the 'natural' grip.

Rees felt that playing golf was a difficult enough task without making things more difficult still by giving up the use of a finger. It can be an advantage of this grip that having the little finger on the shaft takes some emphasis away from the right forefinger. If the last three fingers of the left hand are the most important, why not those of the right as well?

Dai Rees was born the son of a professional and came rapidly to the fore when he defeated one of the Whitcombe brothers in the Matchplay Championship of 1936. At the time, it was a tournament that in Britain ranked little below the Open in stature. It was to be an event in which Rees produced many of his best performances over the years. Two years later, he again reached the final and came through, this time against E.R. Whitcombe's son.

These were Dai Rees's major successes before war came, though he also won the *Yorkshire Evening News* tournament in 1939 and made his first Ryder Cup appearance in 1937 at Southport and Ainsdale, where he was one of only two British winners in the singles, beating the great Byron Nelson by 3 and 1. He was selected for the 1939 match, which was cancelled because World War II had begun.

During the war, Rees served as a driver to Air Vice Marshal Sir Harry Broadhurst in the Middle East and returned quickly to assume a leading role in post-war British golf. Arguably he was second only to Henry Cotton and was the leading figure once Cotton had virtually retired from tournament play after his victory in the 1948 British Open.

During this phase of his career, the Ryder Cup was perhaps of more importance than it is today. It was not at that time suffering from the preponderance of American victories which have since built up and, as the war ended, the score in matches stood USA 4, Great Britain and Ireland 2. The series was in fact level, if the two matches that came before Samuel Ryder's presentation of a cup are also taken into account (the US lost the 1926 match by $1\frac{1}{2}$ to $13\frac{1}{2}$, being a total of 41 holes down in the ten singles!).

In the first post-war match in the USA, Rees lost in both his matches but fought well. The overwhelming defeat by 11 to 1 was partly discounted in Britain at the time. It was felt that Britain was doing badly in all sports, mainly because not enough red meat had been going down British throats.

There were signs of recovery at Ganton in 1949, when the Americans lost the foursomes by 3 to 1, but then went on to win the match as a whole by taking six of the eight singles. Rees was himself heavily defeated.

Another heavy defeat followed in the 1951 match in America, Rees losing his singles only because of a brilliant spell from Jimmy Demaret when behind.

By 1953, the war was long over and diet could no longer be a British excuse. Britain lost the foursomes by 3 to 1 and Rees, playing number one in the singles, lost to Jack Burke. Britain then pulled back, winning four of the next five matches to finish. Alas, this was the year Peter Alliss took four to get down from behind the last green at Wentworth while Bernard Hunt three-putted and the match finished $6\frac{1}{2}$ to $5\frac{1}{2}$ in the Americans' favour.

Hopes had, however, revived. In the next match on British soil at Lindrick, Rees, with Ken Bousfield, facing Art Wall and Fred Hawkins, were the only foursomes winners but on 5 October 1957 there followed the best British assault on the Americans since the war. Golf may be an individual game but it did not seem so that day at Lindrick. American after American collapsed and the British team established an almost total ascendancy. Two matches were won by as wide a margin as 7 and 6. One of these was by Dai Rees, playing Ed Furgol, the 1954 US Open champion. Captain for the second time, it was recognised that the Welshman had played an inspirational role in the $7\frac{1}{2}$ to $4\frac{1}{2}$ victory. Part of his reward was to be voted BBC Sportsview Personality of the Year and to be awarded the Golf Writers' Trophy.

On US soil in 1959, when Rees was captain, another heavy defeat followed,

Dai Rees

with only Eric Brown winning his singles. British hopes by this time were mainly centred on matches on British ground. At Royal Lytham and St Annes in 1961, the format extended to two sets of foursomes and two singles. Rees, at the age of 48, beat both his opponents, Jay Hebert and Doug Ford to complete his Ryder Cup career as a player, having played in nine matches, a record for either side at the time. His success rate was 41.66 per cent for 18 matches played. Though this may not sound particularly impressive, it ranks high amongst those who have played several or more events.

The length of Dai Rees's Ryder Cup career is some illustration of how long he remained at the top of British golf. In the first full post-war season, 1946, he won the Silver King tournament (the name refers to the well-known make of golf ball at the time) and had his first close run at the Open. At St Andrews that year, he set a course record with a 67 in the second round and went into the last round as, with Henry Cotton, the most likely British winner. Rees was on 215, Cotton 216. Level with Rees were Sam Snead and Johnny Bulla. Snead had a 75 and, surprisingly, this was good enough for a comfortable win. Bulla took 79, as did Cotton, while Rees started disastrously and improved too late, finishing with 80.

Rees made several other strong attempts at the Open and earned the reputation of being the best player in post-war golf not to win it. In 1950, he went into the last round level with Bobby Locke, eventually finishing joint third and he had his chances in Hogan's year, 1953, finishing joint second. The following year, he was once more tied for the lead into the last round with Syd Scott and Peter Thomson. The Australian edged in by a stroke for his first championship, Rees again finishing second.

The Welshman's last chance came at a time when most would have long have abandoned hope. By 1961 Rees was 48. Nevertheless he entered the final round of the gruelling 36 holes then played on the last day only a stroke behind Arnold Palmer. There he finished but he was secure in second place by three strokes.

In tournaments of lesser stature Rees built a record that has never been clearly bettered by a British golfer, ranking with the tournament winning achievements of Bernard Hunt, Henry Cotton and Tony Jacklin. He ran up a total of 28, most of these in Britain but he also won in Europe, Australia and New Zealand and that in times when golfers were not so keen on world travel. He twice won the Dunlop Masters, in 1950 and 1962 and took the Vardon Trophy for lowest stroke average in 1955 and 1959. A remarkable strokeplay achievement came at Barnton, Edinburgh in 1973. Rees had rounds of 72, 70, 67, 71 in the Martini International to be second. He was sixty years old.

If the Matchplay Championship had been the scene of Rees's rise to the top of British golf it was also a theme that ran through his career. He beat Henry Cotton in the 1949 final and repeated his victory the following year, this time with Frank Jowle as the victim. His total of four wins equalled James Braid's record, which was later matched by Peter Thomson.

Rees reached three more finals. The first was 1953, when he was beaten by Max Faulkner. The second came in 1967, when at the age of 54 he was there again, beaten this time by Peter Thomson. Two years later, he reached the final yet again, going down to Maurice Bembridge.

Rees's last success came at the age of 62, when he won the South of England PGA. This is not a recognised Tour event but has a very good class field.

Why did Rees's game last so well? The prime reason was enthusiasm. There was also a liking for competitive golf, which for so many is a matter of overcoming almost unbearable tension until the nerve can stand it no more. Dai Rees throughout his career relished the challenge of competition and even at the age of seventy still does.

Doug
Sanders

Born Cedartown, Georgia, USA, 1933

'No one remembers who finished second', said Walter Hagen, an observation true of all sports and particularly so of golf. There can be exceptions, though. Nicklaus's second places in the 1977 British Open and the 1982 US Open will be remembered more often than many of his major championship victories and Roberto de Vicenzo's relegation to second place for a card-signing error in the 1968 US Masters has earned him more footnotes in golf history than Bob Goalby from his by no means undeserved win.

Sanders's place in the footnotes comes from events at St Andrews in the 1970 British Open. Because his current record was not good, Sanders had to pre-qualify and then opened with a 68, good but not outstanding on a low-scoring first day. After two rounds, he lay three behind Trevino, who had begun with a pair of 68s, with Jacklin and Nicklaus on 137. The wind had got up and was to be an increasing factor as the tournament continued.

After the third round, Trevino still led by two, followed by Nicklaus, Sanders and Jacklin. (It was three weeks after Jacklin's US Open win.) Surprisingly, Trevino fell away in the final round, not helped by having played to the wrong flag on the 567 yard 5th hole but, like everyone else, affected by a wind that gusted up to 60mph.

After the low scoring of the first day, no one broke 70 in the final round, the best score of 71 coming from a veteran, Scotsman John Panton. Sanders played steadily throughout and near the end played a master stroke that seemed to have won him the title. At the dreaded Road Hole, the 17th, he was bunkered on the left of the green and had to play a shot of some delicacy, the one most feared by players from sand. It had to rise just above the steep face in front of him and then die quickly on the green. Sanders brought it off to perfection and was left with a putt of little more than a foot.

He came to the last, about the easiest hole at St Andrews, needing to cover the 358 yards in a par 4. Sanders drove well and was faced with a routine shot to the green. All week he had chosen to play running pitches but at this tense moment he chose a high-flying pitch, perhaps influenced by a depression, the Valley of Sin, before the last green.

His ball did not seem to fly as high as one would have expected, indicating that he had struck the shot a little thinly. It came down well past the flag. He was now faced with a long downhill putt to get close to ensure the championship. His ball pulled up about 3½ft short.

Sanders surveyed the putt, which broke from left to right, more, the locals say, than the player usually thinks. Sanders squared up to the putt, as tension rose in the vast crowd and even more in the player. Dissatisfied, he backed away, settled again, and missed.

He had now suffered the recurrent golfing nightmare being in a position of being able to win the Open, with one stroke, but failing to do so.

All was not lost. He would play off with Nicklaus over 18 holes on the Sunday and the great man's star was not in the ascendant. He had not won a major championship since the 1967 US Open and during that period his other results had fallen away, if only a little, leading to speculation that the best of Nicklaus might already have been seen.

The next day, Sanders three-putted the 3rd to fall behind and was in the rough on the next to give Nicklaus a two-stroke lead. That position was

Doug Sanders, St Andrews, 1970

maintained to the turn with Nicklaus out in 36 to Sanders's 38. On the 11th, Sanders took two to get out of a bunker and dropped another shot on the 12th to trail Nicklaus by an apparently decisive four strokes. He then counter-attacked bravely, having birdies on the 14th and 15th while on the 16th Nicklaus thundered a long iron through the green and could not get down in two more. The margin was down to one with the 466 yard Road Hole and the last to play, the wind behind on both. Both drove safely and Sanders followed with a running 5-iron to about 6 yards while Nicklaus drew a 7-iron in towards the flag and finished with the advantage. Both failed with their putts and moved to the last tee, Nicklaus's narrow lead intact.

Because of the following wind, Sanders knew Nicklaus could reach the last green and flung himself full out into the shot, finishing very much off-balance. Nevertheless the drive was straight but did not reach the green, coming to rest in the Valley of Sin some 30 yards short of the flag.

Nicklaus now allowed himself the grandiose gesture of taking off his sweater and there was a rustle in the crowd. A golf ball was about to travel a rare distance. Nicklaus actually contemplated using a 3-wood, fearing his drive might go through the green but took out the driver. His ball skipped past the flag and on, coming to rest in thick rough. The odds shifted in favour of Sanders catching him. This time he chose to play a run up and his ball coasted to about 4ft from the hole for a near-certain birdie. Nicklaus had to play his run-up of some 20 yards with delicacy into a gentle downslope. His ball finished 7 or 8 feet short. He had that putt for the Open.

Nicklaus did not stroke his putt impassively into the middle but his ball just caught the edge of the hole — and dropped in. He flung his putter high and both cowered as it came down again. Sanders became remembered as the man who finished second.

Sanders produced strong performances in other British Opens. In 1972, at the age of 39, he came in fourth behind the Trevino-Jacklin-Nicklaus placings, and was closer still in 1966, another Nicklaus year. He produced the steadiest scoring in the field with rounds of 71, 70, 72, 70 at Muirfield. Nicklaus led him by four after two rounds but then faltered over the closing holes of the third round to a 75, allowing Sanders to come within a stroke.

Nicklaus then went to the turn in 33, Sanders making no impression on him even with an eagle from some 60 yards on the 9th. However, Nicklaus dropped shots early in the second half before finishing steadily and Sanders was joint second with Dave Thomas, only a stroke behind.

Sanders further showed himself to be one of the best players not to win a major championship in the USA. He was second in the 1959 PGA and third in both 1960 and 1961. In the US Open at Oakland Hills in 1961 he had perhaps his best chance of a major championship with a round to go. He was three ahead of Gene Littler, one better than Bob Goalby and Mike Souchak with the young amateur Jack Nicklaus, second the previous year, four behind. Sanders produced a final 72, good enough for second place. Gene Littler had played one of the best rounds of the championship, a 68, and came in a stroke ahead.

As regards winning, therefore, Doug Sanders' main achievements came on the US Tour, beginning with one of his greatest feats, winning the 1956 Canadian Open while still an amateur. His best year was 1961, when he took five events and finished 3rd on the money list with the now paltry total of some $57,000. His peak years were 1961-7, when he was five times 7th or better in the year's money list. He then declined, though he revived in 1972, when he won his last title and over $100,000 for the second of two years. Altogether, he won twenty US Tour events; he still makes infrequent appearances on the Tour.

Sanders was not reknowned only for his golf. He attracted much attention by his golf attire, being likely to turn out from toe to neck in contrasting shades of lavender and the like. Less elegant, but equally worthy of note, was his golf swing. This was easily the shortest ever in top class golf. The clubhead came little above shoulder height after a great number of indecisive shuffles of the feet and with so little space in which to generate clubhead speed on the downswing he was apt to heave and throw himself into the ball on long shots. He had, however, a deft short game and enjoyed life, as his book *Come Swing with Me* demonstrates. The swinging had little to do with golf.

Gene
Sarazen

Born Harrison, New York, USA, 1902

It is quite something to be the man responsible for the two most famous shots ever struck on a golf course. The second was on a sentimental occasion. Gene, at the age of seventy-one, was competing at Troon in the 1973 Open. At the 8th hole, the 128-yard 'Postage Stamp', he gave the ball a little punch with a 5-iron. There was a bounce or so and into the hole it went. The TV cameras saw it all and the world applauded. (The next day Sarazen punched his 5-iron into a bunker, so no hole in one this time. Instead he took out a sand iron and put it in from the bunker. On his farewell appearance in the Open he had thus played the hole twice without needing a putt.) Sarazen on this occasion was over from America to renew acquaintanceships and despite his successes at the Postage Stamp he did not qualify for the third day.

In the spring of 1935, the second Augusta National Invitational was played, the contest which within a few years was to be known as the Masters. After three rounds, Craig Wood held a three-stroke lead on Sarazen and the field. When Sarazen reached the tee of the 15th, a par 5 with the shot to the green over water, he learned that the position was unchanged. He calculated that he would need to find three birdies over the concluding holes to tie.

His drive at the 15th was good and it was possible the green was reachable. (Remember that though Craig Wood, for instance, still holds the record for the longest drive ever hit in a major event (430 yards in 1933 at St Andrews), players on average were shorter off the tee than they are today. The 15th at Augusta would normally be tackled by a drive, a mid iron up to the water and a pitch over.) Sarazen decided that this was a hole he had to birdie. He took his 4-wood and, as he later said, 'rode into it with everything I had'. The shot flew long and straight. Bobby Jones was strolling down to watch the finish. He and the other spectators saw Sarazen's ball pitch and run on into the cup. It was an event far rarer than a hole in one — there are around 40,000 of those in America alone every year — a double eagle. With the shot Sarazen had caught Craig Wood, the equivalent of three birdies on a single hole.

Both played out the remaining holes in par and there was a play-off over thirty-six holes the following day. Sarazen took it comfortably. It was Sarazen's last victory in a major championship in a competitive career that lasted well over fifty years though in only some twenty of those was he a serious contender.

It had all begun with the kind of overnight success that Ballesteros found in 1976, Ouimet in 1913 or Young Tom Morris in the early morning of championship golf. At Skokie Country Club in Illinois, Robert Tyre Jones Junior from Atlanta, Georgia was the youth that everyone's eyes were upon. Though he was just twenty years old, Jones was already recognised as a great player. It was just a question of time before he began winning major championships. Already, at nineteen, he had finished equal fourth in the US Open. With a round to go he was a stroke better than Hagen, and an unheard-of golfer from California, John L. Black (who indeed was never to be heard from again). Wild Bill Mehlhorn was level with him. The question was, would Jones be able to stand up to the professionals Hagen and Mehlhorn?

Sarazen had been playing steadily for 72, 73, 75 and this, as the final found began, put him four behind Jones. In the event, Jones, Black, Mehlhorn and Hagen all returned good scores in their final round, but the problem was that Sarazen, finishing with the flourish of a birdie on the last hole, had done a very great deal better. He had become the first player in the history of the US Open, with his 68, to break 70 in the final round. The 68 equalled the US Open record and was only the 9th time that a sub-70 round had been achieved in the US Open.

He was on his way. At the age of eighty he accepted an invitation from the Royal and Ancient to play round nine holes with Henry Cotton during the Troon 1982 Open, something he already does with Byron Nelson in the US Masters at Augusta, Georgia. In between that beginning in 1922 and the 1982 twilight, Sarazen has lived a brim-full golfing life and alone of the greatest players has continued in tournament play during seven decades, though he was not a serious contender for long after 1940, when he tied for the US Open and lost the play-off to Lawson Little. It is almost always the orthodox player with a stress-free swing who survive, where others make headlines for often no more than three or four years and are then heard from no more. Not so in Sarazen's case. True, the swing in his best years was both full and rhythmic. As one writer put it: 'Gene Sarazen was the simplest golfer I ever saw. He stood with both feet rooted to the ground, grasped the club firmly in both hands with a couple of inches of shaft showing at the top and gave the ball a tremendous elementary thump.' To assist that thump, the 5ft 5in Sarazen (shortest of all major golfers) built up hands, wrists and forearms by swinging a heavily weighted club and in play used a driver that tipped the scales at no less than 15 ounces. In order to hold on to the monster, he built up the grip where his left hand fitted to about $1\frac{1}{2}$ times the normal thickness. A little unusual perhaps, but most tournament golfers have experimented with grip size and have then usually settled for something nearly normal. However, it was the way Sarazen arranged his hands on the grip that would cause even a competent club golfer to dismiss the possibility that the man could be anything other than a high handicapper. At address and impact, for instance, the back of the left hand should face the target, with the golfer himself being able to see only one or two knuckles. Sarazen set this hand so that he could see all the knuckles; at impact, his left hand was in an ideal position for a karate chop and most of his shots *ought* to have whistled low and very sharply left into the long grass just in front of the tee, while the stress on his left elbow *ought* to have enforced retirement before he had truly begun. What of the left thumb? Surely at the top of Sarazen's backswing there was the prospect of a dislocation?

Sarazen had the simplest of answers here: he just let it dangle in space. Though a strategem not to be recommended, not using that thumb at all does enforce what so many of golf's teachers have stressed: the need for the last two fingers of the left hand to have the firmest grip of the lot.

Of his right-hand position there is nothing to relate. It was entirely orthodox, with the palm on target as all the books say it should be.

Perhaps the oddity of Sarazen's grip is the clue to the mystery of why his career falls so neatly into two phases. First there was the confident, even cocky, youth who, after taking the US Open at the age of twenty, easily the youngest of the moderns, then quickly showed he could do it in matchplay as well by winning the US PGA the same year. 'But', they said, 'Walter Hagen wasn't playing.' In 1923, however, Hagen was entered and they met in one of the most closely contested finals of them all. Sarazen won on the 38th. This was the last time Hagen was to lose for five years as he won the event four years in a row, beating twenty-two opponents, and establishing the reputation of being incomparably the greatest matchplayer ever.

After this major victory, came decline. At the 1923 British Open at Troon, Sarazen's first, he failed to qualify and declared he would be back even if he had to swim across. In the

Gene Sarazen

US Open, he finished equal 5th in 1925, equal 3rd the following year, 3rd in 1927, equal 6th in 1928, equal 3rd in 1929 and equal 4th in 1931. In the same period, he once reached the final of the PGA, losing to Tommy Armour, and finished second in the Open at Royal St George's to Hagen after taking a 7 at the Suez Canal hole. Three years later at Carnoustie he had the worst of the weather and came in two strokes behind Tommy Armour.

Of the tournaments that have been mentioned, Sarazen took just one, the 1930 Western, which at that time ranked below only the Open and PGA. He won many minor events that did not necessarily command top fields. His 'second coming' was now at hand.

The hook had proved a threat during these years but Sarazen had been far more concerned about his bunker play. With the sand wedge not invented, the most usual technique was to take the ball clearly off the sand and, if today's splash shot from sand is just about the easiest in golf, to nip the ball out clean requires more precision than even the great can muster. Sarazen decided to devise a new club, one that would ride through the sand because the leading edge was set higher than the rear of the flange that he proceeded to set on the sole by means of the trial-and-error process of adding solder.

At the end of a winter he could claim to have invented the sand wedge. At much the same time, Edwin Kerr McClain, a Texas cotton broker, was working along similar lines and Horton Smith used the resultant 23-ounce bludgeon in 1930. Sarazen's appeared a little later and it was his model that was soon to be copied, for McClain's was banned as it had a concave face which was held to produce at least the suspicion of a double hit.

Confident now that he could get out and down in two from greenside bunkers, Sarazen sailed for England and Prince's, Sandwich. He began 70, 69, 70 and with a round to go was four ahead of his closest pursuer (Arthur Havers, who had a 68 on the final morning) and eight or more ahead of such others as Macdonald Smith, Charles Whitcombe and Percy Alliss. In the afternoon, Sarazen faltered but only to a 74 and took the championship by a clear five strokes, with Mac Smith in second place. His 283 was not beaten until Bobby Locke won at Troon in 1950.

The US Open followed shortly after at Fresh Meadow Country Club in New York State, a course that Sarazen knew well, having been pro there for several years. He began 74, 76, and was five behind José Jurado, the man who threw away the 1931 British Open and Phil Perkins, an emigré Englishman. After eight more holes, Sarazen was seven behind, having dropped four more shots to par. He took only thirty-four more strokes for the round. Then he went out again in the afternoon and improved on his record 68 of 1922. This time, it was a 66, a US Open record round, which stood as the record for a winner's last round until Arnold Palmer took the US Open of 1960 with a 65. Sarazen was pleased and in 1950 entitled a chapter of his classic *Thirty Years of Championship Golf,* 'Twenty-eight holes in a Hundred Strokes'.

Sarazen was truly on top once more and commanding exhibition fees that rivalled the fading Hagen's. The following year he won the PGA Matchplay for the third time and finished one behind Densmore Shute and Craig Wood for the British Open after he had failed to get out of a fairway bunker with two attempts. In 1934, at Merion, he finished second in the US Open. Then, a year later, came that once in a millenium shot in the US Masters. As a result, Sarazen became the first man to win each of the major championships (only Hogan, Nicklaus and Player have since joined him on that particular Olympus).

It is argued that the great players of today are better than those of Sarazen's era; that the scoring is lower and the competition much sharper. My own feeling is that the second rank players of today may be so, but Gene Sarazen's rounds of 73, 73, 70, 72 at the age of fifty-six around Royal Lytham and St Anne's was matched by few indeed thirty years his junior.

Eight golfers have won more than six major championships and Eugene Saraceni (no sort of a name for a professional golfer he thought) is one of them.

Sam
——— *Snead* ———

Born Hot Springs, Virginia, USA, 1912

When the talk turns to assessments of the greatest golfers of all, the names that recur are Hogan, Vardon, Nicklaus and Jones. There will also be those who argue for Nelson, Hagen and Palmer, amongst others. Were longevity to be made the prime criterion all arguments would have to cease, as there would be no rival to Samuel Jackson Snead of West Virginia.

Sam Snead turned professional in 1934 and stayed in his home state for the next couple of years. In the summer of 1936 he decided to match his game against the name players. He drove 300 miles to Hershey in Pennsylvania and was immediately invited to join in a practice round. His first drive was out of bounds into a sewage farm; the next attempt sliced into a factory. Snead, still tense from the long drive, made himself take a slow smooth swing, and hit the green about 350 yards away. He had arrived.

The following year, he won five tournaments, was runner-up in the US Open and made the Ryder Cup team. In 1938 he took eight tournaments and was runner-up in the US PGA. Successes at this level continued, though his number of tour wins fluctuated, but it was not until 1962 that he failed to win a US tournament: twenty-five years after his first victory. His last tour win came three years later when Snead was fifty-two, and the oldest player to win such an event.

How then did Snead come to last so long, so that his only rival may prove to be Gene Littler? One particular thing that they do have very much in common is a natural, full and rhythmic swing and in Snead's case elasticity of body and power as well: he was the first great golfer regularly to drive more than 275 yards.

Most great golfers have with the passing of time, and wear and tear on the nerves, become extremely bad putters: they know full well how to do the thing but the backswing is an involuntary jerk and the movement towards the ball convulsive. Late in their careers, Jones, Hagen, Vardon, Palmer and Hogan, all reckoned at their peak to be masters on the greens, became victims of what is variously known as the twitches, jerks and yips. How did Sam Snead avoid this fate?

The answer is simple. He did not. Sam suffered them for at least three spells. After a highly successful year in 1946, Snead went to play Bobby Locke in a 16-match series in South Africa. Bemused by the nap on the greens that makes them so difficult to read and bewildered by the putting brilliance of Locke, Snead went down in all but two of those matches and returned home with the yips. On that occasion, he says, they lasted a couple of years until he came across a putter which he felt might manage to get the ball into the hole. It did and the yips went away. Snead's best years followed until he broke the putter in 1952. The yips returned but were kept at bay to some extent by his adopting a less wristy stroke and changes of putter. In 1966, he was leading the US PGA when there was a sudden return which caused Snead to jerk after the ball and hit it twice. He tried in tournament play something that he had previously kept out of the public gaze: croquet style.

With this method, Snead had the ball between his legs, gripping with the left hand at the top of the shaft and his right well down, pushing with an arm and shoulder action. The putts started to go in once more, until the US Golf Association changed the rules of golf and decreed that in every golf stroke both feet must be on the same side of the line. Snead thought that his career, already some thirty years on, was over at last.

However, he came up with a solution that was within the rules but was still based on the croquet method. Once again, he stood facing the hole and grasped the putter in much the same way, but with the ball placed to the right of his feet rather than between. He was back in business. (It should be mentioned that with neither of these methods was Snead as good a putter as he had been, using a conventional side-on approach, but once again he was competent and had no dread tendency to stab and jerk.)

He went on to further competition achievements at an age when many club professionals are thinking of retirement from the less stressful tasks of running a shop, giving lessons and keeping the club captain happy. Amongst his autumnal achievements, were victories in the World Seniors title a record five times and the US PGA Seniors a record six times. He is also the only man to beat his age in a tour event when he had rounds of 67 and 66 in the quad Cities Open in 1979 when he was sixty-seven years old. The previous year he had scored 65, but in a minor event. In 1974, he had been second in the Los Angeles Open and the following year third in the US PGA.

At the age of seventy, Sam is unlikely to add much more lustre to his record. The wonders are likely to relate to age and continuing majesty of swing rather than winning: he is certain not to add to his unparalled 84 wins on the US tour and unlikely to improve on variously estimated 135 to 165 wins worldwide. With this let us leave the topic of the greatest 'old' golfer ever and go back to the years when Snead was at his peak, that twenty-year span between the late 1930s and 1950s.

Sadly, the most remembered fact of all about these two decades is, alas, that the world's greatest golfer never could manage to win a US Open. Yet very early in his career, he had so nearly achieved the feat which became more and more troublesome to him. In the 1937 Open at Oakland Hills, his first, he finished second, two strokes behind Ralph Guldahl. Two years later at the Philadelphia Country Club, things went even better. Snead stood on the last tee needing a par 5 in the 558 yard hole to win. His playing partner, Ed Dudley, knew this and Snead did not.

Club golfers fall into two categories: those who in competition like to know what scores they need over the closing hole or holes, and those who are paralysed by fright if they are told that just a one over par will do well enough on a rather easy last hole. There is no evidence at all that Sam fell into the second of these categories, but the two playing with him felt the wisest course was to keep their mouths shut.

Unfortunately Sam did have information of a kind: he thought he had to birdie the par 5, final hole, influenced a little by the fact that he had just three-putted the 17th green. He would have to reach the green in two strokes. After a 30 minute wait, while the crowds were cleared, he went flat out with the driver and reached the corner of the dogleg, and some light rough. No problem. Sam could have picked out a medium iron and knocked it a long way down the fairway and then lofted a wedge onto the green. The odds were, however, against this producing a birdie. Sam took out his brassie and thinned his shot into the face of a bunker some 160 yards away. Again going for length, he decided on an 8-iron rather than a simple splash out with a sand iron. Again he caught the bunker face and with his next attempt was out but into another bunker. At this point he was told that he had two shots left to tie Byron Nelson. His fifth stroke was on the green but the 1939 US Open was gone. Sam three-putted from 40ft to put the seal on the most famous 8 ever scored in a major championship.

The number 8 turned up again the following year. At lunch time on the last day after three rounds completed, Snead was once more in a challenging

Sam Snead

position, only to drift to an 81 that left him right down in sixteenth place.

Perhaps doubts were now beginning to disturb his mind for certainly the only reason that the most dominant golfer of his time (with the exception of Ben Hogan between 1947 and 1953) did not win the US Open is that at some time he began to know that he would never do it.

In 1947, at St Louis, he went round in 72, 70, 70, 70 for 282, three clear of everyone except Lew Worsham, who also had 282. Snead was in his first play-off for the title, against a man who was to win just seven US PGA tournaments in his career. After seventeen holes they were level and on the last green. Snead had a putt of about 2½ft, a little more than Worsham's — both for a 69 and the second 18-hole play-off that would follow. Snead settled down to putt and Worsham interrupted to request that the distances of both balls from the hole be measured. They were and, indeed, it was Sam's putt. He missed; Worsham holed.

By now, Snead was into the era of Ben Hogan's grasp on the US Open but in 1949 Hogan, temporarily crippled in his car crash, was not playing. Snead went round Medinah Country Club in steady style: 73, 73, 71, 70. Cary Middlecoff began and finished with a 75s, but in between had a 67 and a 69, good enough to be champion by a shot.

During the Hogan years, Snead only once threatened to win. In 1953, at Oakmont he was only one behind as the field entered the last round. Hogan, as it seems nearly thirty years on, was marked out by fate to win everything that year and he duly did so here, finishing in 71 to Snead's 76, a score which still left Snead three strokes clear in second place. This was Sam's last chance even though he was to finish third in 1955, but this time with no winning chance after an opening 79.

It is an irony then, that Snead did win a major Open, the British, but regarded it as 'just another tournament'. He played in 1937 because he was in Britain anyway for the Ryder Cup and finished well behind Cotton in eleventh place. His next visit was in 1946, when the first post-war Open was held at St Andrews, hastily tidied up with the help of German prisoners-of-war. Snead hated the course on sight, together with British food and hotels, which he described as being 'just camping out'.

He began strongly with 71, 70 and then weakened to 74, 75, a performance that would have left him well down the field in a US Open of the time. Others in contention weakened far more: Johnny Bulla in third place had a last round 79, as did Henry Cotton fourth, while Dai Rees also fourth did no better than 80. Sam, unimpressed by both course and country, won by four clear strokes and his mood became no more sunny when he saw what was written on his cheque: £150. He decided not to return and in fact only played once more, on a sentimental journey in 1962, when he shared sixth place at the age of fifty.

So far then, Snead is seen as by far the most prolific tournament winner of all time and, most would agree, still the most naturally talented golfer who has yet swung a club, but with a flawed record in major championships. If we turn to the other majors, the US PGA and the Masters, the picture alters. When the US PGA was a matchplay event, Snead was twice runner-up before winning in 1942, his first major championship win, which he repeated in 1949 and 1951. After the change to stroke play in 1958, Snead was three times third, including 1974 at the ripe age of sixty-two!

His record is even better in the Masters. Here he has been third on three occasions, second twice and was champion three times between 1949 and 1954. In all then, Snead won seven major championships, a record beaten only by Nicklaus, Jones, Hagen, Hogan, Player and Palmer, and one which Snead would certainly have improved but for his distaste for camping in the British Isles.

This does of course bring into question the status of the various majors and golfers achievements in them. Only jet travel has made it possible for the superstars to compete in all the majors every year. Jones, for instance 'only' won the British Open three times, but he played in it just four times. Henry Cotton on the other hand, never competed in the US PGA or Open and only once in the Masters. The truth of it is that all the majors have been parochial until recent years. Few overseas players even today compete in the three US majors and it can be argued that the international nature of the British Open field make it the nearest thing golf has to a world championship. Yet this was not the case until Palmer and Nicklaus established the event as one in which every great player had to enter if he aspired to immortality. Snead felt that he had won it once and that he could be making money in a normal US tour event rather than spending it on a lengthy trip to Britain.

Possibly money is at the root of Sam's relative failure to establish a major championship record that might have been on a par with Nicklaus and Jones, for he seems to be the one golfer without a flaw in his method. It has, for instance, been said that Vardon had a tendency to lift the club back; that Jones's grip was loose; Hogan's swing a precarious balance of compensations; Trevino's made up of a series of eccentricities that just happen to work for him; and that the great Nicklaus is not supreme in any department of the game but merely quite good at the whole range of shots from full drive to short putt, with these two extremes being the weakest features of his game.

Perhaps Snead then was more interested than these to make money out of the game, without the burning need and egotism that has driven the Hogans and Nicklauses to want to show the world that they are the best, and to prove that status in golf and major championship wins are pre-eminent.

Sam, in his peak years, did make a great deal of money out of the game, but a pittance compared to what is available today. It is estimated that his tournament winnings approached $700,000, a total that Tom Watson was able to equal in a couple of profitable years. Indeed Snead's best year came when he was sixty-two in 1974, winning $55,000. Of course tournament cheques are not the whole story. By 1965, for example, Snead headed seven corporations and his earnings were thought to be around $200,000, still not in the class of Nicklaus's $5 million to $6 million, but quite acceptable for the year! In a hundred years, when the money is forgotten, and the question is asked 'Mirror, mirror on the wall, who was the greatest of them all?' the answer is likely to be 'Jack Nicklaus — but Sam Snead had the most powerful rhythmic swing and he's still playing well'.

J.H.
Taylor

Born Northam, Devon, England, 1871

J.H. Taylor is the only one of our masters of golf to be known by his initials, which reflects the liking of Englishmen of the past to use initials and surname, not Christian name in full to identify a sportsman. As 'J.H.', this golfer was one of the best known sportsmen in England, his fame dwarfed only by one other: William Gilbert Grace, the great cricketer, 'W.G.' to the English-speaking world.

Both came from the west of England but whereas Grace came from a middle-class environment, Taylor's origins were very different. His route to the top of professional golf is interesting when compared with today's heroes, most of whom turn professional after amateur successes lead them to think they can make a career, and perhaps wealth, out of golf.

J.H. was born into a labourer's family and left school at the age of ten. He became a caddie at Royal North Devon Golf Club, a short walk from his home, which had been founded in 1864 as the first seaside course in England. The year Taylor became a full-time caddie there it cost 1 guinea to become a member and 2/6d a year thereafter. Westward Ho! (as it is more usually known) had 300 members, making it one of the largest clubs in Britain and substantially behind only the Royal and Ancient, Royal Liverpool (at Hoylake) and perhaps also the Honourable Company of Edinburgh Golfers, then playing at Musselburgh.

For the next four or five years, J.H. developed his skills at golf when he had the opportunity, but when he had to give up the caddie role at fifteen years of age, did not take to professional golf. Instead, he worked as a gardener and also a bricklayer's mate, playing in the artisans (working men) section when he could and gaining a low handicap.

He was soon offered a job on the greens staff and in 1891 got the post of professional/greenkeeper at Burnham Golf Club in Somerset. The following year, having beaten the celebrated Scots professional Andrew Kirkaldy in a challenge match, he replaced him as professional at Winchester.

By now, J.H. knew he was a golfer of talent and, having won more challenge matches against other professionals, entered the 1893 Open at Prestwick. He produced the then remarkable score of 75 in the first round to lead, but could not maintain form thereafter and finished out of the running.

The following year, he became the first Englishman to win the championship. At Sandwich his scores of 84, 80, 81, 81 gave him victory by five strokes. A little further down the list, in joint 5th place, there was another young man, up from Bury St Edmunds in Suffolk, named Harry Vardon.

In 1895, the Open was back in Scotland, at St Andrews (the Sandwich Open was the first to be staged outside Scotland). Taylor began with 86 and followed with the excellent scores of 78, 80, 78 to win by four over Sandy Herd, making up seven strokes on him in the last round.

Taylor's scoring in his first two Open wins was of course high by modern standards, mainly the result of three factors: balls, clubs and courses. The gutta percha ball carried far less far than the rubber-wound Haskell ball which was soon to replace it; clubs were comparatively clumsy implements; and courses were relatively ill-kept, the greens especially so in comparison with later standards.

In these conditions, with very few rounds under 80 on championship courses, it would be about right to knock ten strokes a round off Taylor's

J.H. Taylor

score per round to equate his performance with modern players. Nevertheless, under the spur of an increasingly high standard of competition, scores began to fall.

Some of the key features of J.H. Taylor's game were now becoming apparent. He was, for instance, an exceptionally reliable straight hitter, perhaps the first golfer to have that old chestnut about marker posts being the only hazards he found on a course applied to him. He was outstanding with the mashie (about a modern 5-iron) for shots to the flag and manipulated the clubface for a variety of shots: open for high cuts and closed when playing into a wind. He was certainly the first player whose pitching ability became recognised as masterly and a steady putter, much the superior over the years of Braid and Vardon.

This pair were now about to challenge J.H.'s supremacy over British golf. Late in 1895, Braid halved with him in a 36-hole match and, before the 1896 Open, Vardon trounced him at Ganton, the latter's new home club. In the Open that year, Vardon took over as champion after a play-off with Taylor. (Pictured together before the Muirfield clubhouse before that play-off, it can be seen that both were shod in hobnailed workingmen's boots; a further area, then, in which equipment has drastically improved.)

For the next few years Taylor did not win another Open, though he was fourth in 1898 and 1899, well behind Vardon both years. However, in 1900 he gave a dominant performance at St Andrews, beating Vardon into second place by no fewer than eight strokes, closing with an excellent 75 when the championship was already in his pocket. He broke 80 in each round while others in the top six that year managed this only three times in all. He had lowered the winning score he made in 1895 at St Andrews by seventeen strokes.

The Great Triumvirate of Braid, Vardon and Taylor was really established with the general public in 1901, for they finished in that order in the year's Muirfield Open and in 1898-1914 the championship was only four times won by an 'outsider'. Always, one or more of them finished in the top two.

Taylor was second in 1904-7 and in 1909 was again champion, at Deal, where he produced the remarkably steady rounds of 74, 73, 74, 74 and won by four strokes from James Braid. Hoylake in 1913 gave him some of his finest moments. He began 73, 75 to be one behind Ted Ray, 1912 champion, but for the 36 holes of the last day the winds got up. Mike Moran, for example, who was in close contention after his 76, 74 start, scared to 89 in the third round; yet such was the scoring that he still finished joint third with Harry Vardon. Taylor played what he himself considered one of his greatest rounds, a 77, followed with 79, and was champion for his fifth and last time by eight strokes from Ted Ray, who had finished 81, 84.

The year 1914 marked the end of an era in many areas of activity; it certainly meant the end of the Great Triumvirate. Before the Prestwick Open that year Braid, Vardon and Taylor had five Open Championship victories each. Though Vardon, the founder of the modern golf swing, was recognised as the greatest of the three at the time, perhaps history would not have agreed had he not won this last championship, fought while all three were in early middle age.

Primarily it was a duel between Taylor and Vardon. The latter began with a 73, closely pursued by J.H.'s 74. He increased his lead to two after the second round. J.H. then overtook with a 74 to Vardon's 78. In the final round, he missed a short putt to increase his advantage but at the 4th was in various kinds of trouble, emerging with a 7 to Vardon's 4. Said Taylor: 'For the remaining holes, I played like a beaten man.' Vardon became the only man to win six opens, the five-time winners being Taylor, Braid and Peter Thomson.

When World War I was over, it was perhaps not quite recognised that the deeds of the trio belonged to the past. Vardon came within reach of the US Open in 1920, while Taylor still produced strong performances in the British. In 1922, at more than fifty, he led the eventual champion, Walter Hagen by three after one round and with one to go was one ahead. Hagen produced a strong last round for his first Open win and J.H. was four behind in 6th place. In 1924, he again outscored Hagen for 36 holes, but finished in 5th position. That was his last time in contention and he retired from competitive golf after Jones's 1926 Lytham win. Because of his better putting, J.H.'s game had lasted the best of the members of the great trio.

Though Vardon's influence on the playing of the game was far greater than Taylor's, J.H. was a greater force for the development of the professional game, influential in the founding of the Professional Golfers Association, captain in 1909-10, 1913-14 and chairman in 1923-4 and 1936-7.

He ended his days as president of the Royal North Devon Golf Club and lived to the age of 92 at 23 Windmill Lane, Northam, enjoying what he thought was the best view in the world.

Peter
Thomson

Born Melbourne, Australia, 1929

Ben Hogan came to Carnoustie in Scotland in 1953 and conquered. The feat of winning on British soil dotted the final 'i' of his reputation and there was nothing more to prove. Yet Peter Thomson won the British Open five times in eleven years, a striking rate only beaten by James Braid, who also had five wins between 1901 and 1910. Compare either of these achievements in the Open with those of incomparably the greatest golfer of our era, Jack Nicklaus: he has competed 20 times for his three wins.

So why is it that Thomson today is not ranked as a supreme golfer of this or any other time? He failed in the United States of America. The failure is only comparative. Thomson played little in the US and he has an occasional achievement to his credit but in a minor key: 4th in the 1956 US Open, 5th in the 1957 Masters and a win in the Texas Open. Doubtless, if he had played more, he might have taken a major championship and would certainly have made more than small change on the US Tour; he did finish in the top ten money winners after his most determined campaign year, 1956.

Thomson had little relish for the way golf was, and is, played in America. Especially in the 1950s, many of the tournament courses demanded just three abilities of a player: that he could stand on a tee and hit the ball in the general direction of the green — accuracy was by no means always needed; that he could fire soaring short iron shots in at the flag; and could then hole the putts.

Peter Thomson had never seen the game of golf in this way. He took an easy swing at the ball, often using a 3-wood from the tee, and away it went, low and not outstandingly far. For shots into the green he thought much in terms of a pitch and run, of where to land his low iron shots for the ball to run onto the green and up to the hole. At his peak, many thought him dull to watch for he made the game seem easy and the drama of recovery shots from remote parts of the course was entirely absent. First came the drive, then a low running iron shot and a couple of putts to round the whole thing off.

Thomson would indeed have agreed that the game is easy and is one of the very few major golfers not to produce an instructional book. Like Sarazen before him, he thought there was not enough to say about it. However, a conversation with Henry Longhurst at one Open Championship did produce one of the simplest and best instructional articles yet written. Thomson considered that you should measure your distance from the ball with an extended but relaxed left arm and then be extremely careful how you put your right hand to the club. Many

Peter Thomson

golfers, he though, brought their right shoulder forward in the effort to reach the club rather than what was essential: to reach *under,* which then brought the right shoulder down so the shoulders tilted from left to right and square to the target. What about the backswing? No technicalities at all for Thomson here. You just draw it back and thereafter let nature take its course. End of instructions!

However, there was more to the Thomson game than this and, despite its simplicity, it had some technically interesting features. His grip was 'stronger' than the norm, with three knuckles of the left hand showing and the right turned so that the V pointed at the right shoulder. On the backswing there was considerable lateral sway and a pronounced hip slide into the ball. Off form, his head movement and right-side release came too early. Henry Cotton feels that Thomson always let the shaft slide a little in his right hand on the backswing, perhaps a result of his belief that a player should hold the club very lightly indeed, as lightly as an axe (which does slide in the right hand) and the grip naturally tightens in the hitting area.

Peter Thomson finished leading amateur in the 1948 Australian Open and turned professional the following year, and this time was 2nd. He first came to Europe in 1951 and competed in the Open. The 6th place he took then was his worst performance until 1959 for Locke and Thomson established a stranglehold on the championship. In the next two years Thomson finished 2nd then became the only golfer after Young Tom Morris, when the entry list was fewer than twenty, to win three successive titles. He followed up by finishing 2nd again and a 4th victory came in 1958. Therefore in a stretch of eight years he finished either 1st or 2nd, a sequence unparalleled in Open Championship history.

Although he continued to be a frequent winner in Europe at times his main interest seemed to be to help in the development of a Far East circuit and in campaigning for a world championship event, to be held, of course, outside the USA.

In 1965, the Open returned to Royal Birkdale, where eleven years previously Thomson had won his first Open. The interest centred on other men. Could Player follow his US Open victory the previous month? Was Palmer about to add to his two victories? Tony Lema had played dominantly at St Andrews the previous year and was highly favoured again. Above all, surely the Open Championship could not resist the might of Jack Nicklaus another year?

Lema jumped into the first round lead with a 68 and after a 72 the next day shared the lead with a coming star, Australian Bruce Devlin. Palmer was close behind and Nicklaus still lurking but not at centre stage.

Thomson began with a 74 and followed with a 68, equal best round of the day. On the Friday, thirty-six holes were played for the last time in an Open. Thomson, by a happy chance, was paired through that long day with his main opponent, Tony Lema, and the conditions were to Thomson's liking. The course was long, at more than 7,000 yards, but firm and the rough profuse. The wind was strong. Thomson's lack of length from the tee did not matter on fast running fairways and his low pattern of shot would be little affected by the wind.

After the first nine holes of the day, Thomson led the championship and by the end of the morning his 72 had proved the best round of those in strong contention. In the afternoon, the wind moderated and Thomson went to the turn in 34. Early on the final nine he missed putts of between 2ft and 8ft on four successive holes but came to the final two holes, both par 5s, needing to birdie one to beat the rest of the field, while Lema needed to have two 4s to catch Thomson. He finished 5, 6, while Thomson drove straight and long enough at each and then struck two low running 3-irons to the greens. He won by two strokes.

This was the last time that Thomson threatened to win an Open but it was the win that pleased him most, for by 1965 it had become a kind of world championship of golf, with easily the most representative field to be found in the four major championships. This time Thomson had beaten all the best Americans, leaving the likes of Nicklaus and Palmer nine and ten strokes respectively in his wake.

Lee
—— *Trevino* ——

Born Dallas, Texas, USA, 1939

Lee Buck Trevino is the outstanding example of the success of a left-hander in golf. Of course, as we all know, the man does not stand that way round. The left-handedness comes in with his unparalleled stress on the importance of the left side for shots of all length from full drive to short putt.

All this derives from the fact that for approaching twenty years Trevino has been potentially the worst hooker in golf. Nearly all professionals are frequently much occupied with technical thoughts concerning what little adjustment to make to grip or stance to feel assured that the ball will not suddenly begin to curve disastrously to the left. In Trevino's case 'adjustment' is hardly the word.

Having taken a 'strong' grip on the club, he reaches the top of the backswing with the clubface in a very closed position, nearly square to the intended line of flight rather than the classical toe-down-the-line placement. If from there he produced a normal swing down into the ball, it would not hook; rather it would go sharply left, perhaps at times even endangering his left kneecap.

There is no doubt at all that Trevino was a hooker in his early years, but long before he made his late appearance on the tournament scene in 1966 he had found the answer. It was oddest swing from a major championship winner ever seen until then and it produced a consistent slice. That consistency, and the superiority of fade over draw, made Trevino suddenly one of the great players of the last fifteen years.

Trevino had found two remedies to his hooking problems, other than simply change his grip to a weaker position as most of his contemporaries have done. The first was his stance. Just about every competent player stands with left foot withdrawn just an inch or so from the line for his full shots. Not Trevino. So open is his stance, (approximately 45 degrees to the intended line of flight) the casual onlooker might well imagine the talkative Trevino had so lapsed in concentration that he was about to play the wrong hole. No one, other than Locke, has aimed so far off line. He was the reverse case. A natural slicer as a young man, the South African adopted a number of remedies for the sake of the extra length that hooking brings. He ended up aiming 45 degrees to the right but his banana-shaped shot unerringly brought the ball back from deep in the rough to the fairway.

Despite Trevino's typical slicer's stance, however, he still had to get the clubface to the ball in a square position. Shut at the top normally means shut at the bottom unless something drastic is done.

This is where Trevino's left-handedness comes in. The whole drive into the ball comes from the left side pulling the clubshaft, the hands well ahead and the legs driving strongly. One aspect of the modern golf swing is that the club is pulled into the ball rather than, as earlier, pushed at the ball with hands and arms. No one pulls more than Trevino does.

The scene of his arrival was the US Open of 1968 at Oak Hill. A few close observers of the US Tour had heard of him. He had finished 54th in the 1966 US Open, his only event that year, and in 1967 had improved his own opinion of his ability to live on the US Tour by finishing fifth, still a substantial eight strokes behind the winner, Jack Nicklaus, who set a new US Open record. A year later, Nicklaus was second to Trevino, who had equalled that new mark, and become the first man to break 70 in all four rounds.

Of course there is no doubt at all that the winning of a major championship is an enormous boost to a man's career but it is not, as is so often stated, the entry to immediate wealth. Think of Orville Moody, who was to win the same event the following year, picking up a handsome enough cheque. In his case, he did not go on to win anything else of note and his personality was generally found to be colourless.

On the other hand, Trevino was immediately popular with the press. It soon became aparent that he is the most talkative golfer of all time and also a ready source of quotable material. Here also, at last, was a major golfer who kept up an almost non-stop flow of back-chat with his galleries, rather than presenting the stern and even agonised countenances that prevail in tournament golf. Trevino was almost immediately in demand for the exhibitions, endorsements and clinics that can make up far more of a golfer's income than his prize money.

His appeal was immediately recognised; no one, including I suspect Trevino himself, rated his golf swing at all highly. Indeed, it was described as being that of 'a weekend hacker', 'more suitable for scything grass with', 'totally untutored' and containing 'a whole handful of basic errors'.

Trevino did not follow his entry to the world golf stage with a string of victories as did Severiano Ballesteros, but played well enough to win the Hawaiian Open later that season and finished 6th on the US Tour money list. His results were similar in the year that followed, but 1970 was the year of real consolidation.

He won two US Tour events, led the British Open into the last round before finishing joint third but, more important, showed such consistency on the US Tour that he won the Vardon Trophy for the year's lowest stroke average and was the year's leading money winner, despite having won only two events.

People were now beginning to take notice of Trevino. The man with the 'hacker's' swing was being found more meritorious. It was a swing which got Trevino's tee shots into the fairway consistently and held them there. He had also proved himself an excellent wind player. Unusually for a man who fades the ball, Trevino's flight was low and less prey to the wind, a product of the way his hands are well ahead of the clubhead into the ball. This counteracts the tendency of faded shots to fly high.

Once it became recognised that Trevino was a masterly driver, more attention was perhaps paid to his shots into the greens as well. Many top professionals rely on a standard shot which, more often than not, is a fairly straight high-flying iron.

Lee Trevino (right), Ryder Cup, 1981

Trevino, however, had a far greater variety of shot in his arsenal. Was there a strong left to right wind? Trevino might sometimes choose to hit a draw, using the wind to work his ball against with, let's say, a 7-iron. Or by contrast, he might aim off left and hit a low fade with a 5-iron. However, the fade being his stock in trade, he usually chose to vary the height and line of his normal left-to-right game. Added to this, Trevino has always been an excellent sand and short game player, though his putting is good, rather than outstanding.

The consistency continued. Trevino won the Vardon trophy three times in a row, a feat only otherwise achieved by Tom Watson in the period 1977-9. Trevino did it again in 1974 and 1980. On the US Tour he had five wins in 1971, his best year in this respect.

The year of 1971 was also outstanding as regards his major championship performances. In the US Open at Merion, a tight course favouring Trevino's accuracy, he began 70, 72, 69 to be two strokes behind Jack Nicklaus and four behind an amateur, Jim Simons, who led going into the last round. The amateur faded out to a 76 and Trevino outscored Nicklaus 69 to 71 for them to go into an 18-hole play-off. Here, Trevino again did the trick with 68 to 71. The play-off showed the contrast between the two driving styles. Nicklaus's soared upwards and pitched and stopped; Trevino's were low-flying, pitched well short of the Nicklaus mark but ran on for many yards to leave little difference in the distance achieved. Eventually Trevino's winning margin was mainly made up of two bunker shots that Nicklaus left in the sand, perhaps a reason for Trevino saying years later that all golfers lacked some essential ability and that Jack 'wasn't born with a sand iron'.

A few weeks later, he was at Royal Birkdale for the British Open, having in the meantime picked up the Canadian Open. His first three rounds were 69, 70, 69, which gave him a lead of one on 'Mr Lu' of Taiwan and Tony Jacklin. Trevino made the result sure by going to the turn on the last day in 31 and had only to cruise home. But the cruise was a rough one. He began to drop shots and had a 7 on the 17th hole, finding himself at that point needing to par the last to win. He did so and had won three national championships in a June to July spell.

Jacklin had finished third, two strokes behind. The scene was in a sense set for a return duel at Muirfield a year later, which is discussed in the Jacklin entry. Undoubtedly Jacklin was unlucky to be faced by such a stream of long putts and chips holed in the closing holes of the third round. It was, however, the par 5 17th that will be remembered on which Jacklin took four to get down from about 40 yards while Trevino ran in a chip shot of about a dozen yards. Later that season, in the World Matchplay at Wentworth, Jacklin, after his revenge, told Trevino that he didn't wish to talk during the match. Said Trevino: 'You don't have to talk. Just listen.' Talk or not, Jacklin saw Trevino go into a 4-hole lead by the lunch break. In the afternoon, there was a quiet start in which both parred the first three holes. Jacklin then launched one of the most thrilling counter-attacks ever seen in this event. He eagled the 4th, birdied the next two and had another birdie at the 8th to draw level and then sank another short putt on the 9th to go ahead. Trevino had reached the turn in a one under par 35 while Jacklin had used only twenty-nine shots, golf even better than his scoring to begin the 1970 British Open. The psychological advantage was all against Trevino at this point yet he retaliated with birdies on two of the next three holes to draw level again. The following holes were halved up to the last, a par 5. At this point of crisis, Trevino hit the green in two and Jacklin didn't. The American had withstood a 63 from Jacklin in the afternoon with a 67 of his own.

By this time, Trevino had won four major championships. Oddly, he has never been optimistic about his chances in the US Masters, feeling that the course favours hookers, long hitters and high shots. Sometimes, he has decided not to compete in the event and his best performance is no better than 10th in 1975. He has, however, won the US PGA. This victory came in 1974. Again Nicklaus was the victim, after Trevino had given him a four stroke advantage with his first round 73. However, he caught up with 66, 68 and won by a stroke with a last round 69.

Since that time, Trevino has rarely been in contention in major championships and it is likely that his putting nerve, in particular, is not quite what it once was. He did, however, look a likely winner of the 1980 British Open after two rounds but, like everyone else, was buried by Tom Watson's 64 in the third round.

In tournaments, it has been a different story and one of continuing success. He has won the Canadian Open three times in all, the Tournament Players Championship and the Tournament of Champions on the US tour, all events that rank only a little below the major championships. In all, by the end of 1981, he had totted up twenty-six Tour wins and added to these are other victories in various parts of the world where Trevino is a highly popular figure and attracts large amounts in appearance money. For several years, he has suffered with lower back pain and has to do loosening-up exercises daily to avoid the muscles going into spasm. The problem became acute during 1982 and he enjoyed little success before an operation to dull the pain from a pinched nerve appeared to be successful. At the end of the year he was just a stroke off tieing for the Sun City $1 Million Challenge and began the new season in the US hitting most of the fairways once again.

Harry *Vardon*

Born Grouville, Jersey, 1870

If you would know the truth about Vardon, examine the photograph by George Beldam on page 173. Taken in the early years of this century, it remains, to me, the supreme depiction of a golfer at the follow-through. The upper body reveals that the attack on the ball has been gloriously free and the overall poise shows that the whole performance was carried out without stress. Balance at the finish is perfect.

Memories of Vardon today are those of old men and those are old men who saw the great player long, long after his best years, which ran from 1896 to the first few years of the present century. Thereafter, Harry Vardon remained a great player but one who contended with tuberculosis and regularly went off for a 'cure' at a Norfolk seaside sanatorium.

As a very young man, Henry Cotton played with him and noted the famous 'bent left arm', the opposite of the Cotton method, but wrote 'no player hit the ball more cleanly with all clubs. He could pick up a ball cleanly and hold it straight in its flight in a full shot with any iron club.' At a time when the taking of divots in iron play had become the norm, Cotton was surprised but probably concluded eventually, as have many since, that it requires less skill, and hence a more consistent result, if the ball is struck with the club on a downward path, rather than precisely skimmed from the turf.

Vardon was still good enough at the age of fifty in 1920 to come very close to winning the US Open at Inverness. With scores of 74, 73, 71, he led the field with a round to go and increased that lead in the final round until a storm sprang up. Vardon, with seven holes to play at the time, could have won with a score little better than level 6s but his long game inevitably suffered more than that of younger men and on the greens he dropped shot after shot, three-putting three holes in a row. In the end he was joint second behind Ted Ray, who thus became the last British player to take the US Open until Tony Jacklin fifty years later.

Putting had always been Vardon's weak spot. As early as his first Open victory in 1896, the *Times* correspondent remarked that 'in putting he seemed very weak'. Photographs from this time show that he bent double over the ball and gripped low on the club; both symptoms of anxiety and making a cramped stroke more or less inevitable. His contemporaries felt that he was an excellent long putter but was never convincing in the 2ft to 4ft range. Eventually, he suffered from what he himself called 'the jumps' at this distance and when playing exhibitions and friendly games would pick up his ball, remarking 'too difficult'.

Few players can have risen to the top of golf with so little practice as Harry Vardon. The histories of the great men of golf echo with accounts of how many golf balls a day they struck, how young they began (about six seems to be today's average!) and when they first realised they might make something of themselves as golfers. Harry thought he first played a form of golf at about the age of seven, using a club made from a branch and a marble for a ball. He was, however, probably more interested in football and cricket and after leaving school worked as a gardener, playing golf just a little on public holidays.

It was his brother Tom who caused Harry to become a professional golfer. Tom went off to England to learn the trade and had some minor successes in tournaments (he was later to finish second in the Open Championship — in 1903 at Prestwick when he was six strokes behind Harry). Harry knew that he was the better player of the two so when Tom told him of a job going at a Ripon golf club, Harry moved to the mainland in 1890.

There, of course, he played often and his game improved rapidly, his first Open entry coming in 1893. The following year, at Sandwich, the name 'Vardon, H., Bury St Edmunds' (his new club) was first seen amongst the top players. He began 86, 86, and improved to 82, 80, finishing eight behind the champion, J.H. Taylor, but only three adrift of the second place man. The scoring will seem high, only two of the top seven finishers broke 80 even once and the champion not at all. To Vardon, it was proof that he had the game to compete with the best. In 1895, he led after the first round and eventually was 9th.

He moved to Ganton Golf Club, near Scarborough in Yorkshire, and there, a short time before the 1896 Open, beat Taylor heavily in an exhibition match by 8 and 6, a confidence-builder to him.

The venue, Muirfield, had been lengthened for the occasion, one of the Honourable Company of Edinburgh Golfers having had the scant respect to play the second nine in 31 during the 1894 Spring Medal. At the Open that year, it probably measured about 6,200 yards, an increase of a thousand yards on its length for Harold Hilton's 1892 win. There was no par for the course or individual holes but the 'standard of the green' was reckoned to be 78. The venerable figure of Old Tom Morris, thirty years after his last Open win, went round in 101, Vardon in 83, showing 'weak putting' and 'usual accurate long game'. The talk of the day was a 72 from Sandy Herd, made by good pitching and putting, and it was wondered if such a score 'had ever been accomplished before'. It gave him a five stroke lead on Tom Vardon's 'magnificent score' of 77, equalled by J.H. Taylor's 35/42.

The next day, Herd came back to the field with an 84, while Taylor moved into the lead with a 78. Vardon did not lose ground with a 78 but he still lay well down the list.

On the final morning, Vardon took an unimpressive 42 to the turn but made his first real move for the championship by coming home on the much lengthened second half in 36, very likely the best on this nine in the championship that year. He had moved to within three strokes of Taylor, while Sandy Herd, who had a 79, led Taylor by one.

In the afternoon, Taylor finished in 80 for a total of 316, having played a very consistent championship, while Vardon still had a few holes to play. On the last, he knew he needed a 4 to win. At 382 yards it required, Vardon later wrote, 'a good drive and a real good brassie'. The brassie had to carry severe cross bunkers fronting the green and Vardon played short to make sure of his 5 and a tie.

Before this became sure, however, Vardon had to wait it out while a very gifted young amateur, Freddie Tait, attempted to catch both of them. Playing inconsistently, he had recorded 83, 75, 84 but played finely in the last round, needing to finish the last six in an average of 4s. He made a good start to the home stretch with 3, 4 but closed 6, 5, 5 for third place.

Because Taylor and Vardon had other commitments, the play-off was delayed for four days. With birdies on two of the first three holes, Vardon went two in front and after eight holes had a commanding six stroke lead.

Harry Vardon

Taylor fought back and after fifteen the margin was back to only one. At the last, Vardon tried to carry the feared cross bunkers with his brassie and failed. However, he came out well and ended the morning's activities two strokes ahead: 78-80.

His lead went immediately after the break, when his cleek to the 204 yard 1st hole was out of bounds in a wood. But at this point in his career, Vardon later wrote, 'I had not known what it was to be nervous. I had everything to gain and nothing to lose.' Despite the shock of having a good lead whittled away he was again three in the lead with four holes played and the position was the same after eleven. On the 390 yard 12th, Taylor went for the green while Vardon did not and the margin was back to two strokes. The next four holes were all halved and Vardon virtually assured himself of the championship at the 330 yard 17th: he birdied from about 12 yards to step onto the last tee three ahead. Taylor's only chance was to go for the green over those bunkers, make a 3 and hope Vardon met disaster. However, it was Taylor in trouble in the bunkers, having to play out sideways. Vardon came in champion by four strokes.

An era had begun. For the next few years he was considered well-nigh unbeatable. Though professional tournaments were few, and are remembered today only by golf historians, exhibition matches were frequent and highly popular. People wanted to see how the great players fared on their own club courses against their own professional or a top amateur. Challenge matches were sometimes on a par in the public interest with an Open championship. This might indeed be so today but the top players tend not to relish the blemish to a reputation of being beaten in a challenge match. They prefer their fame should rest on strokeplay performance over 72 holes.

The match that Vardon himself is said to remember most fondly took place over 72 holes, the opponent Willie Park, and was played over the West Course at North Berwick and Ganton, for the vast sum of £100 in 1899 (at the time, 1896, the Open Championship was worth £40 to the winner — £30 in cash and a gold watch worth £10). Vardon won by 11 and 10 against the best putter certainly and probably the best matchplayer of the time.

Another famous match was the 'great foursome' between Vardon, partnered by J.H. Taylor, and James Braid and Sandy Herd: or England *v* Scotland. The match was played over four courses for £400, Vardon and Taylor winning.

Vardon's dominant form was reflected to the end of the century in the Open Championship. He lost the title to amateur Harold Hilton in 1897, Hilton playing his home course, Hoylake. At Prestwick, the following year, he won it back with rounds of 79, 75, 77, 76, the first winner to have all his rounds below 80. He had been closely pursued by Willie Park, who also broke 80 each time, and Hilton.In 1899 he won again at Sandwich, by five strokes, from Jack White.

Scoring by now was coming down in the Open, the other golfers perhaps reacting to the new standards Vardon was setting. His Sandwich winning total was sixteen strokes lower than Taylor's in 1894 and his Prestwick total fifteen lower than Willie Auchterlonie's 1893 championship.

In 1900, Vardon embarked on a long tour of the USA to promote a ball called 'The Vardon Flyer' for its manufacturer. While there he showed the gulf between standards in Britain and America by winning the sixth US Open at Chicago Golf Club by two from J.H. Taylor, also in the US to promote sales of his own clubs. The first American-based player was nine behind Vardon.

It is said that the wear and tear of incessant train journeys, and being expected to play his best every time he stepped on the first tee of immature courses, made its mark on Vardon; that he was never quite so supremely dominant a player again. Spasmodic illness set in from 1901.

However, he won his fourth Open at Prestwick in 1903, setting a new championship record of 300, with scores of 73, 77, 72, 78. Thereafter, none followed for some years, Braid being the dominant figure of Open Championship golf in the years 1901-10. In 1904-10, Harry Vardon only once finished in the top three.

Although he played as much golf as ever, perhaps frail health and suspect putting were the main causes of the decline. Perhaps it was the transition from easy superiority to closer competition. Perhaps, also, he found it hard to adapt to the ageing process as the swing became less free, and reactions slower.

Whatever the reasons, he was himself again in the Opens from 1911 to the First World War and never out of the first three. At Sandwich in 1911 he tied with the Basque Arnaud Massy, champion of 1907, but beat him conclusively in the play-off (Massy conceding defeat on the 35th hole). He was second the following year, third in 1913, while in 1914 came the final battle between him and J.H. Taylor at Prestwick. Vardon, with a 73, led by one after the first round and by two the following day. However, Taylor, with a 74 to a 78 took a two-stroke lead into the final round but faltered. Vardon won by three strokes, at the age of forty-four.

In everyday golfing talk, he is remembered for the Vardon Trophies competed for in both Britain and America; but more so for the grip which bears his name. Vardon did not invent the device of overlapping the little finger of the right hand to help make the two hands act as one but, as he was easily the most imitated of players, he came to get the credit. More important, however, was the influence of two of the main features of his swing. Although he was a powerful striker for his times, he made the whole performance look unstressed and rhythmic. Golfers were forced to recognise that golf was a matter of timing and acceleration rather than savagery. Just as important was the plane on which he swung the club. The tradition was for a long, flat slash at the ball, often known as the 'Carnoustie' swing from the hosts of golfers that derived from there and spread the game of golf, particularly in America. Vardon was far more upright, as are almost all the great players who have followed him. He also showed that it is highly useful to have large hands — his own were huge — and varied his flight of shot by manipulating the clubhead rather than choosing a different club. In his peak years he carried only seven: driver, brassie, putter and the equivalent of irons 2 to 5, approximately. With the mashie (5-iron) the most lofted, he had to produce the short pitch shots by opening the face and cutting across the ball, rather than letting the loft of a wedge do the work for him. Most significantly of course, he had no broad-soled club with raised rear edge to play from bunkers; the sand wedge did not appear until the early 1930s to save good golfers perhaps a couple of strokes a round by allowing ease and accuracy of recovery play to the flag.

Yet Vardon won only one more British Open than did Taylor and Braid which makes it seem almost chance that he is recognised as much their superior. Despite Vardon's lean years, it seems that they too gave him pride of place, as did all his contemporaries.

After thirty-four years as professional at South Herts Golf Club, he died in 1937 and is buried at Totteridge parish church.

Roberto
De Vicenzo

Born Buenos Aires, Argentina, 1923

To many players from outside Europe, the British Open has only in recent years become an event they automatically write in on their itinerary. Sam Snead, when he won it in 1946, called the Open 'just another tournament', while Ben Hogan competed just once and did not choose to enter again. But for Roberto de Vicenzo, the greatest golfer that South America has ever produced, the championship became a personal Odyssey. As the years passed, he usually appeared and as often as not he finished high. After some twenty years, he had almost as good a record in contending for the British Open as Jack Nicklaus. Unlike Nicklaus, however, he did not win it.

His first entry was in 1948 and his start of 70, 73 at Muirfield was well up with the leaders — except for one, Henry Cotton, who had a 66 in the second round. That, in days of higher scoring, was good enough to ensure victory if Cotton could merely produce steady golf over the final 36 holes. He did and Vicenzo was joint third. The following year, his opening 68 was one of the leading rounds of the Sandwich Open but he followed with 75, 73 and eventually came in third, two strokes out in the play-off between Harry Bradshaw and Bobby Locke. In Troon in 1950 he stood level with Locke and Dai Rees after three rounds and finished on 281, a total that would have won any previous British Open but, alas for Roberto, Locke set a new Open record on 279 and the Argentinian was second.

In 1953, there came one of the Opens of legend. The great man Hogan decided to enter, hoping to dot the final 'i' of his reputation by adding the British title to his US Masters, Opens and PGAs. After the third round, Vicenzo was level with Hogan and ahead of the rest, but it is said that he broke down and wept in his hotel room before the last round. He knew that his putting was too unsound to survive the stress to come. Hogan had a 68 to Vicenzo's 73. The Argentinian was fifth.

By 1956, the Thomson era was at its peak but after two rounds the Australian led Vicenzo by one only. Roberto then went round Hoylake in 79 to end his chances, though a last round of 70 pulled him up to third place, four behind Thomson.

What happened in the Centenary Open at St Andrews in 1960 ought to have finally destroyed Roberto. He put in the finest start to an Open since Cotton's 67, 65 in 1934. With a pair of 67s he led Kel Nagle by two and the new man, Arnold Palmer, by seven. Again, his putting collapsed, once he had missed a tiny putt at the beginning of his third round. His scoring went up to 75, 73 and again he was third, four behind Nagle, whose putting had been magnificently solid throughout.

Of course, the story of Vicenzo at this time was not by any means wholly concerned with his performances in the British Open. He had become a winner in the Argentine Open in 1944 and was eventually to total nine wins in this, a championship that attracted a strong field. Amongst its champions up to this time in Roberto's career had been Henry Picard, Paul Runyan, Jimmy Demaret and Lloyd Mangrum of overseas players and such very good South Americans as Pose, Bertolino, Cerda, Ruiz and de Luca.

Internationally, Roberto de Vicenzo was more successful than any other golfer except Sam Snead and altogether is estimated to have won over 140 tournaments and the national championships of some sixteen countries, the latter an unparalleled achievement.

Roberto De Vicenzo

He was also a winner on the US Tour, taking nine events in all from 1951. Nevertheless, for a long time his aim was to be the first South American to take the Open, a feat that his compatriot José Jurado had come close to in 1931.

So the long saga continued. In 1964 at St Andrews he was third behind Tony Lema and Jack Nicklaus and fourth in 1965, Thomson this year winning his fifth championship. In 1967, the championship returned to Hoylake, scene of his disastrous third round 79 eleven years before. De Vicenzo was no longer considered a serious contender at the age of 44. The names on everyone's lips were Nicklaus, Player, Devlin, Sanders and Thomson.

Roberto had incorporated two key changes into his game by this time. A majestic driver of the ball, with his power concealed by fluid rhythm and exact striking, who averaged a measured 275 yards from the tee, he was also liable to hit destructive hooks. He changed his grip with the left hand so that only one knuckle showed and set the shaft more in the palm. Both, for a handicap golfer, would be useful recipes for a disastrous slice but for Roberto, as for Ben Hogan when he had made a similar adjustment, the hook became a thing of the past. He also made himself a less wristy putter. His stroke became more reliable, though he was never to be entirely comfortable on the greens.

He began the 1967 Open 70, 71, good enough to put him a stroke behind the defending champion, Jack Nicklaus, and two ahead of Gary Player. The South African and he then both had 67s to Nicklaus's 71 and the final day would, it seemed, be decided by one of the three. Few favoured Vicenzo. He had failed too often and in Nicklaus and Player he was facing perhaps the top two world stars at the time (Nicklaus was defending champion and Player was to win the following year).

Vicenzo was paired with Player and began by saving his par twice early on with deft chips. Player began to drop shots and was soon out of it after the first nine. Ahead, Nicklaus birdied the 16th and 18th for a 69. Vicenzo needed par over the last three holes of Hoylake's feared finish to win. He managed to get home in two into the light wind at the 529 yard 16th and needed only 9-irons into the last two greens, both holes over 400 yards. Perhaps no major player has tried for so long before succeeding at the age of 44 years and 93 days, the oldest winner this century. He had three-putted only once.

Amongst Roberto de Vicenzo's international achievements, some of his performances in the World Cup — when the nations were entering their best players rather than those who could be persuaded to go along — were outstanding. With Tony Cerda in 1953, it was won for the Argentine, while Vicenzo was individual winner in both 1962 and 1970, on the last occasion setting a record at 269. In all, he made more than twenty appearances for his country.

However, more than all his successes, it is a failure of Vicenzo's that has most earned him fame and has indeed gone down into golfing legend. In 1968 in the last round of the US Masters he played one of the greatest rounds seen at Augusta, a 65. He seemed to be the winner. It now seems to be remembered through a slight distortion caused by time, that Vicenzo was disqualified for a mistake for which he signed his card. This is not exactly so. Vicenzo's 65 was sufficient only to earn him a tie with Bob Goalby and then to play off. It was then discovered that Vicenzo's birdie 3 on the 17th had been written down as a 4 and he, thinking only of a dropped shot on the last had signed his card as correct, but with a 4 on the 17th his 65 became a 66. On TV millions had seen his wedge shot on the 17th settle close to the hole, and Vicenzo hole the putt. Bobby Jones other Masters organisers met hurriedly, in fact anxious to find a way round the rule that a player is responsible for checking his score. They decided that this morally could not be done. Goalby was declared the winner, with Vicenzo second by a stroke he had never played.

Though the longevity of Vicenzo's career cannot (yet) be matched with Sam Snead's, he can bear comparison with anyone else: that smooth, rounded swing has a rhythm and lack of apparent effort that lasts. He won both US and World Seniors titles in 1974 and was still accustomed to finish high up in Open events, having a tie, for instance, in the 1979 Brazil Open, when he was 56: sixteen years older than Nicklaus when people began to assert that he was 'over the top'. It was appropriate that when the US Golf Association decided to organise a Senior Open Vicenzo should be the first champion and another great player, Arnold Palmer, the second.

Vicenzo now competes on the US PGA's Senior Tour though for him it has come a little late. All golfers must decline with age and it is undoubtedly better to be a fifty-year-old competitor than sixty, the age he reached in 1983.

He now totals almost 170 tournament wins, a professional record.

Lanny
Wadkins

Born Richmond, Virginia, USA, 1949

A round of golf used to be something that four competent club golfers got through in little more than two hours. They walked up to their ball through the green, having already decided what club was required for the next move and hit it. On the green there was a quick glance to see just where the hole was and if any severe slopes complicated the matter and away went the putt.

Then came TV. The club golfer quickly realised that all these years he'd done everything wrongly. The good player should walk up to his ball and first do nothing at all while his companions go through their motions. When it is his turn to take centre stage, he should pace out at least part of the distance to the green (to reassure himself that the committee haven't slyly carried out any drastic course re-design overnight), return to his ball, select a club, make several practice swings, pause to test the wind and at last he is ready. Or is he? No, perhaps it should be the 8-iron with that breath of wind barely perceptibly disturbing the tree tops. Most of the process can then be repeated, though the walk to the green might be considered excessive.

On the green there are a wealth of opportunities to turn that hurried two hours on the golf course into four of gentle perambulation. A glance at the hole and away at you now? Certainly not. At the very least the line of the putt must be surveyed from both fore and aft. Sideways also will do no harm at all. Then there is the lie of the grass to be minutely examined; which way it was cut that morning can be detected by an examination of the inside of the hole. By now the job is almost done, with a final delay for a little dangling of the club at arm's length, known to the cognoscenti as 'plumb-bobbing'. The player then proceeds to scrape the ball about 2½ yards short of the hole and about as far off line.

Instead of indiscriminate TV watching, he should observe Mr Jerry Lanston Wadkins. The man belongs to that long dead school that meant by 'going to the golf club' 18 holes in the morning, a quick lunch, another 18, tea and a few holes 'just for fun' thereafter. You can do all that only if you play quickly and Lanny Wadkins is as fast as they have ever come.

His rise to the top was as brisk as his pace of play. In the period 1968 to 1970 he captured most of the prestige American amateur events, including Southern Western and Eastern Amateur Championships and was US amateur champion in 1970, in the process setting the strokeplay record at 279. He played for America in the 1970 World Team Championship and on the 1969 and 1971 Walker Cup sides. The 1971 team was one of the very few to go down to defeat against Great

Lanny Wadkins, St Andrews, 1978

Britain and Ireland but Wadkins was little to blame. Playing number 1 in both singles he beat Charlie Green and Michael Bonallack.

A professional for the full 1972 season, Lanny Wadkins won $116,000, at that time a record for a first year player. For an encore in 1973, with $200,000, he eclipsed previous marks for a second season golfer. He also gave his first good performance in a major championship, coming in third in the US PGA, behind Jack Nicklaus and Bruce Crampton.

At twenty-four, he had now reached the age that can be decisive, for good or ill, to many golfers. Many grow up, for example, with a hitting action that is not faultless but for which youthful reactions can make instantaneous adjustments. Others have limited ambitions; early success can sometimes seem to be enough and they lose the appetite for new glories. The boldness that has brought success can be replaced by caution and calculation, the flaw that Nicklaus had to overcome before the achievements of his later career. Whatever the reasons (and these included ill-health) Wadkins virtually disappeared for three years, winning no tournaments and dropping from his 5th placing for the 1973 season as low as 88th in 1975.

Full revival came in 1977 in the duel with Gene Littler for the US PGA at Pebble Beach, a tragedy for Littler but triumph for Wadkins. Three weeks later there came the World Series at Firestone. The event had been changed from its previous format of being a kind of exhibition of the year's major championship winners playing two rounds of golf, to a far broader and worldwide selection of the most successful players. Wadkins won by five strokes, setting a new record at 267, thirteen under par. He finished the year 3rd on the money list.

There followed a poor 1978 season but in 1979 came perhaps his finest performance to date at Sawgrass, Florida, in the Tournament Players Championship. This is an event that the US PGA would dearly love to see elevated to major championship status. It now carries prize money of some $700,000, more than any other world event except Sol Kerzner's $1 million extravaganza at Sun City, Bophuthatswana.

Over the 7,083 yard course, Wadkins's start of 67, 68 gave him a three stroke lead. Then the weather changed the championship to a test of who could play in high winds. Wadkins returned 76, 72 to beat Tom Watson by five strokes. His scoring does not sound good but can be compared, for example, to the strangely named Kermit Zarley. His 66 led after one round but he followed up with 79, 78, 82. Jack Nicklaus finished 82, 78, and the coming man Craig Stadler's 81, 82.

Again Wadkins backed out of the limelight for two seasons, though he did win events in Canada and Australia, and can now be seen as a 'streak player', one capable of the heights when the spirit moves. 1982 was another good year. His first achievement came in January in the Phoenix Open, which he won by six strokes with rounds of 65, 70, 63, 65, and followed with a three stroke margin in the Tournament of Champions. This brought him to 5th in the money list and he remained there to the end of season, adding another win in the Buick Open and topping $300,000 for the year.

In 1983, Wadkins for once did not follow a good season with an indifferent one. By the end of May, he was leading US money winner with more than $260,000 banked. He had begun strongly with second place finishes in both the Tucson and Los Angeles Opens and went on to take the Greater Greensboro' by five strokes. A little later in the same month, April, he won the important Tournament of Champions to bring his total of US Tour victories to twelve. With the lowest per round stroke average on the US Tour, he also led the points list for Ryder Cup selection. All this tends to support Wadkin's claim that his bad years have been largely due to ill health or injury rather than inconsistency. A major championship victory to add to the two he has already achieved would not surprise me — provided he can cope with the certain Spaniard who defeated him in the 1982 World Matchplay.

Tom
Watson

Born Kansas City, Missouri, USA, 1949

In June 1982 Tom Watson hit the most important shot of his career. It was by no means as spectacular as Gene Sarazen's 4-wood, holed towards the end of the 1935 Masters to catch Craig Wood, but its consequences were no less far-reaching.

Watson came to the 17th at Pebble Beach in the US Open needing two pars to finish level with Jack Nicklaus and earn a play-off. On this long par-3 he had an iron shot of 209 yards to the flag, took a 2-iron and was exactly right in his judgement of length. He had, however, slightly pulled the shot. Although only 5 yards from the flag he had missed green, fringe and light rough. His ball stopped in uncut rough about 5 inches deep.

However, he enjoyed the essential luck that made the next shot possible. Instead of his ball settling down in the grass, it lay exposed. Nevertheless he was faced with the problem of popping the ball up in the air cleanly and the impossibility of putting enough backspin on the ball for it to bite on the green. His playing partner, Bill Rogers, later said that Watson's ball would have run 10 feet past but was nevertheless a superb shot.

But Watson's ball was stopped by the hole itself. He had a birdie 2 and suddenly needed only to par the last to win the US Open. Nevertheless, the last hole had still to be played, one of the most spectacular par 5s in golf. It stretches 548 yards with the Pacific Ocean all along the left, making it possibly the biggest water hazard in the world, especially from the tee shot if the player pulls, hooks or attempts to take too much of a short cut from the angled tee. Watson played the hole conservatively with a 3-wood from the tee, followed by a cautious iron further up the fairway and a final 7-iron to about 15 feet.

By the green waited Jack Nicklaus. Watson had gone into the last round three strokes better than Nicklaus, who had begun by dropping a shot on the first hole, parring the second and then producing one of the great runs of modern golf. He birdied five holes in a row, three-putted the 11th but was generally rock-steady thereafter. He did, however, give his supporters qualms on the last when he went firmly for his birdie putt and drifted some 4½ feet past the hole — not the maestro's best length — but, in the end, all was well. Nicklaus, at that point, must have felt sure of at least a play-off and then of victory when Watson pulled his tee shot on the 17th.

With Nicklaus's chance of a record-breaking fifth US Open now gone, Watson added the minor wound of putting cautiously up to the hole on the last but seeing the ball drop in for a birdie and a two-stroke victory, against which the odds would have been a thousand and more to one just minutes before.

The following month, in a scrappy championship, Watson found himself in possession of the British Open. Unlike at Pebble Beach, he had not so much won the event but been given it by the collapse of Bobby Clampett in the third and fourth rounds and similar play from the South African Nick Price over the closing holes.

That was Tom Watson's seventh major championship which gives him the following standing among the great players of golf history:

Nicklaus:	19	Hogan:	9	Snead:	7
Jones:	13	Player:	9	Vardon:	7
Hagen:	11	Palmer:	8	Watson:	7
Ball:	9	Sarazen:	7		

If we decide that in modern times the US and British Amateurs are not quite worthy of major championship status, as once they certainly were, Watson looks even better:

Nicklaus:	17	Watson:	7	Snead:	7
Hagen:	11	Jones:	7	Vardon:	7
Hogan:	9	Palmer:	7		
Player:	9	Sarazen:	7		

There is a special magic in the major championships which has increased rather than diminished with time. One reason for this is very simple: the names don't change. If we look at the rolls of tournaments both past and present we can come across these names: Jeyes, Colgate, Reschs Pilsener, Dixel, Tam o' Shanter, Arlington Hotel, Thunderbird. They don't strike a chord in every case. Often golf tournament sponsorship is an enthusiasm of the chairman of the board. The enthusiasm may wane or the chairman himself be the object of a putsch, in which case his successor may have to do many things differently; his predecessor's golf tournament probably having to be sacrificed.

To put it another way, the oldest sponsored British tournament was the Dunlop Masters, played for the last time in 1982 after 37 years. In America, apart from the major championships, only the Western, Texas, Los Angeles and Pensacola Opens have a history starting before 1930 and a majority derive from the last twenty years.

In recent years, a Nicklaus-Watson duel has whetted the appetite more than any other prospect. The 1982 US Open was one of several such confrontations and the most emphatic in its climax but the 1977 British Open at Turnberry had a climax hardly inferior and the confrontation was face-to-face and sustained over thirty-six holes.

Watson came to Scotland as leading money winner for the year and current Masters champion (after a duel with Nicklaus he had won by two strokes); Nicklaus was to be second in the money list and won the Inverrary Classic, the Tournament of Champions and his own Memorial.

The relatively unknown John Schroeder, son of a Wimbledon and US Open tennis champion, led the first day with a 66 but then fell away with a 74. Roger Maltbie led after 36 holes with 71, 66 but eventually finished well down the field after a last round 80. Nicklaus and Watson had begun precisely the same: 68, 70,

Tom Watson

and were paired for the third round. On the first half, Nicklaus took a lead, holing long putts to go to five under, having a 2 to Watson's 4 on a short hole. Thereafter, Watson fought back and Nicklaus missed some short ones. They came to the last each needing a par 4 for a 65. Nicklaus was through the back in two but played a masterly run-up to 6 inches while Watson only narrowly missed his long birdie putt.

They were now jointly in the lead at 203 and seven under the par of 70 for the three rounds. One player remained in range, Ben Crenshaw, at 206 after rounds of 71, 69, 66. A new star, he was given a very good chance and the following day was to increase his run of holes without dropping a shot to 35 holes before he was suddenly gone, dropping two on the 9th and then another on the 10th.

This final day was fought out in a fresh westerly breeze that increased the difficulty of scoring well. For instance, of the first nineteen players out, only Bob Charles played the first nine in level par. All day, only six players broke the 70 par.

On the first hole, a 355 yard par 4, Watson drew first blood by hitting a drive some 300 yards while Nicklaus was in light rough to the left. Watson put his second shot a couple of yards away, but missed the putt and the hole was halved in 4.

On the 428 yard second, Nicklaus took the lead, holing a 3 yard putt for a birdie while Watson's second shot ran off the left of the green and he then made a worse mistake, leaving his little pitch shot 20 feet short of the hole. Nicklaus down 8 under, Watson up to 6 under par.

On the 4th, Nicklaus increased his lead with another birdie but Watson then made his move, having birdies at the 5th, 7th and 8th to draw level. He then dropped a shot on the 9th to give Nicklaus back the lead.

They continued to match each other closely until a turning point came on the par 3 15th. Nicklaus was safely on the green with Watson short and left by about four yards in short rough. From there, he took his putter and holed out a shot of 20 yards or more and suddenly they were level again at 10 under for the championship. The 409 yard 16th, which is closely fronted by a burn, saw a superb drive from Watson, while Nicklaus pushed his right into the rough, giving him a difficult line in to the flag, having to just clear the water to get close. Eventually the hole was halved.

The 17th was a par par of 500 yards, but very easily in reach of two shots on the day. It saw another good Watson drive but Nicklaus, who had been less reliable with his driver throughout, now launched a huge one. Watson followed with an iron past the flag and waited while Nicklaus chose what looked like only a 7-iron. He then made a series of errors against Watson's cast-iron birdie. He hit the iron a little heavily and came up 20 yards short of the green on the right but had a run-up that presented no problem. He failed to get it as close as he would have wished. He was 1½ yards past the hole and then saw Watson putt dead. Nicklaus now hit his putt off line and missed on the left.

For the first time Watson was in the lead, at the right time at that, with just a hole to go. The last is a par 4 of 431 yards; many had found difficulties on the hole, not being able to get up in two having taken an iron for safety off the tee. Watson nevertheless chose an iron and struck truly down the middle of the fairway while Nicklaus, needing a birdie, spared nothing with his driver but, as he later said, 'hit it with my belly' and cut the ball well right, only 2ft from a patch of gorse. Watson then produced another superbly struck iron, a 7 this time, his ball finishing only about 2 foot from the hole. Surely the Open was his? Not quite. Nicklaus managed to get his iron on the green some 8 to 10 yards from the hole. Hope was almost gone and Watson no doubt ready with a 'Bad luck Jack' and having two for the Open, Nicklaus then holed out. That this may have been a blow to Watson was only shown by the fact that he putted quickly, not giving himself time for his nerves to become taut. In it went for Watson's 65, victory by one over Nicklaus, a new Open record by eight strokes and a margin over the third place man, Hubert Green, of no fewer than eleven.

I think there can be few to argue against this being Watson's greatest major championship performance, coming at a time when Nicklaus was still the unchallenged number one, while Watson had less than a dozen tournament wins and had yet to finish leading money winner on the US Tour.

He accomplished that by the end of 1977 and followed with three more consecutively (four in a row is the record, only Hogan and Nicklaus having done it three times consecutively).

The British Open has continued the arena of his greatest success. After his Troon win in 1982 he had won four time in eight entries, a striking rate only improved on in modern times by Peter Thomson's four in five years in the period 1954-8. He has also taken the Masters twice (and lost a play-off) and the US Open once. The US PGA has so far escaped him but he has got to a play-off in that one also, in 1978.

The major championship tables earlier in this piece give clear illustration of how high Watson's status now is and the chances strongly favour his going higher. Certainly he now starts as favourite in major events.

What has made Watson perhaps the greatest current performer? Nerve must be rated as highly as anything and this in a man who was early thought, almost certainly correctly, to crack in the final round of tournaments. (He led the US Open in 1974 going into the last round and came in with a 79. Worse followed in 1975, when he led after one round with a 67 and then equalled the US Open record for 36 holes with 135 and a three-stroke lead over Ben Crenshaw. Watson then finished 78, 77 for joint 9th place; the champion was Lou Graham, who had been eleven strokes behind at the 36-hole stage.)

Though Watson now shows some tension when he plays, he has the Nicklaus ability to hit some of his best shots when, as Nicklaus puts it, 'under the collar'. Trevino sees just one weakness in his armoury, the lack of a 'soft' shot. The result can be seen in the way Watson appears to hit every shot, even a putt on lightning Augusta greens, firmly. Even in short putts there is the feel of a forearm punch in the stroke, restrained though it must, of course, be on such putts. He is indeed one of the great putters in golf history, though this has not yet been fully recognised. Many of his wins, however, have hinged on the occasional long putt holed and more on resolute, even inevitable, holing out in the 3ft to 6ft range.

More than anyone else since the arrival of Jack Nicklaus he has proved himself fit to rank with the greatest. It will be a continuing drama to see how that story continues during the 1980s.

Tom Weiskopf

Born Massillon, Ohio, USA, 1942

What makes a man a major championship winner? The answer is by no means as simple as 'He must be a very good player indeed.' Some of the great players have seemed able to go into a kind of overdrive for the great occasions of golf. They move from being outstanding tournament players, yet happy enough to feel they've had a good week if they come in tenth, to being able to impose themselves on international fields. Think of Bobby Jones, a very infrequent competitor in tournaments, who could switch from friendly fourballs with cronies to winning Open Championships. Or Walter Hagen. He was beaten 18 and 17 by Archie Compston in a challenge match one week, yet British Open champion the next. Or Jack Nicklaus, able to come from a disastrous 1979 season, which 'proved' he was finally finished, and then win the US Open and PGAs the following year. Watson too, in the last year or two, has seemed to find a new dimension in his game when a major championship is involved, even more so if the address is Scottish.

How have these, and other, players been able to do this? Undoubtedly the primary factor has been that rare ability to raise their games for the greatest occasions. They also have a passion to win, at its most intense when the great event is involved.

Amongst these, Tom Weiskopf is an enigma. It could not be said that anyone has more natural talent for the game. His full swing has always attracted admiration wherever it has been on display, while at the other extreme of golf he had an admirably steady putting stroke. He used to have a weakness from near the greens. A perfectionist, Tom expected to be on with every shot — that's what a golfer was supposed to do. If he missed with his approach, he felt that he ought to drop a shot. Of course, in the end he buckled down to this vital 'tidying up' part of the game and is competent enough nowadays.

With this chink in the armour filled, why has Tom Weiskopf not won a clutch of major championships to add to his fifteen US Tour wins and half-a-dozen international successes?

Passion may be the answer to my question. Tom Weiskopf has said that he plays the US Tour as a job which enables him to do what he likes best, which is hunt wild mountain sheep. To do this, Tom Weiskopf has once withdrawn from a US Ryder Cup team. Although the match itself is usually a foregone conclusion, being selected to represent the United States is in itself usually incentive enough, as the only occasion when the top group of Americans represent their country in professional golf.

However, there is no moral imperative that states a player should have a passion to win major championships. It is fair enough, surely, if he lives life in the way he prefers. Nevertheless, in Britain we have seen pressure put upon Tony Jacklin to win tournaments and the Open. His failures to achieve much in the later 1970s were made to seem as if he had betrayed the nation!

Weiskopf achieved passionate intensity on one notable occasion: the place Royal Troon, the occasion the 1973 British Open. He was encouraged by the kind of start that can suddenly make a golfer feel that he can win. He missed a birdie putt from 3ft on the first hole but then birdied the next three and reached the turn in 33, and kept going on the homeward half, more difficult because some of the holes were played into a stiff breeze. His 68 led the field.

The next day he aimed to play conservatively, to make sure of pars as far as possible rather than strain boldly for birdies and take risks. The end result was a 67. His long game had been excellent, his drives usually being in the confined fairways and his exceptional length showed to advantage on the par 5s: he birdied all of them. During this round, his putting was excellent. He used only thirty and throughout the championship did not once three-putt.

So, after two days he had a lead of four strokes on Johnny Miller, fresh from his remarkable winning 63 at Oakland Hills in the US Open.

For the rest of the championship, he was paired with Miller and it became a matchplay situation as in the later 1977 battle between Nicklaus and Watson at Turnberry.

With victory for Weiskopf looking an odds-on chance, he started his third round badly, dropping shots and in little more than half an hour Miller had caught him, and then went ahead with three consecutive birdies.

In such a situation Weiskopf has sometimes seemed to lose interest or lose control in rage but he had a birdie or two of his own and the championship as a whole may have swung on the 8th, usually known as 'the Postage Stamp'. With the honour from the tee, Miller hit his short iron only about 4ft away. At this crisis, Weiskopf responded by hitting even closer and both birdied the hole.

On the par 4 9th both drove long but Weiskopf's ball tailed off into gorse and he decided that it was unplayable. He had then to drop his ball close by, still in gorse, or go back towards the tee until he reached more favourable ground. He had to give up some 100 yards of distance before he found it and eventually took 6 to be out in 37 to Miller's 32. Miller led the field by one from Bert Yancey and two from Weiskopf.

Through wind and rain they made the return to the clubhouse, now matching each other shot for shot, but by the end Weiskopf had gained two strokes on Miller and again led the championship with his 71 to Miller's 69. Gone was Jack Nicklaus, who had followed two good rounds with a 76. Of course he came out the next day with all guns firing and got round in 65 but was too late. So the last day was very much between Miller and Weiskopf, only Bery Yancey being not more than five away from Weiskopf's 206.

It was Miller's turn to falter early and Weiskopf had increased his lead to three by the turn. Miller had openings on the return half but then could not hole the necessary putts. Weiskopf won by three from Miller and Neil Coles, who had made up much ground with a spirited 66. Weiskopf, with his 276 total, had

Tom Weiskopf

equalled the Open record, his rounds being 68, 67, 71, 70. He celebrated by driving a car in the USA with a number plate featuring the letters TROON.

Altogether, it was an outstanding year for Tom Weiskopf. On the US Tour he took four titles, which included the Canadian Open, and also the World Series and South African PGA Championship. At the time, there was much comment that Tom had 'pulled himself together' following the death of his father. Previously, it was felt that he had not made the best use of his superb talents.

Tom became a professional in 1964, having won the Western Amateur, one of the US's most prestigious tournaments, but nearly gave up tournament golf because of poor results that even affected his health. He improved steadily, however, and broke through to the top in 1968, when he finished third in the US money list and won twice.

Ever since, Weiskopf has piled up the money each year and by 1981 had become only the fourth man to reach $2 million on the US Tour. Worldwide, by the end of the following year he had passed $2½ million. On the US Tour he stands fifth on the all-time money winners list and is seventh worldwide.

Yet his career did not go on to greater things after his British Open Championship. Although Tom continued to win a lot of money and add a tournament win most years, another major championship has not come his way.

Nevertheless, he has a good record in major events, not as a winner but as a consistent contender. He 'ought', for instance, to have won the 1975 US Masters, when his ship was sunk by a huge curling putt from Jack Nicklaus on the 16th hole of the final round. As recently as 1980, he began the US Open with a record-equalling 63. But so did Jack Nicklaus. He followed up with 71, 70, 68 to win, while Weiskopf's scores were 75, 76, 75, which gave him only 36th place. He had a fairly daunting experience also in the 1973 US Open. He went into the last round five ahead of Johnny Miller and completed the championship creditably enough with a 70; but Miller had his 63 to win.

He has made other strong challenges in the US Masters, a course that favours his length from the tee (270 yards or so average), drawn drives and high-flighted irons. Besides the 1975 disappointment, Weiskopf has been second on four other occasions: 1969, 1972 and 1974. Augusta was also the scene of a strange Weiskopf performance in 1980. In that year, he took 13 on the par 3 12th and followed that with a 7 the next day. Tom has not always managed to control his temper and the high scoring in each case was almost certainly the result of some irritation after he had put his first attempt into water.

On other occasions Tom has knocked his ball along backhanded, refused to sign his card or walked off the course. However, is temper quite so disastrous as it is usually considered to be? Sam Snead, for instance, thought that a golfer should always be 'cool mad', which I take to mean that he should play with controlled temper. Certainly a couldn't-care-less merry smile is not the attitude that brings success in golf.

Finally, it is not Weiskopf's anger that has held him back but lack of concentration and desire. Tournament golf is not the most important thing in life, but it helps if the golfer thinks it is.

Craig Wood

Born Lake Placid, New York, USA, 1901

Being second is always a lot better than finishing nowhere but it is a diet that can jade the palate. It is worse if God seems to be against you. Craig Wood first came to Britain in 1933 and could have gone into legend as the man who won the Open at his first attempt. He tied for first place and then lost the play-off over 36 holes by five strokes. Fair enough, he may well have thought. At least he had established a record that still stands for the longest drive hit in a major competition, a fully authenticated drive of 430 yards on the 5th at St Andrews into — bad luck again — a bunker.

The next year was a little bit worse; second in the first Masters ever played and beaten on the 38th hole in the US PGA final by Paul Runyan, the shortest hitter who ever won anything.

Worse was to come. In 1935, players in Bobby Jones's Invitational event turned up once again at the new Augusta course and spectators, unlike today, were sparse: in the first year they had turned up to watch Bobby Jones, retired from competitive play for a full four years, prove that he was the best. Jones did not in 1934. He finished 13th for his best Masters finish as the yips had got him. However, the 4,000 or so that were there on the last day were mostly watching Craig Wood, who, with four holes to play, had a lead of three strokes on Gene Sarazen. Nobody was watching Sarazen except his playing partner Walter Hagen, Jones (who just happened to have strolled down towards the 15th green) and an estimated seven others, excluding caddies, who were probably rather weary and so remained turgidly around the 15th green. Sarazen then proceded to hit the most famous golf shot ever hit. He toed in his 4-wood slightly for extra length and went for the green over water at the 485 yard 15th. All went well and he cleared the water and after a bounce or so the ball went into the hole for a 2. Very nice indeed for Sarazen, who is reputed to have told all and sundry all about it for the next 40 years, but for Craig Wood it meant a three shot lead suddenly plucked away. There was a 36 hole play-off and Craig lost that.

Three years passed, and it was the 1939 US Open. This time fortune seemed to smile on Craig and on Byron Nelson and Densmore Shute alike. It was the year of Sam Snead's 8 on the last hole when a 5 would have won the championship for him.

The three of them tied on 284. The play-off the next day was over 18 holes and Craig Wood was at his best. His 68 left Shute eight strokes in arrears but unfortunately Byron Nelson repeated his last round 68 also.

With Shute out of it, another 18 holes began between Nelson and Wood. In the end, Wood finished with a very respectable 73 during which he had played to just about the same standard as Byron Nelson; but once more there had been a happening: Nelson had holed a full 1-iron shot for a 2, had finished in 70 and was US Open Champion.

Wood came back the next year to see what Fate had to offer this time in the US Open and finished 4th, a couple of strokes behind the winner. He did nothing else of particular note, but at least he was still trying.

In the 1941 Masters he began with a 66 which should have put him clearly in the lead. This in itself must by now have been a surprise to Craig Wood. He followed with a 71 and still led. Then came another 71 and still he was leading. His final round was a 72 and there were one or two 68s, but when it was all over Craig Wood had become the first man to lead the Masters throughout and win, by three shots.

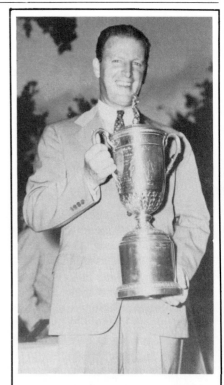

Craig Wood, US Open, 1941

He went on, somewhat encouraged, to the 1941 US Open. His back was giving him considerable pain though a brace helped a bit. At one point he was three over par, in a ditch and there was a storm to add to disenchantment. Tommy Armour persuaded him to carry on. Wood's scores were 73, 71, 70, 70 and no-one who mattered knocked the ball into the hole from unreasonable distances. By three strokes he was US Open Champion, still one of only four golfers to win both Masters and US Open the same year.

That really was the end for Craig Wood. Never again did he feature in a major championship and it is easy to speculate that he felt it was enough to have stopped being incessantly second. This is, perhaps, an over-simplistic view.

In later years, spectators at an exhibition match noted that Craig hit his tee shot, knocked the second onto the green and then picked up. They may well have thought that putting was beneath the attention of a former Masters and US Open Champion, but this was not the case. Craig had the yips and did not wish to be embarrassed by jerking the ball to and fro to little purpose; the same reason that Hogan ceased to compete when his long game was still supreme.

However, there was one more second place to come. He finished there to Jack Grout in the 1947 Spring Lake Invitational. It was the only tour event that Grout won, though he was much later to achieve fame as the mentor of Jack Nicklaus.